Churchill's
D-Day

THE BRITISH BULLDOG'S FATEFUL HOURS
DURING THE NORMANDY INVASION

Richard Dannatt

and

Allen Packwood

DIVERSION
BOOKS
NEW YORK

To all those under Allied Command
who lost their lives in the Normandy Campaign

Diversion Books

A division of Diversion Publishing Corp.

www.diversionbooks.com

Copyright © 2024 by Richard Dannatt and Allen Packwood

Published in association with Churchill Heritage Ltd

Diversion Books and colophon are registered trademarks
of Diversion Publishing Corp.

For more information, email info@diversionbooks.com.

First Diversion Books Edition: May 2024

Hardcover ISBN 978-1-635-76959-3

e-ISBN 978-1-635-76928-9

Book design by Beth Kessler, Neuwirth & Associates, Inc.

Printed in the United States of America

1 3 5 7 9 10 8 6 4 2

Diversion books are available at special discounts for bulk purchases in the US by corporations, institutions, and other organizations. For more information, please contact admin@diversionbooks.com.

Contents

Part One

Planning

Map of D-Day beaches showing British and Canadian objectives, 1944.
(Selwyn-Lloyd Papers, SELO 3/43)

Chapter 1

Hindsight Is a Wonderful Thing

*"Are you going to lay there and get killed,
or get up and do something about it?"*

IN THE EARLY MORNING OF TUESDAY, JUNE 6, 1944, AS BRITAIN SLEPT, Company Sergeant Major Stan Hollis of Sixth Battalion Green Howards clambered down the scrambling nets on the side of the cargo ship *Empire Lance* and into the landing craft taking him the final sea-sickening miles to Gold Beach. As Hollis's craft lurched toward shore, he saw a German position in the middle of the sector toward which he and his men were heading. Seizing a Lewis gun from another soldier, Stan gave the pillbox two magazines of automatic fire. No fire was returned. A few minutes later, having sprinted up the beach, Hollis discovered his "pillbox" was only the tram shelter for the local light railway. (The "Hollis Hut" is now in the proud possession of his regiment.)

The much awaited Allied Second Front in the West, codenamed Operation Overlord, had begun to take shape. From 06:30, the early summer sun had illuminated the landings from the greatest armada of ships ever assembled. Overnight, paratroopers from the British Sixth Airborne Division had secured the eastern flank of the landing zone while the US Eighty-second and 101st Airborne Divisions had seized the western flank to reduce the risk of German counterattacks. Ironically, the unseasonal bad weather, which had already forced a twenty-four-hour postponement of the amphibious assault, had persuaded the German High Command that the weather was too bad for the Allies to launch their assault that day. Field Marshal Rommel, in command of Army Group B in the Normandy sector, had returned to Germany to celebrate his wife's birthday while senior officers from Seventh Army were gathering in Rennes for a study day to review their anti-invasion plans.

As the day commenced, HMS *Belfast* (now maintained in the Thames by the United Kingdom's Imperial War Museum) began its bombardment of the German defenses above Gold Beach onto which Stan Hollis's Green Howard soldiers were storming ashore. Farther west, the assault by the US Fourth Infantry Division had secured Utah Beach at a cost of only 197 casualties, but the fighting on Omaha Beach still hung in the balance. The untested US Twenty-ninth Infantry Division assaulted the western half of the eight-kilometer beach while the battle-hardened First Infantry Division was allocated the eastern sector. The beach was overlooked by rising bluffs defended by the experienced German 352nd Infantry Division recently reassigned to Normandy from the Russian front. The intensity of the fighting is captured in the opening sequences of Steven Spielberg's film *Saving Private Ryan.* The specter of disaster hovered as casualties mounted. An unidentified US lieutenant is credited with cajoling reluctant infantrymen: "Are you going to lay there and get killed, or get up and do something about it?" The fighting on Omaha Beach came closest to realizing the Allied leadership's nightmare of the failure of Overlord. There was no plan B, only evacuation.

The British people awoke to the news of the landings on their radios. Prime Minister Winston Churchill entered the Chamber of the House of Commons at three minutes to twelve and was quickly called to the dispatch box. According to the MP Harold Nicolson, he looked as "white as a sheet," and Nicolson feared that he was "about to announce some terrible disaster." The excited chatter of the waiting MPs was replaced with an expectant hush. Churchill had two pieces of news to impart. He started, not with the Normandy landings, but with an account of the liberation of Rome on the previous Sunday, heaping praise on British general Harold Alexander, the Italian theater commander, whose name was greeted with a tremendous cheer by the assembled politicians. The prime minister then proceeded to detail the recent phases of the Italian campaign, from the Anzio landings of January 22 to the Allied entry into the eternal city (coincidentally, the fourth anniversary of Churchill's famous "Never Surrender" speech).

No doubt there was an element of theater in delaying mention of Normandy. Churchill was a consummate parliamentary performer. He knew that his audience was hanging on his every word, waiting anxiously for the first report of the landings. But by delaying, he was also emphasizing the equal weight he attached to events in Italy, where the Allied armies were under British command. He saw this "memorable and glorious event"—the capture of Rome—as vindicating his continuing support for operations in the Mediterranean. Operations that he was keen to stress were ongoing, reporting that "the Allied forces, with the Americans in the van, are driving ahead, northwards, in relentless pursuit of the enemy." Churchill remained keen to maintain combined British American operations in the Italian peninsula but feared that the Americans would now give primacy to France and Overlord.

Having made his point, he came to the day's main announcement about the landings. His remarks were short, simple, and factual. Obviously, there was much he could not say. The situation was still evolving. The fog of war hung over events, and, mindful of security, he did not want to prejudice the landings by giving helpful information to the enemy. Even so, it is worth printing his remarks here in full:

> I have also to announce to the House that during the night and the early hours of this morning **the first** of the series of landings in force upon the European Continent has taken place. In this case the liberating assault fell upon the coast of France. An immense armada of upwards of 4,000 ships, together with several thousand smaller craft, crossed the Channel. Massed airborne landings have been successfully effected behind the enemy lines and landings on the beaches are proceeding at

various points at the present time. The fire of the shore batteries has been largely quelled. The obstacles that were constructed in the sea have not proved so difficult as was apprehended. The Anglo-American Allies are sustained by about 11,000 first line aircraft, which can be drawn upon as may be needed for the purposes of the battle. I cannot, of course, commit myself to any particular details. Reports are coming in in rapid succession. So far the Commanders who are engaged report that everything is proceeding according to plan. And what a plan! **This vast operation is undoubtedly the most complicated and difficult that has ever occurred. It involves tides, wind, waves, visibility, both from the air and the sea standpoint, and the combined employment of land, air and sea forces in the highest degree of intimacy and in contact with conditions which could not and cannot be fully foreseen.**

There are already hopes that actual tactical surprise has been attained, and we hope to furnish the enemy with a succession of surprises during the course of the fighting. The battle that has now begun will grow constantly in scale and in intensity for many weeks to come and I shall not attempt to speculate upon its course. This I may say, however. **Complete unity prevails throughout the Allied Armies. There is a brotherhood in arms between us and our friends of the United States. There is complete confidence in the supreme commander, General Eisenhower, and his lieutenants, and also in the commander of the Expeditionary Force, General Montgomery. The ardour and spirit of the troops, as I saw myself, embarking in these last few days was splendid to witness. Nothing that equipment, science or forethought could do has been neglected,** and the whole process of opening this great new front will be pursued with the utmost resolution both by the commanders and by the United States and British Governments whom they serve.

The passages in bold highlight themes to which this book will return: the complexity of the operation, the use of deceptive measures to contain the element of surprise and convince the enemy that this might be the first of several assaults, the unity of the American and British commanders, and the morale and training of the troops. Churchill was right that all were essential for a successful operation on this scale.

This first reaction may seem rather short and muted, especially when compared with his famous oratory from 1940. There is no great peroration, no references to "finest hour," no promises of "blood, toil, tears and sweat," no exhortations to "never surrender." Churchill spoke only for a few minutes before promising to return to the House, perhaps before it adjourned later that day, to give an update. This was an interim statement, made at a moment when the outcome of the battle was still unknown.

Given the unique circumstances, the prime minister's remarks were received by the House without debate or criticism. Now was not the time for speeches or disunity, though two longtime Churchill opponents did make comments. The veteran communist politician Willie Gallacher expressed "my own feeling, and I am sure the feeling of every Member of the House, that our hearts and thoughts are with these lads who have gone across to the Continent and with their mothers here at home." While the socialist firebrand Aneurin Bevan asked whether the prime minister would be framing a message from the House to the people of France. Both may seem innocuous interventions, but they surely served to remind Churchill of the huge responsibility he was bearing for the lives of both British soldiers and French civilians—two groups that were suffering casualties at that very moment.

Churchill's statement stands in marked contrast to the way in which he would later describe this same moment, the launching of the assault, in his wartime memoirs. In 1950 and 1951, revisiting the events of D-Day, he would write:

The immense cross-Channel enterprise for the liberation of France had begun. All the ships were at sea. We had the mastery of the oceans and of the air. The Hitler tyranny was doomed.

That quote, taken from the penultimate paragraph of *Closing the Ring*, itself the penultimate book in his epic six-volume history of *The Second World War*, could not be more confident, concluding, "Nor, though the road might be long and hard, could we doubt that decisive victory would be gained."

But it is a quote that sums up the problem we have when talking about Operation Overlord, namely the luxury of knowing that it worked. With hindsight it is easy for us to sit here and say that it is clear that this was the right strategy, one that brought the war to an end in a fast and decisive manner and ultimately secured the freedom of Western Europe from both fascism and perhaps communism. In spite of what he wrote later, it was not so easy, simple, and predictable for Churchill or for the American president Franklin D. Roosevelt, General Dwight D. Eisenhower, and the other British and American political and military leaders in 1944.

By the time the relevant volume of his war memoirs was published in 1952, Churchill was back in 10 Downing Street as a peacetime prime minister, and General Eisenhower, the Supreme Commander for the D-Day operation, was about to become president of the United States. The reputation of both men had been assured by victory, and their story had become synonymous with the triumph of the West; a story that now deliberately downplays the role of their former Soviet allies—turned Cold War enemies—and that already viewed the events of 1944 through a different lens; one that was colored by nostalgia, influenced by new postwar realities, and composed with the benefit of hindsight. D-Day was already becoming the stuff of myth. It is a trend that would only accelerate, fueled by Hollywood movies like *D-Day: The Sixth of June* (1956) and *The Longest Day* (1962).

Strip away those layers of hindsight, look afresh at the events as they appeared to Churchill and his contemporaries at the time, and a less confident, more confusing story emerges. This volume will identify the complex factors that came together to make D-Day successful. In so doing, it will examine the criticism that has been leveled against the Allied leadership and against Churchill in particular, both in his lifetime and since. Namely, that he deliberately delayed and then obstructed attempts to stage the cross-Channel invasion at an earlier date, and, as a result, by crossing the Channel in 1944 rather than 1942 or 1943, the duration of the war was prolonged, causing unnecessary deaths in other theaters, and extending the misery of countless millions in Europe.

It is a complicated history that can only be understood in the context of British defeat and weakness in the first years of the Second World War. It involves weaving together different strands; of shifting political alliances, conflicting military strategies, evolving tactical needs, and huge logistical challenges. Events will take us to Downing Street, Parliament, the White House, and the Kremlin; to North Africa, Greece, Italy, and France. We will meet an incredible array of characters, some of them already well known to history: national leaders such as President Roosevelt, Marshal Stalin, and General de Gaulle; military commanders like Generals Alexander, Brooke, Eisenhower, Marshall, Montgomery, and Patton, and Admirals Cunningham, Mountbatten, and Ramsay. But we will also introduce others who are not such household names, a cross section of the diverse range of men and women who made D-Day possible by doing their jobs, sometimes in the face of danger, often in secrecy and under great stress. They include servicemen and -women like Company Sergeant Major Stan Hollis of the Sixth Battalion Green Howards; John Anthony Hugill—known as Tony—of Thirty Assault Unit; Wren officer Christian Oldham (later Christian Lamb); Canadian bomber pilot Roland MacKenzie; and American paratrooper TL Rodgers; organizers and administrators like the young Joan Bright (later Joan Astley), who sat in the middle of the Whitehall information web, General Frederick Morgan, the man charged with developing the D-Day plan, and Commander "Jock" Hughes-Hallett who helped prepare the naval assault force; deception experts like Colonel John Bevan and the novelist Dennis Wheatley; scientists and innovators like Geoffrey Pyke and Major-General Percy Hobart. The list goes on. The success of June 6, 1944, depended on the contribution of so many.

But at the heart of our narrative sits the British prime minister. Sixty-nine years old in June 1944, Winston Leonard Spencer-Churchill was already a man with a long and complex history. A powerful orator, professional writer, and amateur painter, he had enjoyed a roller coaster of a political career. First elected to Parliament in 1900, he had served in many of the major offices of state. Highly conscious of his lineage as a descendant and biographer of the great eighteenth-century British general John Churchill, first Duke of Marlborough, he had served in the army and had previously exercised ministerial responsibility for all three armed services. Unafraid to court controversy, he had changed political parties twice (moving from Conservative to Liberal in 1904 and back again twenty years later in 1924) and had established a reputation as a vocal defender of the British Empire and a bellicose opponent of both communism and fascism. For the decade prior to the Second World War, he had been out of office and for much of the 1930s was viewed by many as a maverick, an opportunist or a relic of a previous age. But his fiery oratory, consistent opposition to the appeasement of Hitler, and calls for British rearmament had seen him return to prominence and secure the premiership.

By June 1944, Churchill had been prime minister for a little more than four years. With his bulldog scowl, spotted bow tie, two-fingered V for Victory salute, and ever-present cigar, he had become one of the most famous and instantly recognizable figures of his age. In some respects, his prime ministerial office was not unlike a modern Tudor court, where his own eccentric band of special advisers rubbed shoulders with family members, civil servants, politicians, and military commanders. By creating for himself the new position of minister of defense and combining it with the office of prime minister, he made sure that the political and military leadership reported directly to him, chairing the War Cabinet, the Defence Committee, and meeting regularly with the chiefs of staff (the military heads of the army, navy, and air force). Never one to lack self-belief, he was confident in his own abilities as a strategist and, as we shall see, had brought strong views to all phases of the debates about the nature and timing of D-Day.

How Did Churchill Run His Wartime Government?

Churchill created a very strong, centralized administration run out of his Downing Street Private Office. By making himself not just prime minister, but also minister of defense (a new role that he created), he made sure that he controlled both policy and strategy. His was a national coalition government bringing together members of the main political parties: the Conservatives, the Labour Party, as well as the Liberal Party, the National Liberals, and National Labour. There was an informal understanding that this super coalition would continue for the duration of the wartime emergency (in practice until the end of the war in Europe), but Churchill could not assume that this would automatically remain the case. The member parties could opt to leave and a successful vote of no-confidence in the government by parliamentary backbenchers might lead to his removal at any point—as had happened to his predecessor, Neville Chamberlain. This meant that Churchill was not entirely free to choose his own government ministers, as he had to make sure that his coalition partners, particularly the Labour and Liberal Parties, were rewarded with some of the key offices of state.

He chose to govern primarily through a small inner War Cabinet. Its composition changed between 1940 and 1945, but it initially consisted of just five ministers: Churchill, Chamberlain, his erstwhile rival the Foreign Secretary Lord Halifax, and the Labour leaders Clement Attlee and Arthur Greenwood. Halifax was sent to America as ambassador and was replaced by Anthony Eden as foreign secretary in December 1940. Clement Attlee became deputy prime minister in 1942. Others came and went. Churchill deliberately kept the three service ministers—the First Lord of the Admiralty (Royal Navy), the secretary of state for war (Army), and the secretary of state for air (Royal Air

Force)—out of the War Cabinet, summoning them only when needed—as was the case with all other government ministers.

This allowed him to exercise more direct control over the military by having the chiefs of staff report into him directly as minister of defense. The chiefs were the military heads of the three services, the senior British commanders, comprising the First Sea Lord (Navy), the chief of the Imperial General Staff (Army), and the chief of the Air Staff (Royal Air Force). Churchill chaired the important Defence Committee, which decided on important operations, and his military chief of staff, General "Pug" Ismay, represented him at the regular chiefs of staff meetings. As prime minister, he created a powerful War Cabinet Secretariat, including the Cabinet Secretary, the Downing Street Private Secretaries (male career civil servants), and a military secretariat under Ismay. To this he added his own team of personal secretaries (nearly all female), an assortment of special assistants and advisers, his own map room, and a statistical unit to help research, analyze, and interpret information. He also sought direct access to the Joint Planning Staff.

Yet, even with all this support and centralization, Churchill had to prioritize and delegate. He chose to concentrate on military strategy, security, and foreign policy, allowing other ministers considerable independence on domestic affairs and the economy (both at home and around the Empire). He had to work closely with the Dominion governments, on which he was dependent for troops and resources and regularly allowed their leaders or senior visiting representatives to attend War Cabinet meetings. The war was being run through a huge number of ministries, departments, and committees, some public, some secret, and however hands-on he might want to be, Churchill could only do so much.

Orpen portrait of Churchill, 1916.
(William Orpen / National Portrait Gallery)

But to what extent was that strategy influenced by the ghosts of his past? It is common for the dining halls of Oxford and Cambridge colleges to be covered with the portraits of their former distinguished fellows and alumni. In contrast, the dining hall of Churchill College, Cambridge, built as the British national and Commonwealth memorial to Sir Winston, holds just one picture. It is of a younger Churchill, thinner, more angular, and still sporting the remnants of his youthful red hair. Depicted against a somber black background, with bags beneath his eyes, this is a dark, stark portrait. It captures Churchill in 1915 at age forty. The original was painted by William Orpen and still belongs to the Churchill family. The version that hangs in Churchill College is a specially commissioned copy by the artist John Leigh-Pemberton. It was recommended by Churchill's widow, Clementine, as one of the truest depictions of her husband, and it captures him not during his "finest hour" but rather at his lowest ebb, after losing office over the Dardanelles Campaign.

Churchill had started the First World War as the First Lord of the Admiralty, the civilian minister in charge of the largest navy in the world. The fleet had been modernized and mobilized, and his stock was high. But hopes for a decisive naval battle between the British Grand Fleet and the German High Seas Fleet had failed to materialize. Faced with the stalemate of trench warfare on the Western Front in France and

Belgium, the navy was relegated to the less glorious role of protecting British trade routes and blockading Germany. Casting around for ways to relieve pressure on the Allied armies, Churchill focused on opening up a new front against Turkey, Germany's weaker ally. He quickly became the leading advocate in the Cabinet of a plan to use ships to force the Dardanelles Straits, the narrow waters that led into the Sea of Marmara and were guarded by the Gallipoli Peninsula. The aim was to force open a passage through the Straits, besiege Constantinople (now Istanbul), and knock Turkey out of the war, while in the process providing new supply routes for Britain's ally, Russia. The problem was that the Straits were heavily protected by forts and mines. When the naval expeditionary force under Admiral Carden and then Admiral de Robeck failed to clear a way through, losing three battleships, the War Cabinet made the fateful decision to use troops to seize the Gallipoli Peninsula. British, French, Australian, and New Zealand forces landed in April 1915, but—faced with heavy Turkish resistance from entrenched positions in the mountainous terrain overlooking the landing grounds—they were unable to break out of the beachheads and were evacuated in January 1916. The casualties were considerable, about a quarter of a million Allied dead or wounded. Among the survivors were those who would go on to play a prominent role in the Second World War, including young captain William Slim, later commander of British forces in Burma (now Myanmar), and Clement Attlee, who would become leader of the Labour Party and later Churchill's deputy prime minister and Britain's postwar prime minister.

The immediate aftermath of the initial failed naval operation was a complete breakdown between Churchill and his First Sea Lord (senior naval commander) Admiral Lord "Jacky" Fisher. When Fisher left his post in protest in May 1915, Prime Minister Asquith took the opportunity to restructure his government, bringing in conservatives who had not forgiven Churchill for his defection to the Liberal Party in 1904 (he would not rejoin the Tories until 1924). Their price was Churchill's removal. Winston found himself demoted to the lesser position of Chancellor of the Duchy of Lancaster, facing hostile criticism from the press and public and unable to defend himself while military operations were ongoing.

The Orpen portrait captures Churchill at this moment of crisis. It looked to many as though his hitherto promising career was over. His father, Lord Randolph Churchill, had enjoyed a meteoric political rise but had thrown everything away with an ill-judged political resignation at the age of just thirty-six. History seemed to be repeating itself. Clementine thought her husband would die of grief. Ultimately, Winston would claw his way back to the political front rank, but it would take time. Resigning from the government, he chose to restore his personal honor by serving for six months in the trenches of the Western Front, commanding a battalion of Royal Scots Fusiliers. There was then an anxious wait for the report of the Dardanelles Commission of Inquiry, which largely exonerated him, before he could write his own comprehensive justification for his actions as part of his multivolume history of the First World War, titled *The World Crisis*, published in the 1920s. But even then, the stigma of failure at the Dardanelles continued to hang over him, becoming a staple of critical cartoons and hostile heckles.

Books have been written on the reasons for the Allied failure at the Dardanelles, and debate still rages. It is often said that it was this failure that made Churchill extremely cautious about D-Day. The film *Churchill*, starring Brian Cox in the title role and released in 2017, opens with the British prime minister walking on a beach in 1944 and recoiling as, in his mind's eye, the waters run red with the blood of British troops. The suggestion in the movie is that, unlike Eisenhower and the military commanders of the day, he had seen this before at Gallipoli and was therefore determined to do all he could to prevent it from happening again. It is a script that depicts him trying to obstruct the landings with only days to go. The question of Churchill's opposition to D-Day and the extent to which he actively interfered by attempting to prevent or delay the operation forms one of the major themes of this book.

What lessons did Churchill take from the Dardanelles Campaign? It certainly made him aware of the political risks associated with advocating major operations. He felt he had been made a scapegoat and unfairly brought down, given his inability to influence events on the ground. Without complete control, "Men are ill-advised to try such ventures. The lesson had sunk into my nature."

He was also clearly aware of the difficulty inherent in such large amphibious operations, trying to coordinate naval, ground, and air forces belonging to independent countries all under their own commanders. The importance of establishing clear command structures with good communications based on the very best intelligence is obvious in his reflection that:

> Without the title deeds of positive achievement no one had the power to give clear brutal orders which would command unquestioning respect. Power was widely disseminated among the many important personages who in this period formed the governing instrument. Knowledge was very unequally shared.

But this did not stop him from continuing to think about the challenges of seizing an enemy-held shoreline or of promoting other similar operations.

When writing about the origins of Overlord in his Second World War memoirs, he chose to highlight a paper on *Naval War Policy* that he had created for the attention of Prime Minister Lloyd George almost twenty-seven years before D-Day on July 7, 1917. Then, his aim had been to show how the Royal Navy could retake the offensive in the First World War. One of his main suggestions had been to seize the Heligoland Islands of Sylt and/or Borkum, located just off the German coast, for use as a forward base for an attack against the enemy.

The operation he described in his paper certainly had some similarities with the later 1944 cross-Channel assault. It required mastery of the seas, would be preceded by a heavy bombardment (albeit primarily naval in an age before air warfare), and would culminate in:

> The landing under cover of the guns of the Fleet, aided by gas and smoke, of the troops upon the island, from torpedo-proof transports by means of bullet-proof lighters. Approximately 100 should be provided for landing a division. In addition a number (say) 50, tank landing lighters would be provided, each carrying a tank or tanks, fitted for wire-cutting in its bow, which, by means

of a drawbridge or shelving bow, would land under its own power, to prevent the infantry from being held up by wire when attacking the gorges of the forts and batteries. This is a new feature, and removes one of the very great previous difficulties, namely the rapid landing of field artillery to cut wire.

Winston also anticipated the need to establish an aerial base "sufficiently powerful to hold its own air" and the "establishment of oilers and storeships in the anchorage" for the landing of the necessary stores. This paper illustrates his grasp of the challenges to be faced and proves that, less than two years after the Dardanelles Campaign, he was already prepared to champion other similar attacks from the sea. He appreciated that the wars of the future would involve combined operations, and he was also aware of the difficulties, particularly if conducted at scale. As it turned out, his interwar career would take him in different directions, and it fell upon others to try to develop the equipment and tactics for combined operations in an atmosphere of austerity, retrenchment, and disarmament.

More broadly, the war of 1914–1918 certainly had a profound impact on Churchill's life and on his thinking. Friends had been lost, his career had almost been destroyed, and his worldview challenged. The British Empire had been severely weakened, and the fabric of ordinary British life ripped apart, with war memorials appearing in almost every village. As wartime prime minister since 1940, he could not contemplate the cost of another bloody stalemate in Europe, writing:

[T]he fearful price we had had to pay in human life and blood for the great offensives of the First World War was graven in my mind. Memories of the Somme and Passchendaele and many lesser frontal attacks upon the Germans were not to be blotted out by time or reflection.

But there is another interrelated criticism of Churchill, namely that he did not want to fight in France in 1942 or 1943 because he was prioritizing the defense of the British Empire. Much has been written about his imperialism. He was certainly a lifelong supporter of the British Empire and, in November 1942, would famously assert that he had not become the king's first minister (i.e., prime minister) to preside over its liquidation. His was a worldview built on a belief in the superiority of the Western democracies and the white European races. Yet Britain was also dependent on its Empire for men and materials; a global power with colonies, linked dominions, and mandates. No British prime minister would have been willing or able to walk away from those responsibilities in 1940, and that meant keeping forces in Africa, the Mediterranean, and the Pacific, as well as maintaining supply lines to Britain across the seas and oceans. Britain had no choice but to fight in several theaters, and this book will look at the decisions that were made with regard to priorities versus resources and their impact on the timing and nature of D-Day.

Churchill was certainly not alone in wrestling with these problems. Another recurring question within this book is the extent to which he could or did act independently. He was undoubtedly a powerful prime minister, but he was running a coalition government within a parliamentary system and presiding over an enormous civil bureaucracy and military services that had their own long-standing structures and systems. General John Kennedy, who became assistant chief of the Imperial General Staff, described it as "essentially a government of committees.... Winston is of course the dominating personality, ... Yet Winston's views do not often prevail if they are contrary to the general trend of opinion among the service staffs." From 1941 onward, he was also a partner with the United States and the Soviet Union in an international alliance against fascism, an alliance that was increasingly led from Washington, DC, and Moscow. There was no doubt that France and northwestern Europe were most easily liberated from the offshore base provided by the United Kingdom, but it was equally evident that Britain could not undertake that liberation on its own.

Churchill was certainly sensitive to criticisms about his reluctance to open a Second Front in Western Europe and very keen to rebut them, writing in volume II of his war memoirs:

In view of the many accounts which are extant and multiplying of my supposed aversion from any kind of large-scale opposed-landing, such as took place in Normandy in 1944, it may be convenient if I make it clear that from the very beginning I provided a great deal of the impulse and authority for creating the immense apparatus and armada for the landing of armour on beaches, without which it is now universally recognized that all such major operations would have been impossible.

This book will look in detail at exactly what that role comprised, but to fully understand what was at stake for Churchill and the British chiefs of staff in 1944, it is necessary to go back in time to the desperate first years of the Second World War and follow the long evolution of Overlord, to explain the broader Allied strategy from which it emerged and show how it was the culmination of years of planning, preparation, and effort (of blood, toil, tears, and sweat).

In keeping with its aim to focus on events as they were seen at the time, this book reproduces carefully chosen contemporary documents and uses them to provide insights into the story. It also uses breakout text to provide further insight into some of the military questions faced by Churchill. The authors hope that our selection will further illuminate key personalities and debates. This is not intended to be an academic book, but we have given the citations for major quotations in the notes and included a select bibliography for those who wish to delve further.

10, Downing Street,
Whitehall.

I spoke the other day of the colossal
military disaster which occurred when the French High
                        failed
Command ~~neglected~~ to withdraw the Northern armies from
Belgium at the moment when they knew that the French
Front was decisively broken at Sedan and on the Meuse.
This delay entailed the loss of ~~at least fifteen~~ French
Divisions and threw out of action for the critical period
                          and 120,000 French troops
the whole British Expeditionary Force. Our Army ~~indeed~~
no doubt ~~escaped~~, but with the loss of all ~~its~~ cannon, vehicles
              modern
and/equipment. This inevitably took some weeks to repair,
and in those weeks the ~~great~~ battle of France has been
lost. When we consider the heroic resistance made by the
French Army at ~~enormous~~ odds in this battle, and the
~~enormous~~ losses inflicted upon the enemy, and the exhaustion
of the enemy, it may well be thought that these twenty-five
Divisions of the best troops might have turned the scale.
However General Weygand had to fight without them. Only
~~the equiv~~ two British Divisions or their equivalent were

Annotated page from Churchill's speech and broadcast after the fall of France,
June 18, 1940. (Churchill Papers, CHAR 9/140A/132)

Chapter 2

Dealing with Defeat

"He spoke in English, and evidently under stress. 'We have been defeated.' As I did not immediately respond he said again: 'We are beaten; we have lost the battle.'"

IT IS ONE OF THOSE EXTRAORDINARY COINCIDENCES IN HISTORY THAT the date of May 8 during the Second World War loomed large. It was on May 8, 1940, that Winston Churchill summed up in the House of Commons for the government in the no-confidence debate called by the Labour Opposition after the disastrous Norwegian Campaign—a debate that set him on the path to 10 Downing Street. It was also on May 8, 1945, that the war in Europe finally ended. What happened in those intervening five years has become the stuff of legend. Legends require heroes—Winston Churchill became that hero. But his rise was not inevitable.

His appointment with destiny rested on securing the keys to 10 Downing Street. At the beginning of May 1940, Winston Churchill was First Lord of the Admiralty, the civilian minister in charge of the navy in Neville Chamberlain's conservative government. After Churchill spent ten years in the political wilderness, his vocal opposition to Hitler had seen him brought back into the Cabinet with the outbreak of war.

As criticism of Chamberlain's war leadership mounted, Churchill was increasingly seen as one of the contenders to replace him, but it was far from a fait accompli.

The May 4 entry from the diary of Aubrey Leo Kennedy, diplomatic correspondent of *The Times*, provides a rather unflattering snapshot of Churchill on the eve of his premiership:

> After this Norway breakdown there is of course a lot of criticism of Gov[ernmen]t & general despondence. M.P.'s are all especially discontented. There is a drive against Chamberlain. I can't quite see who can advantageously take his place. Curiously enough what is really needed is that Winston should be made to take a rest. He is overdoing himself and taking the strain by stoking himself unduly with champagne, liqueurs etc.; Dines out and dines well almost every night. Sleeps after luncheon, then to the House O' Commons, then a good and long dinner, and doesn't resume work at the Admiralty till after 10 pm, and goes on till 1 or 2 am. He has got into the habit of calling conferences and subordinates after 1 am, which naturally upsets some of the Admirals who are men of sound habits. So there is a general atmosphere of strain at the Admiralty which is all wrong. Yet Winston is such a popular hero and so much the war-leader that he cannot be dropped. But he ought somehow to be rested!

Churchill had two major problems to overcome. First, he was still seen by many, especially within his own Conservative Party and the British establishment, as an unstable maverick and opportunist. Second, he was a leading member of Neville Chamberlain's Cabinet and heavily implicated in the military failure that now threatened to bring down the prime minister and his government. The "Norway breakdown" referred to by Kennedy was the Battles of Narvik, a hastily and poorly planned British intervention in Scandinavia in April 1940.

Rearming very late in the 1930s after the failure of the policy of appeasement, Britain and France began the war in 1939 with the same broad strategy with which the Great War had ended—to blockade

Germany in a long war and starve her of resources, leading to eventual surrender. The battlefield lessons of the Hundred Days Campaign in 1918 were largely forgotten by both the British government and her army, although they were studied carefully by Germany, where the High Command knew that they could never win a protracted war. It led them to develop their blitzkrieg capability, of mobile armor supported by airpower, which had defeated Poland between September 1 and October 6, 1939. Notwithstanding that illustration of modern warfare, the British Expeditionary Force that deployed to France in the autumn of 1939 joined the French Army under the operational belief that the power of the defensive, delivered by the extensive fortifications and firepower of the Maginot Line in northeastern France, would contain Germany, while the strategy of blockade would deliver ultimate success.

Consistent with this misplaced strategy, plans began to be formulated in London for the mining of neutral Norway's territorial waters to prevent the export of iron ore from Gällivare in Sweden to Germany through Norwegian ports. There was a well-founded belief that if the supply of Swedish iron ore to Germany could be interdicted, German industry would come to a stop in a very short time, possibly measurable in weeks. Winston Churchill, as the new First Lord of the Admiralty, saw the blocking of this iron ore supply as a strong move to take the war to Germany, rather than relying on the passive defensive posture of the armies in France. As in the First World War, he was always looking for ways to take the offensive to the enemy. At Chamberlain's request, he had taken over the chairmanship of the Military Coordination Committee from Lord Chatfield, but his strong personality and constant interventions had failed to bring harmony at the top. According to Ian Jacob, a member of the secretariat charged with administering the meetings, "Churchill was so much larger in every way than his colleagues on this committee that it ran like a coach with one wheel twice the size of the other three, and achieved very little with much friction."

Churchill's voice was only one among many in the higher direction of the war, and—as yet—perhaps the loudest but not the most powerful. His attempts to impose his views on the Cabinet, the Army, the Royal Air

Force, and the military commanders, without the authority or machinery to control the operation, contributed to the ensuing failure.

Norway 1940: The Epitome of a Muddle

The Norway Campaign from April 8 to June 10, 1940, was characterized, disastrously, by muddled thinking and poor planning at the strategic, operational, and tactical levels of war. Its failure was a deep embarrassment for Britain and her Allies, a catastrophe for the Norwegians, and another military success for Nazi Germany.

At the top of the strategic chain of command was the Supreme War Council, set up under the terms of the Anglo-French Alliance. Below that was the War Cabinet of nine members, which included the three single service ministers. From October 1939, there was also the Military Coordination Committee charged with ensuring coordination between the three services. Unfortunately, its chairman, initially Lord Chatfield and then Churchill, was given no executive powers. The fourth level of decision-making was the Chiefs of Staff Committee, chaired by the chief of staff who had been longest in post. At the start of the war, this was Air Chief Marshall Sir Cyril Newall, the chief of the Air Staff, the service least involved with the Norway Campaign.

To illustrate the problem, in April 1940, the first month of the Norway Campaign, this cumbersome structure resulted in no less than ninety-four meetings: the War Cabinet meeting thirty-one times, the Military Coordination Committee twenty-one times, and the Chiefs of Staff Committee forty-two times. In addition, the chiefs of staff (or a deputy) attended all ninety-four meetings. Were they capable of rational or clearheaded thought? Against this must be contrasted the dictatorial command arrangements in Germany, which saw Adolf Hitler's hands on all the principal levers of power and decision-making.

When democracies face dictatorships, time is not on the side of consensus. Neville Chamberlain was not a Winston Churchill.

If the British machinery directing the war at the strategic level was inefficient, the arrangements at the operational, or campaign, level were equally deficient. There was no overall joint commander for the operation, nor an integrated staff. Each element of the proposed plan was to be commanded by a senior officer from each respective service. The landing force was to be commanded by Major General Pierse Mackesy, and the naval units by Admiral of the Fleet William Boyle, the Earl of Cork and Orrery, two ranks senior but not in overall command. This unsatisfactory situation was compounded by the eventual inclusion of troops from France and Poland and the need to coordinate with the Norwegians themselves. Another measure of the dysfunctionality of the command arrangements was that the two senior officers met for the first time on the quarterdeck of the admiral's flagship in the Norwegian port of Harstad, only after the operation had already begun. It was reported that both men, having saluted respectfully, then fitted their monocles to look at each other. It was only at this point that Cork, who had received no written orders but had been briefed personally by Churchill on the short car journey from the Admiralty to the House of Commons, discovered that Mackesy had been ordered not to make an opposed landing. Cork had been briefed in a diametrically different way.

Space does not allow for detailed discussion of the orders, counterorders, plans made and discarded that characterized the planning and preparation for the British involvement in Norway. Sadly, as deficient as were the command-and-control arrangements, so was the intelligence surrounding potential German operations in Scandinavia. On April 8, 1940, as the Royal Navy began to lay mines in Norwegian waters off the northern port of Narvik, the German military prepared to launch Operation Weserübung—its attack on Denmark and Norway. This took the British completely by surprise. On April 9, German paratroopers dropped on Danish soil and the

Kreigsmarine landed soldiers in Copenhagen. Denmark surrendered very quickly. Simultaneously, German paratroopers captured the airfields at Oslo and Stavanger. Unfortunately, the Royal Navy interpreted this German naval activity as a precursor to the German navy breaking out into the North Sea and threatening both the security of the United Kingdom and that of the sea-lanes of communication to the United States. The British troops, embarked to secure Narvik and show solidarity with the Norwegians, were hastily disembarked as the fleet set to sea to contain the Kreigsmarine. They were left on the dockside in a confusion of manpower and logistic stores. Too late, it was realized that the German operation was focused on controlling Norway itself.

In haste, troops were reembarked, with one of the brigades landing in a different port from its commander. From that moment on, the Allied troops were always at a disadvantage—often without air and artillery support, certainly outnumbered, and struggling to agree to a common cause with their Norwegian hosts and common colleagues. Narvik, the focus of the iron ore export trade, was initially held but then abandoned by the British and her allies when the overall Norway Campaign proved unsustainable and defeat in France became inevitable. Norway was then condemned to a five-year occupation by Nazi Germany.

British attempts to forestall a feared German advance by occupying Norway quickly ended in defeat, bringing about the very Nazi occupation that they had hoped to prevent. The Germans simply outmaneuvered the British. Ironically, while Adolf Hitler celebrated this victory, the failure of the Norway Campaign propelled Winston Churchill into 10 Downing Street. He was the architect of Hitler's eventual demise—little did Hitler know—though, in the short-term, it was not immediately apparent to Churchill either.

To many at the time, this failed amphibious operation was only too reminiscent of another Winston-led project. History seemed to be repeating itself, and Churchill continued to be haunted by the ghosts of Gallipoli. General Ironside, the chief of the Imperial General Staff, felt that in Norway "we have muddled things in every way. Always too late. Changing plans and nobody directing." Had nothing been learned?

Both Ironside and General Ismay, Churchill's military adviser and chief of staff, were clear that amphibious operations of this type were incredibly difficult. Ismay would later reflect on this operation:

Amphibious operations are a very specialised form of warfare. . . . They require highly trained personnel, a great variety of technical equipment, a detailed knowledge of the points at which the landings are to take place, accurate information about the enemy's strength and dispositions, and perhaps above all, meticulous planning and preparation.

He clearly felt the campaign in Narvik had failed because none of those elements were in place. To this day the Joint Services Command and Staff College use the failures at Gallipoli in 1915 and 1916 and in Norway in 1940 as object lessons on how not to construct and conduct an amphibious operation against a peer enemy. The book *Anatomy of a Campaign: The British Fiasco in Norway* by John Kiszely—himself a former director of the higher command and staff course at the Army Staff College, Camberley—is an enduring indictment of the British failure. Like Gallipoli, the Norwegian Campaign was born of Churchill's best intentions. In both cases, he had wanted to progress rapidly the conduct of the wars against Germany—in 1915 to find an alternative to the trench deadlock on the Western Front and in early 1940 to tighten the economic pressure on Germany by interdicting the supply of Swedish iron ore to Germany, on which her industry so heavily depended. However attractive both aspirations were in grand strategic terms and however bravely British troops fought at the tactical level on the ground in both campaigns, the absence of sound preparation and planning at the operational—or campaign—level doomed both ventures to failure.

Despite the strategic muddle and the operational level confusion, the British soldier on the ground, the sailor at sea, and the airman aloft did all that their country could have demanded. A snapshot illustrates the consequences of the muddle and confusion. Stan Hollis's regiment, the Green Howards, sent its First Battalion to fight in Norway. After six months on the Maginot Line in France, it was suddenly recalled to England on April 17, then transported to Scotland and, with no winter warfare equipment or training, found itself dispatched on four Royal Navy ships to Norway on April 26. Disembarking at Andalsnes, well south of Narvik, fierce battles were fought by the battalion, sometimes in three or four feet of snow, stemming the German advance down the Gubrandsdalen valley toward the town of Otta, where casualties were heavy among officers and men. Amid further confusion about the operational plan, the battalion was reembarked at Andalsnes on May 2, arriving in Scapa Flow the next morning. We talk about a week being a long time in politics, but what about a week in the life of a British infantryman? The final evacuation of some 29,000 British servicemen was complete by June 10 when the situation in Norway, exacerbated by events in France, was deemed hopeless and the survival of the British Army for another day became paramount. King Haakon VII of Norway would ultimately become colonel in chief of the Green Howards, in honor of the First Battalion's heroic defense of Otta (an honor continued through King Olav V to King Harold V, until the Green Howards were amalgamated with other regiments in 2006), but all this lay far in the future for Stan Hollis in 1940.

In the immediate term, the ensuing parliamentary debate on the failures of the campaign quickly became a test of Chamberlain's government. Churchill was now walking a deadly tightrope. He had to wind up the debate for the government. He needed to defend the action while also preserving his reputation as a potential prime minister in waiting. On November 15, 1915, the failure at Gallipoli had cost him his job as First Lord of the Admiralty. Now, almost a quarter of a century later, he found himself defending the same post and a similar action as he endeavored to explain the failure in Norway to a fractious House of Commons. Fellow MP Harold Nicolson felt he managed to achieve this "almost impossible task . . . with absolute loyalty and apparent sincerity while demonstrating by the brilliance of his personality that he has really nothing to do with this confused and timid gang."

He was helped by the fact that those leading the charge against Chamberlain, men like Admiral Sir Roger Keyes and Leo Amery, had no interest in bringing Churchill down. The various opposition groups were only united in their desire for a more vigorous and efficient prosecution of the war. Churchill's long vocal campaign against the appeasement of Hitler meant that he was considered so much the war leader that he could not be dropped. But that did not mean that he would automatically become prime minister. The debate became a vote of confidence in Chamberlain. The embattled prime minister appealed to his friends to support him, but when the government majority was slashed from 213 to just 81, it was clear that his government would have to be reconstructed.

It was external factors that facilitated Churchill's survival and transformed his prospects. Neville Chamberlain may have weathered the storm of criticism over his failed appeasement policies, but the early months of the war had demonstrated that he was no war leader, nor indeed did he have either the ability or appetite to be so. There was a growing, if grudging, acceptance by many in the Conservative Party that change was needed and that a national cross-party government should be formed. The new prime minister would need to be a Conservative, as they remained the largest party in the House (an election while fighting in Europe being out of the question). The Labour Party refused to serve under Chamberlain. Lord Halifax, the foreign secretary, was the preferred choice of many in the establishment, including the king and Chamberlain, but he was in the House of Lords. The power was in the Commons. More a man of diplomacy than war, Halifax had the sense to see that he would struggle to control MPs in their current belligerent mood. The crucial meeting to determine the succession happened on the evening of May 9 (though Churchill later placed it on May 10). Chamberlain, Churchill, and Halifax gathered in a private conclave. There was an awkward silence. Then Halifax ruled himself out.

The stars were already coalescing around Churchill when fate intervened. Early in the morning of May 10, the Germans launched Fall

Gelb—Case Yellow (also known as the Manstein Plan)—their attack on Holland, Belgium, Luxembourg, and France.

It was against this background that Winston Churchill found himself at his moment of destiny. By the end of the day he was prime minister. The criticisms of the Norwegian Campaign quickly paled into insignificance as the disastrous battles in Holland, Belgium, and France unfolded. Numerically superior but operationally outclassed, the Dutch, Belgian, British, and French armies were split by the audacious German thrust through the Ardennes, across the Meuse and toward the Channel. It all happened very quickly.

In the early hours of May 15, Churchill's slumber was broken by a desperate telephone call from the French prime minister, Paul Reynaud:

> He spoke in English, and evidently under stress. "We have been defeated." As I did not immediately respond he said again: "We are beaten; we have lost the battle."

This was far more serious than Norway. British war planning had been built on the foundations of Anglo-French cooperation. The two countries had formed a Supreme War Council bringing together their respective leaders to coordinate strategy. In the event of any major German offensive in northwestern Europe, it was expected that the British Expeditionary Force would fight under the command of the larger French Army. The Royal Air Force would help secure the skies above France while the Royal Navy would keep the Channel open and blockade German ports.

Why Did Things Go So Wrong for the British Army in France, May–June 1940?

The British Expeditionary Force had deployed to France at the outbreak of war in September 1939 and had spent that winter developing the Gort Line (named for General Lord Gort, their commander in chief)—an extension of the French Maginot Line. This was the French response to the First World War, a heavily fortified line of static defenses to protect the fatal avenue—as historian Richard Holmes called it—between Germany and France, and down which the Germans had successfully advanced in 1871 and, nearly to success, in 1914. The French response was reflected in concrete and fixed-gun emplacements—they shall not pass— albeit tempered by the realization that battle tanks had a role in counter maneuvers. The Gort Line, constructed by sweating British engineers and infantrymen during the so-called Phoney War of the winter of 1939–1940, was the British Expeditionary Force's contribution to the renewed entente cordiale.

The Germans and the British had learned different lessons from the battles on the Western Front in 1918—the German spring offensive in March and the Allied Hundred Days Offensive that began in August. The Germans had demonstrated that specially trained troops, breaking through an enemy front line, could cause panic in the rear and lead to a defeatist mindset, and that in any future war such a situation should be exploited by armored troops, not marching infantry, who would quickly become exhausted. They studied the British use of tanks—tanks closely supported by infantry, artillery, and air power—and reflected on the lessons after the war drawn from the Hundred Days Offensive by J. F. C. Fuller and Basil Liddell Hart. These British military theorists expounded the virtues of an armored thrust leading to an expanding torrent of threat into an enemy's rear areas. In Britain, these novel ideas were toyed with through half-hearted experiments involving the deployment of an armored force in the late 1920s and early 1930s, but they were rejected. Financial constraints, the distractions of Empire and Irish Home Rule, an innate conservatism in the military establishment, and a conviction that the First World War had been, or must be, the war to end all wars, meant that the British Expeditionary Force that deployed in 1939 to France was a mechanized army in lorries, but one that would face a German army in tanks, closely supported by air power. The German commanders Heinz Guderian and Erich von Manstein had learned and applied the writings of Fuller and Liddell Hart, but the British had not.

There were a few exceptions. Later, we will meet Major General Percy Hobart. He was one of the few who anticipated the scale and speed of mechanized warfare. He would also play a key role in applying heavy armor on D-Day. Liddell Hart will also make another appearance, though for a rather different reason.

The implications of the fall of France were catastrophic. Defeat on the continent meant the loss of Britain's major ally and brought German forces to within easy striking distance of the UK's shores. What signal would this send to other countries? Would President Roosevelt and the United States view the war in Europe as lost? Might Spain take advantage of British weakness to seize Gibraltar? Would Benito Mussolini bring fascist Italy into the conflict and attack British interests in Malta, Egypt, or the Middle East? What about the French fleet? If allowed to fall into enemy hands and combined with German and Italian naval forces, would it threaten British supremacy in the Mediterranean and Atlantic? Could Japan enter the conflict and move against the British Empire in the East? Such were the questions flashing through Churchill's mind.

He initially refused to accept Reynaud's defeatism. At this stage, Churchill still felt the French defeat was largely psychological. After tense debates in the British War Cabinet, he supported sending further British fighter aircraft for the defense of France. But the reality hit home when he visited Paris the following day and observed the deteriorating situation for himself. The Germans were now expected to arrive in the French capital within hours, where both the French ministry for foreign affairs and the British Embassy were burning their archives. "Utter dejection was written on every face." Determined to support his beloved French ally to the last, Churchill asked the fundamental question of Marshal Maurice Gamelin, the French Army commander in chief: *"Ou est la Masse de Manoeuvre?"* Where were the French operational reserves?

"*Aucune.*" There are none, was the stunning reply.

Churchill must have known at that moment the Battle of France was lost. He told Lady Campbell, the wife of the British ambassador, "This place will shortly become a charnel house."

The Dutch quickly surrendered. After more of a fight, so too did the Belgians, leaving the First French Army and the British Expeditionary Force with the unenviable choice between encirclement and annihilation or evacuation to Britain. Fortunately for the future prosecution of the war, Lord Gort recommended the latter. The so-called miracle of Dunkirk ensued, and the majority of the British Army found its way back home, courtesy of the Royal Navy and the fleet of little ships, albeit without almost all its equipment. For Stan Hollis, the retreat to Dunkirk was a bewildering disaster. As his commanding officer's dispatch motorbike rider, leading counterattacks along with his comrades in the Sixth Green Howards, he was among the last to defend the Dunkirk beachhead and be evacuated, albeit it on a stretcher, having been wounded during the withdrawal. He was recommended for the Military Medal.

But Churchill had not yet given up on France. Edward Spears, a close friend of the British prime minister, now freshly installed as Churchill's personal representative to Prime Minister Reynaud, witnessed Winston's arrival in Paris on Friday, May 31, 1940, and recalled him being as "fresh as a daisy, obviously in grand form. . . . Danger, the evocation of battle, invariably acted as a tonic and stimulant to Winston Churchill." His energy contrasted with the defeatism of the French leadership. No doubt he liked to be at the heart of the action, but it also fell upon him to project an image of confidence. Against the backdrop of the unfolding crisis on the beaches of Dunkirk, he emphasized in his clumsy French that the French and British soldiers would leave the beaches "*bras dessus, bras dessous*" (arm in arm).

In the end, more than 338,000 men (of whom some 140,000 were French and Belgian) were successfully taken across the Channel. This was far higher than initial estimates, but Churchill was still careful in his report to the House of Commons on June 4, 1940, "not to assign to this deliverance the attributes of a victory. Wars are not won by evacuations." Responding to criticism by the soldiers on the beaches about the absence of the Royal Air Force and the perception that they were left exposed to attacks by the Luftwaffe, he argued that the British fighter planes had provided a largely effective cordon. A similar argument could be made in favor of the Royal Navy, which had organized, supplemented, and defended the smaller merchant ships undertaking the operation. The advice that Churchill was getting from his chiefs of staff was that Britain could still resist invasion and reequip its army if it could hold the skies and seas surrounding the country. The power to do both would also be vital to any successful return to France. And it is interesting to note that the naval planning for Dunkirk (codenamed Operation Dynamo) was carried out by Vice Admiral Bertram Ramsay, who would ultimately do the same for Operation Neptune (the naval aspect of Overlord) in 1944. Some of the seeds for D-Day were already being planted in defeat. With the benefit of hindsight, perhaps Winston was right to state that "there was a victory, inside this deliverance, which should be noted."

At the time, victory was less apparent. His speech that day is now best remembered for its lines about defending the United Kingdom "whatever the cost may be" by fighting on the beaches and the landing grounds and in the fields, streets, and hills. But he did not just mean in Britain, defiantly declaring that "we shall fight in France." Even then, he hoped to salvage something from the wreckage of the original Allied strategy. Rescued French forces were quickly repatriated. The Fifty-first Highland Division continued to fight in France before ultimately being forced to surrender. While the Fifty-second Lowland Division and the First Canadian Division were quickly dispatched as a second British Expeditionary Force, only to be evacuated just days later. Under huge pressure from the French to send more fighter aircraft, Churchill's natural instinct was to do just that. His political and military colleagues rightly persuaded him to hold them back.

And yet Churchill still refused to abandon France. As the endgame approached and German forces moved toward Paris, he made repeated attempts to rally the French government, which was now retreating southward. He urged the French to continue the war from their North African empire and to fight a guerrilla campaign in France. He advocated continued resistance by the Allies in Brittany. Despite the clear dangers in flying so close to the front line, he met with Reynaud at Briare on June 11 and at Tours just two days later on June 13.

The accounts of their final meeting could not be more poignant. The British delegation landed on an airport runway pockmarked with bomb craters, with no one there to greet them. They had to borrow a car and persuade a café to open in order to get a meal. When they finally obtained a meeting with the French prime minister, an exhausted and depressed Reynaud saw "no light at the end of the tunnel" and asked to be allowed to make a separate peace with Germany. Churchill, while refusing to agree to this, recognized that there was little he could do to prevent it. He begged Reynaud to make one more appeal to President Roosevelt for an American intervention before pursuing such a course. Then he ended on a characteristically defiant note, confirming that "his confidence that Hitlerism would be smashed and that Nazidom could not and would not over-rule Europe remained absolutely unshaken." It would be four long years, almost to the day, before Winston returned to France in the week following D-Day.

In the interim, some of the Frenchmen he met at those fateful meetings would face German retribution. Georges Mandel, Reynaud's minister of the interior and an outspoken critic of Nazism, would be executed, while Paul Reynaud would be imprisoned. Yet it was also at this time that Churchill first noticed General Charles de Gaulle, then a junior French defense minister and clearly in favor of continuing the conflict. Churchill may or may not have referred to him as a man of destiny, but he clearly identified him as someone with whom the British could work. Spears smuggled him out of France in an airplane just before the armistice and de Gaulle famously addressed the French nation via the radio services of the BBC on June 18. He spoke just after Churchill had made his "Finest Hour" broadcast, urging French soldiers and workers to join him in Britain to continue the struggle against Germany and declaring that the flame of French resistance will not be extinguished. The Free French movement was born.

It was the message of continued resistance that Churchill wanted to promote. He wanted to find creative ways to keep France in the fight even after the fall of France. He had even been prepared to endorse a scheme, promoted by Jean Monnet (a future founding father of European unity, then working in London to coordinate Franco-British war supplies), de Gaulle, and others, for full Franco-British union. It allowed Jock Colville, one of Churchill's Private Secretaries, to joke in his diary that the French fleur-de-lys might soon be restored to the British Royal Standard.

The pooling of national sovereignty would certainly have been a powerful, symbolic gesture. It would also have allowed the transfer of French arms, troops, and gold to British soil, while potentially keeping French North Africa and the French fleet in the conflict on the Allied side. Sadly, it was not to be. The offer was made but only reached France after the collapse of Reynaud's government. The new regime under Marshal Pétain, Laval, and Admiral Darlan was set upon the armistice and obtaining what independence they could still get from Hitler. They were in no mood for unity with Britain. This would have repercussions. Hitler would occupy Paris and northern France, while the Vichy republic would be set up in the south, nominally independent but in reality dependent for its existence on Germany. Britain would be forced to view Vichy France as a potentially hostile power and to look across the Atlantic for a new alliance with the United States. If there was a glimmer of hope, it lay to the West where the fall of France acted to spur American rearmament. President Roosevelt had cause to be anxious. If Britain fell, too, then Germany would have clear access across the Atlantic.

It is against this bleak backdrop that Churchill made his "Finest Hour" broadcast on June 18, 1940. Referring to the offer "to conclude a union of common citizenship" with France, he pledged:

However matters may go in France or with the French Government, or other French Governments, we in this Island and in the British Empire will never lose our sense of comradeship with the French people. If we are now called upon to endure what they have been suffering, we shall emulate their courage, and if final victory rewards our toils they shall share the gains, aye, and freedom shall be restored to all.

Broadcasting over the BBC at 21:00 hours, Churchill had no choice but to respond to the unfolding crisis. He had prepared carefully. The heavily annotated draft notes for his speech show him wrestling with the implications of these momentous events and struggling to find the right response. They are literally a first draft of history. Dictated to his duty secretary, they were first set down in normal typescript for the prime minister to correct. Once the text had been approved, it was then taken away and retyped at a size that fit comfortably into his jacket pocket, and in the blank verse format that he used to aid his delivery.

His peroration was one that still echoes down the ages, helping to secure his place in history. Having noted that, "What General Weygand calls 'the battle of France' is over. The battle of Britain is about to begin," Churchill built up to a dramatic finale, laden with deliberate echoes of Shakespeare's *Henry V*, declaring:

> Let us therefore brace ourselves to
> our duty, and so bear ourselves that
> if the British Empire and
> Commonwealth last for a
> thousand years, men will still
> say,
> "This was their Finest Hour."

Note: The layout of this extract reflects how Winston liked to set out the text of his speeches, in a blank verse format like poetry.

Yet to his Private Secretary, Jock Colville, listening to his boss on the wireless, this was far from a triumph. "It was too long and he [Churchill] sounded tired. . . . He smoked a cigar the whole time he was broadcasting." It was little wonder that Churchill was tired. Few leaders in modern times can have endured the sustained pressure that he had experienced the previous six weeks.

Churchill was a Francophile. His American mother had been brought up largely in Paris, at the court of Emperor Napoleon III. An admirer of French history and culture, he had fought alongside French troops in the First World War and worked with their leading politicians in war and peace. His love of French food and wine is well documented. The south of France is where he had always gone to write, to paint, to gamble, and to recharge his batteries. He had failed to foresee the speed and totality of the French collapse, and he had worked tirelessly to try to prevent it. The diary of his daughter Mary, then just seventeen, provides an insight into the prevailing depression that the French armistice engendered within his personal family circle. Her entry for Monday, June 17, reads:

> Today came the announcement that following Reynaud's resignation and Pétain's assumption of the leadership France asks for peace terms.
> Oh *chère* France—I can never love you one jot less—but why have you failed in this. We have been expecting this—& yet now it has come—we all feel shocked—bereaved of a great & brilliant ally. Now we are alone. . . .

Churchill had embraced de Gaulle and his Free French movement and pledged himself to a policy of restoring what he called the "genius of France." Britain may not have left the continent willingly, but in the short-term, she was in no position to contemplate a return in strength. Now came some very hard decisions. Churchill's promise of comradeship was to be immediately tested by events.

Within days, and on his orders, those elements of the French fleet that refused to surrender to the Royal Navy were engaged by the British and several French ships were sunk. At Mers-el-Kébir in French Algeria, almost 1,300 French sailors lost their lives at the hands of their former British allies. Churchill was moved to tears when announcing the action in the House of Commons, but most MPs cheered. The action sent a clear message to the United States. Britain was not going to go the way of France. But relations with de Gaulle and the Free French were undoubtedly damaged. At a Downing Street lunch, de Gaulle implied that rather than rallying the French behind the British, this action might tempt them to turn their guns against their former allies. His words incurred the wrath of his hostess, the prime minister's loyal wife, Clementine, a fluent French speaker. Relations with France were now complicated.

By the end of 1940, Britain had been forced out of continental Europe. Churchill's immediate priority was national survival. In the coming weeks, the young men of the Royal Air Force and the just-in-time supply of Hurricanes and Spitfires would thwart Hitler's ambition to invade the English coast. Had Lord Halifax, not Winston, succeeded Chamberlain as prime minister then the outcome might have been very different. Halifax favored some form of negotiation to prevent further bloodshed, and his ultimately unsuccessful bid to advocate this course of action while serving as Churchill's foreign secretary provides the inspiration and starting point for the Hollywood movie *Darkest Hour* (2017). It was an argument that Churchill won on the grounds that any German invasion could still be resisted.

Ironically, Britain was protected from enemy invasion by the very same obstacles that prevented an early British return to the continent. It was just as difficult for Hitler to launch a successful amphibious invasion of Britain as it was for Churchill to cross back to France. There was an uneasy stalemate as the two opposing armies fortified the beaches on either side of the Channel. But this did not mean that Churchill had given up on cross-Channel operations. He knew that the defeats in Norway and France had left Britain too weak for a return in force, especially while the Luftwaffe was still bombing British cities and factories. His room to maneuver was severely limited; his political position might not have survived another major defeat. But that did not mean he countenanced doing nothing.

In a brief note to General Ismay, issued on June 4, 1940, the very day of his "fight on the beaches" speech, Churchill wrote:

> The completely defensive habit of mind which has ruined the French must not be allowed to ruin all our initiative. It is of the

highest consequence to keep the largest number of German forces all along the coasts of the countries they have conquered, and we should immediately set to work to organise raiding forces on these coasts where the populations are friendly. . . . How wonderful it would be if the Germans could be made to wonder where they were going to be struck next, instead of forcing us to try to wall in the Island and roof it over!

Resistance in France was to be encouraged. The order went out to set Europe ablaze. A new Special Operations Executive was set up to coordinate operations behind enemy lines. Commando operations were gradually scaled up; starting with small, single-boat attacks led by men like Captain March Phillips and graduating to larger raids, like Operation Chariot, which boldly knocked out the Normandy dry docks at St. Nazaire.

It was into this male-dominated world that a young woman was suddenly plunged, finding herself at "the vanguard of a revolution." Aged just twenty-nine, Joan Bright was efficient and adventurous, glamorous and respectable, sociable and trustworthy. One of five daughters in "an average family with a less than average income," her upbringing may have lacked money, but it was rich in experience. She was born in Argentina to British parents and spent her early years in Spain before returning to England. Actively encouraged by her family to find her own way in life, she trained as a secretary and never looked back:

> With a shorthand pad and typewriter I could be a valuable and mobile interpreter of others' thoughts, a human machine with the power to give and receive confidence.

In the early 1930s, she worked at the British legation in Mexico City. On her return, she turned down roles working for the British Conservative politician Duff Cooper and the German Deputy Führer Rudolf Hess. What she accepted instead was a top-secret job working for a new clandestine unit within the British Secret Intelligence Service. Section D of MI(R) was charged with planning subversion and sabotage behind enemy lines. She joined in the spring of 1939, doing her bit for the British war effort before war had even been declared.

From offices in London's Caxton Street, she helped organize the first guerrilla operations in Norway, in support of the Battle of Narvik. Section D did not last. It was quickly subsumed within Churchill's new Special Operations Executive, with some of its functions passing to Combined Operations, but Joan observed the small beginnings of the fight back that would lead to Normandy in 1944. Her skills had not gone unnoticed. She was moved to the Joint Planning Secretariat at the heart of the British war machine and was soon working and living in the eye of the storm. When the Luftwaffe unleashed its bombs in the Blitz, a concerted bombing campaign to cow London and other British cities, she lived through it all. Her flat was destroyed, colleagues were killed—but Joan kept calm and carried on.

Churchill's response was to promise the people that he would "give it 'em [the Germans] back." One strong strand of that pledge was to step up operations against enemy targets in France. These were to be planned and executed by his new Combined Operations Command; its leaders chosen for their willingness to take the fight to the enemy. He turned first to Admiral Sir Roger Keyes, a veteran of naval raids during the First World War, and then to Lord Louis Mountbatten, a personal favorite with royal connections. By the time of his appointment in 1942, Mountbatten's exploits on board HMS *Kelly* had already been turned into a wartime propaganda movie by Noel Coward. Larger than life on the big screen, Mountbatten was depicted as the sort of dashing commander who would always take the fight to the enemy, described by the historian Correlli Barnett as the "Sam Goldwyn of Combined Operations." This was exactly the image Churchill wanted his commanders to embody.

The Combined Operations Command emerged from the failures of Gallipoli and Narvik. It was a deliberate attempt to coordinate amphibious operations and end interservice muddle and rivalry. Mountbatten was promoted to vice admiral but was also given the honorary army and air force ranks of lieutenant general and air marshal to reflect the unique tri-service nature of his new command. He became a member of the Chiefs of Staff Committee, gaining a place at the top table and direct access to the prime minister. It was clear to Mountbatten that his brief was to facilitate the return to France. But it was also clear that it was going to take time to build up the necessary resources, experience, and expertise. To do so, he set about building a team. The forty-year-old Captain John Hughes-Hallett was an early and eager recruit. He had been running a Combined Training Center in Scotland and quickly established himself as Mountbatten's key naval adviser. But Mountbatten, like Churchill, was also prepared to include more eccentric figures who would challenge the political orthodoxy and military status quo.

They certainly did not come any more unorthodox than Geoffrey Pyke, a hyperactive ideas man and former radical educationalist who cared nothing for his own personal appearance or for obeying orders. Introduced to Mountbatten by Leo Amery, he became director of programs at Combined Operations and proceeded to bombard his chief with long papers suggesting new equipment and stratagems. Mountbatten called these "Pykeisms," and they were often prefaced by their eccentric author with aphorisms, quotes like "The inconceivables of only two years ago are today's realities."

Pyke's response to defeat in Norway was to suggest new ways of continuing the fight. He too advocated for a behind-the-lines guerrilla campaign, but one that harnessed new technology; advocating hit-and-run actions by specially trained troops on fast mobile snowplows, which he now began to design. When challenged about how such equipment could be kept from the Germans, his response was to argue that it should be hidden in plain sight: making the snowplows look German and adorning them with such notices as *"Verboten"* or "Special-Death-Ray Department," which would stop investigations by inquisitive enemy soldiers. It was not to be his only wild idea. The complex preparations for D-Day would require contributions from both experienced service professionals and maverick thinkers.

Yet, as Combined Operations began to contemplate a return to France, the war was already moving to other theaters. The road to D-Day would be a long one that would detour through Washington, DC, and North Africa. Narvik and Dunkirk had been visceral reminders of the difficulties of amphibious operations and the limitations of British military power.

For Churchill, after his inspiring speeches to rally and buttress the morale and will of the British people, came the realization that wars were not won by evacuations but by success on the battlefield. He was personally committed to a policy of waging war until final victory, and victory meant the defeat of the Germans in Europe. But that prospect still seemed a very long way off, if ever possible, in the autumn of 1940.

THE WHITE HOUSE
WASHINGTON

April 3
11 pm

Dear Winston

What Harry ~ Geo. Marshall will
tell you all about has my heart &
mind in it. Your people & mine
demand the establishment of a front
to draw off pressure on the Russians,
& these peoples are wise enough
to see that the Russians are today
killing more Germans & destroying
more equipment than you & I
put together. Even if full

*Letter from President Roosevelt
to Winston Churchill, April 3,
1942. (Churchill Papers, CHAR
20/52/29)*

success is not attained, the
big objective will be.

So to it =! Syria & Egypt
will be made more secure, even if
the Germans find out about
our plans.

Best of luck — make Harry
go to bed early & let him
obey Dr. Fulton U.S.N. whom
I am sending with him as
super nurse with full
authority

As ever
FDR

Chapter 3

Arguments with Allies

"No lover ever studied every whim of his mistress as I did those of President Roosevelt."

"NEVER IN THE FIELD OF HUMAN CONFLICT WAS SO MUCH OWED BY SO many to so few." With those immortal words, Winston Churchill summed up the achievement of the young fighter pilots during the Battle of Britain.

With them, came the awful realization that Great Britain and her Empire were alone and on the front line. The Royal Air Force had secured the skies, the Royal Navy controlled the domestic waters around the British Isles, but the Army at home was still licking its wounds after Dunkirk and gallantly standing ready—along with the Home Service Volunteers, "Dad's Army"—to defend the beaches, should Hitler still be minded to invade. But there was a war to fight and an enemy, now joined by Italy, to be defeated. On, above, and under the surface of the ocean, the Battle of the Atlantic was being fought to secure Britain's strategic lifelines to the United States and the Empire, the first faltering bomber attacks had begun against targets in Germany, and the army in North Africa was enjoying some surprising success against, not the Germans, but the Italians, whose military hubris had exceeded their capabilities.

The two dates that changed the course of the war were June 22, 1941, and December 7, 1941. From those moments onward, Churchill knew that Britain, her Empire and Commonwealth, were no longer fighting alone. When the Wehrmacht launched Hitler's ill-conceived strategic attempt to gain *lebensraum* ("living space") in the west of the Soviet Union for the ethnic German people and secure the oil reserves of the Caucasus and the agricultural resources of Ukraine and Byelorussia, Churchill knew that Stalin and the Soviet Union had become allies in his fight against Germany. Although ideologically odd bedfellows, the old dictum that "the enemy of my enemy is my friend" became the pragmatic foundation of a distrustful but mutually beneficial relationship between Stalin and Churchill. Or as Churchill put it to his Private Secretary, Jock Colville, "If Hitler invaded Hell, I would at least make a favourable reference to the Devil in the House of Commons."

Although Stalin, as well as Franklin Roosevelt later, were suspicious and, at times, critical of Britain's Mediterranean and imperial obligations, it was Hitler's decision to secure his southern flank before launching Operation Barbarossa that probably prevented Stalin's defeat in front of Moscow in the winter of 1941–1942. The British were assisting the Greeks, and an anti-Nazi coup took place in Yugoslavia. Hitler fatally delayed his attack on the Soviet Union from early to mid-summer, pausing to defeat Greece and Yugoslavia first. By the time his much-vaunted panzer armies in their thin summer uniforms had reached the outskirts of Moscow, winter had set in, and the chance of an outright German strategic victory was gone. For Churchill this was the first of those two lifelines.

The second materialized out of a clear blue sky on the morning of Sunday, December 7, 1941, when aircraft from the Imperial Japanese Naval Service attacked the US Pacific Fleet at its moorings in Pearl Harbor, causing catastrophic damage (though it was lucky that the aircraft carriers were at sea). The next day, while the Japanese were also attacking the British colony of Hong Kong, the United States declared war on Japan. By December 11, the United States also declared war against Germany and Italy, made easier by Hitler's declaration of war against the United States. From Churchill's point of view, he had achieved what he had set out to do since becoming prime minister in May 1940—to get the United States into the war against Germany, and Italy, for good measure.

It could be said that if the declarations of war were just the overture, the main movements were to be the agreements over strategy and the sequencing of campaigns to defeat Germany, Italy, and Japan. However, as Churchill was about to discover, waging war with allies who had conflicting strategic objectives and timetables demanded statesmanship of the highest order, ultimately to be played out on the world stage in major conferences over the course of the next three years. Yet, in December 1941, for Churchill and Roosevelt and their military staffs, the initial priority was to hammer out an agreed Western position before sitting down with the Soviet Union's Joseph Stalin. That would come later.

Churchill and Roosevelt spoke on the phone in the immediate aftermath of Pearl Harbor. The American president confirmed events with the words, "We are all in the same boat now." Churchill later wrote that he slept the sleep of the saved and thankful, declaring:

So we had won after all! Yes, after Dunkirk; after the fall of France; after the horrible episode of Oran [the attack on the French fleet]; after the threat of invasion, when, apart from the Air and Navy, we were almost an unarmed people; after the deadly struggle of the U-boat war—the first Battle of the Atlantic, gained by a hand's breadth; after seventeen months of lonely fighting and nineteen months of my responsibility in dire stress. We had won the war.

With the benefit of hindsight, he glossed over the many frustrations he had experienced in courting Roosevelt and the United States. Churchill was half American by birth—his beautiful mother born in Brooklyn, New York—and he proudly asserted that "American blood flowed in my veins." He had visited the United States in 1895, 1900–1901, 1929, and 1931–1932, spending time touring its major cities, meeting its leading people, and writing about its history, culture, and customs. After 1940 he was determined to drag the Americans in, admitting that, "No lover ever studied every whim of his mistress as I did those of President Roosevelt."

He had always believed that this moment would come, that America would not abandon the Western democracies, but his faith had been sorely tested. It had proved a far more protracted and costly process than he had hoped. He had been forced to cede British bases for American destroyers, give up British gold reserves, and accept deferred payments for vital Lend Lease supplies. Roosevelt had inched toward war, gradually assuming an ever-greater role in the defense of the Atlantic, but it was Japanese aggression rather than British diplomacy that had finally forced the United States onto the battlefield.

Churchill's relief at the materialization of the Anglo-America alliance was no doubt real and palpable. It certainly changed the dynamic of the war, creating the grand alliance against fascism that would ultimately make Overlord possible, but it came with its own complications. His confidence that now America was in the harem, Britain could "talk to her quite differently" would prove equally overconfident.

The prime minister certainly moved quickly. He lost no time in visiting Washington, keen to argue that the highest priority for the Western allies was a policy of Europe first or, more specifically, the defeat of Germany first. This was no easy case to make, given American anger against Japan, and was made even more difficult by the news that the Japanese had sunk the two British Royal Navy battleships HMS *Prince of Wales* and HMS *Repulse* on December 10, 1941, when they were embarrassingly caught without air cover. This left Japan as masters of the Pacific and Britain's imperial possessions of Malaya, Singapore, and Burma at great risk. A potential threat to India could not be discounted. At the ensuing Arcadia Conference between Britain and the United States, Churchill managed to achieve agreement that a holding action would be fought against Japan in the Pacific, while the main effort of Allied forces would concentrate on the defeat of Germany first. Thereafter all forces would be concentrated against Japan. For Churchill and the United Kingdom, after more than two years of war, this was a strategic success of utmost significance.

Yet, while that conference agreed on the main muscle movements between the Western allies, it did nothing to placate Stalin who continued to argue strongly at every opportunity for a Second Front to be opened in Western Europe. He urged a return to France by the armies of the United Kingdom and the United States to take the pressure off the Red Army, which had been comprehensively mauled, but not beaten, in the early months of Barbarossa. Yet, in 1942, neither the United States nor Britain was remotely capable of considering such an operation in strength. As in 1917, the US Army was faced with the challenge of expanding its size and capability to become a major participant in the war in Europe and elsewhere. It may already have been growing rapidly, with a million and a half officers and men by the middle of 1941, but it lacked training, combat experience, and equipment. It would take time for the American economy to realize its full production potential. By 1942, the Americans were garrisoning Iceland, but they had less than five thousand men in the United Kingdom and only two divisions en route.

For the British, the problem was one of war weariness and imperial overstretch. By 1942, they were already heavily committed in the Mediterranean and North Africa; stuck in a fight that had begun in late 1940 against the Italians. This had been the one theater in which Churchill had been able to take the fight to the enemy. The Mediterranean Fleet under Admiral Cunningham and the army in Egypt under General Sir Archibald Wavell had initially achieved significant successes against Mussolini's forces, and for a while it had looked as though North Africa might be cleared of the enemy by early 1941. In February, Lieutenant General Richard O'Connor had marked the defeat of Italian forces in the Libyan desert with a very British message (based on hunting terminology), signaling to his superior, General Wavell: "Fox killed in the open." Perhaps O'Connor could have advanced farther to Tripoli and finished off the war in North Africa for good, but Churchill's eyes had turned somewhat prematurely toward defending Greece and fighting in the eastern Mediterranean. During the operational pause in the desert after the Italian collapse, Hitler had dispatched the Africa Korps under Lieutenant General Erwin

Rommel to prop up what remained of his Italian ally in North Africa. The success of Rommel in the desert during 1941 resulted in another torrid year for Churchill, but it also set the scene for the emergence of one of the two leading British commanders in the Second World War— Bernard Law Montgomery. (For the curious, the other was William Joseph Slim, commander of the Fourteenth Army in Burma.)

Of course, fighting in North Africa and the Mediterranean was also about defending the Empire. While Roosevelt and Marshall were wary of entangling American forces in defense of the British Empire, Churchill's administration was an imperial government and had no option but to think in terms of imperial defense. Defeat and withdrawal in the Mediterranean threatened to further erode British supply lines to India and the Pacific (via the Suez Canal), risking vital oil supplies in Iran and Iraq, strengthening the Axis powers and—coming on top of earlier defeats—inflicting a potentially lethal blow on British morale. In the early months of 1942, there was a very real fear among British planners that if the Germans, Italians, and Japanese coordinated their strategy, between them they might be able to besiege and close all the main imperial shipping routes and bring Britain to its knees.

The British were too heavily engaged elsewhere to simply break off and refocus on France.

The Allies, and particularly Britain, were still on the defensive, but the arrival of American men and material in the European theater quickly reawakened the debate about the war in the West and the possibility of operations in France.

Churchill was fond of saying that the only thing worse than fighting with allies was fighting without them. By early 1942, he had not one but two powerful new allies, each coming to the top table with their own agendas and strategies for running and winning the war: the Russians desperate for help, and the Americans keen to defeat Germany in Europe as quickly as possible so that they could turn against Japan in the Pacific. The British and Americans had agreed on a "Germany First" strategy, and President Roosevelt was keen to see US troops in action, but the detail was lacking. Various operations had been discussed. Nothing had yet been decided.

It was at this moment that an important letter was handed to Churchill.

> *The White House*
> *Washington*
> *April 3*
> *11pm*
>
> *Dear Winston*
>
> *What Harry and Geo. Marshall will tell you about has my heart & mind in it. Your people & mine demand the establishment of a front to draw off pressure on the Russians, & these peoples are wise enough to see that the Russians are today killing more Germans & destroying more equipment than you and I put together. Even if full success is not attained, the big objective will be.*
>
> *Go to it! Syria and Egypt will be made more secure, even if the Germans find out about our plans.*
>
> *Best of luck. Make Harry go to bed early, and let him obey Dr Fulton, U.S.N. [US Navy], whom I am sending with him as super-nurse with full authority.*
>
> *As ever*
> *FDR*

Most of the wartime communication between Churchill and Roosevelt was conducted by telegram, via transatlantic telephone, or through intermediaries. A handwritten missive from the president was rare and to be taken very seriously. Written out on green White House paper by the president at 11:00 p.m. on April 3, it was hand-delivered to the British prime minister five days later by Harry Hopkins.

Hopkins was one of the president's closest advisers. Physically, he was not in good shape. Cancer had already led to the removal of most of his stomach. He looked gaunt and often disheveled. To Mary Churchill, Winston's daughter, he appeared "painfully thin with wispy hair." Charles Wilson, Churchill's doctor, painted an even grimmer picture: "His lips are blanched as if he had been bleeding internally, his skin yellow like stretched parchment and his eyelids contracted to a slit." This is why Roosevelt had a US naval doctor accompany him on his mission to London.

But physical appearances can be deceptive. Hopkins was a man of incredible energy. He had worked with Roosevelt throughout the 1930s to combat the Great Depression and, since January 1941, had served as the president's main emissary to Winston Churchill, becoming a leading advocate of American support for Great Britain; famously winning the admiration of the British prime minister by expressing that support by quoting a biblical verse from the Book of Ruth: "Whither thou goest, I will go and where thou lodgest I will lodge, thy people shall be my people, and thy God my God."

This time, Hopkins did not arrive in London alone. He was accompanied on his mission by General George Marshall, chief of staff and military head of the United States Army. Six foot tall, smartly dressed, proper, and precise, Marshall was very different from Hopkins, in character and temperament as well as appearance. To Joan Bright, he was a "very upright man" who would never "have ever trimmed his sails or changed a little bit his position to accommodate the person he was talking to." While the two Americans shared the view that the war would be won or lost in Europe and that Hitler was the main enemy, their approach to Churchill and their British allies was very different. Hopkins used friendship, debate, and humor to gain acceptance into Churchill's inner circle; Marshall maintained a deliberate distance. He arrived skeptical of British war strategy, defensive of American independence and determined to prioritize action in France.

The president's letter was designed to open discussions that would lead to the establishment of a new front in Western Europe. It served as the preface to a second document, a secret memorandum. Titled "Operations in Western Europe," this American military plan— developed by Marshall and his protégé General Eisenhower, delivered by Hopkins and endorsed by Roosevelt—could not have been clearer. The United States wanted a cross-Channel operation and as quickly as possible. The language was unambiguous:

OPERATIONS IN WESTERN EUROPE

1.   Western Europe is favored as the theater in which to
stage the first major offensive by the United States and Great
Britain. By every applicable basis of comparison, it is
definitely superior to any other. In point of time required to
produce effective results, its selection will save many months.
Through France passes our shortest route to the heart of Germany. In no other area can we attain the overwhelming air
superiority vital to successful land attack; while here and
here only can the bulk of the British air and ground forces
be employed. In this area the United States can concentrate
and maintain a larger force than it can in any other. A
British-American attack through western Europe provides the
only feasible method for employing the bulk of the combat power
of the United States, the United Kingdom and Russia in a concerted effort against a single enemy.

            Another, and most significant consideration is the
unique opportunity to establish an active sector on this front
this summer, through steadily increasing air operations and by
raids or forays all along the coasts. This initial phase will
be of some help to Russia and of immediate satisfaction to the
public; but what is most important it will make experienced
veterans of the air and ground units, and it will offset the
tendency toward deterioration in morale which threaten the
latter due to prolonged inactivity.

            Finally, successful attack through Western Europe will
afford the maximum possible support to Russia, whose continued
participation in the war is essential to the defeat of Germany.

2.   Decision as to the main effort must be made now. This
is true even if the invasion cannot be launched during this year.
A major attack must be preceded by a long period of intensive

- 1 -

American paper on Operations in Western Europe, 1942.
(Churchill Papers, CHAR 20/52/33)

Western Europe is favoured as the theatre in which to stage the first major offensive by the United States and Great Britain. By every applicable basis of comparison, it is definitely superior to any other. In point of time required to produce effective results, its selection will save many months. **Through France passes our shortest route to Germany.** In no other area can we attain the overwhelming air superiority vital to successful land attack; while here and here only can the bulk of the British air and ground forces be employed. In this area the United States can concentrate and maintain a larger force than it can in any other. A British-American attack through Western Europe provides the only feasible method for employing the bulk of the combat power of the United States, the United Kingdom and Russia in a concerted effort against a single enemy.

The plan proposed immediate cross-Channel air operations and raids to allow troops to gain experience accompanied by an intensive effort to create an invasion force of 5,800 combat aeroplanes and forty-eight divisions, including some one million American troops. The objective was to seize the beaches between Le Havre and Boulogne. Recognizing that it would take time to build up American forces in Britain, the earliest date for D-Day was estimated as April 1, 1943. But the plan also allowed for an earlier operation if the circumstances demanded. A more limited operation was also advocated to establish a beachhead in France in the event of a Russian collapse on the Eastern Front or a German disintegration.

The delivery of this letter and memorandum, and the discussions that followed, marked the arrival of the Americans in the European theater. This was something that Churchill had been hoping for, and working toward, since May 1940. It might be assumed, therefore, that the contents of this letter would be music to his ears. After all, he had pledged himself very publicly to the restoration of France and the destruction of Nazism in Europe. But British weakness meant that he and the British chiefs of staff now favored a very different policy.

In the short-term, Pearl Harbor had only exacerbated their weakness. This was no moment to risk a return across the Channel. In the Pacific, they had been relying on a strong American presence to deter and, if necessary, counter Japanese aggression. The loss of the American fleet had left the British Empire in the East horribly exposed. Within weeks, this had resulted in the loss of Hong Kong, the capitulation of Singapore (the largest surrender in the history of the British Army), and a Japanese threat to the Indian Ocean and Australia. Worse still, the British were on the retreat again in North Africa. Early 1942 was a bleak time. In July 1942, Harry Butcher, Eisenhower's naval aide, noted that, "Rommel can almost smell the Suez and the Japs are knocking at the door of India."

Defeat followed defeat, with insult added to injury by the escape of two German warships from France through the Channel to Germany. It was almost like a rerun of the disasters of 1940, occurring just at the moment that Churchill wanted to impress his new American and Soviet allies. Alexander Cadogan, undersecretary of state at the Foreign Office, confided his fears to his diary. "Our soldiers seem very incapable." . . . "Our generals are no use and do our men fight?"

It was a refrain taken up by the prime minister. "Have you not got a single general in that + who can win battles, have none of them any ideas, must we continually lose battles in this way?" Churchill fired these questions at General Brooke in front of the Cabinet. The chief of the Imperial General Staff struggled to keep his temper and stiff upper lip, gripping his pencils so tightly that they sometimes snapped. In public, he made a robust defense: In private, he too wondered why the troops were not fighting better and in a low moment conceded that half the corps and divisional commanders "lack character, imagination, drive and power of leadership."

Unsurprisingly, opposition to the government's management of the war effort was rising in the press. Churchill was forced to defend his administration's conduct of the war in Parliament. It was into this atmosphere of self-doubt and recrimination that Hopkins and Marshall breezed with their plan for attacking France.

Joan Bright observed it all from her office in Whitehall and would later recall:

> Well I think 1942 was a horrible year . . . I mean the Battle of the Atlantic was really nearly lost that year. It was a horrible year and things were going very badly in the Far East. We were losing all over the place, we were losing. And the Russians were screaming for us to go . . . and land . . . on the Continent, so the Americans and the Russians were sort of slightly anti our point of view.

British troops were desperately trying to hold their positions in North Africa and the Pacific. Seen from London, the strategy was clear: The Allies must weather the immediate storm, clear North Africa, secure the Mediterranean, and only then could they contemplate a return to France. In the meantime, Combined Operations could continue to plan raids of increasing scale against the French shoreline. But Churchill was faced with a dilemma. Having worked hard to create the American alliance, and ultimately dependent on American men and material for final victory, he could not risk alienating the president and Marshall. He could not simply ignore their plan. And so, an elaborate game of diplomacy began.

Tactically, the British decided to nominally accept the US strategy of focusing on France while simultaneously steering their new ally toward the Mediterranean. Hopkins and Marshall were exposed to the full force of Churchillian hospitality. They were wined and dined by the king and the prime minister. On the evening of April 14, they were the guests at a specially convened meeting of the Defence Committee, called to consider the American plan, with key ministers and the chiefs of staff in attendance alongside the prime minister. Churchill opened proceedings by saying "he had no hesitation in cordially accepting the plan," and he ended the meeting with the observation that "it was clear that there was complete unanimity on the framework. The two nations would march ahead together in a noble brotherhood of arms." But the devil was in the detail, and he also made a point of expressing one broad reservation—"it was essential to carry on the defence of India and the Middle East" where Britain could not face the loss of an army of 600,000 men and the "man power of India." Nor, he pointed out, could Britain abandon the defense of Australia. Ominously, the chief of the Air Staff, Charles Portal, felt that the British fighter force would be wiped out in a matter of months if used to support operations in heavily defended French air space alone, without support from American fighters.

So, behind the scenes, Churchill and the British set about persuading, cajoling, and convincing their American counterparts that any return to France could only happen after the completion of their preferred operations in North Africa. The Americans were initially intransigent. Marshall was insistent. If France was not possible then the Americans might turn east against Japan and fight in the Pacific instead. As Hopkins pointed out in the Defence Committee meeting, "If public opinion in America had its way, the weight of American effort would be directed against Japan."

In fact, anticipating the American position, Churchill had already instructed that plans be drawn up for possible operations in France. Suddenly new codewords abounded in Whitehall as possibilities were explored. How would the necessary forces be assembled for a major assault on France? What would a large-scale operation look like? Might there be more immediate, limited opportunities arising out of existing plans for raids against the continent?

In June, Churchill shot down plans to land a division and armored units on the continent for a raid of just two to three days. While still in favor of small-scale raiding operations, he felt that there should be no substantial landing in France "unless we are going to stay" and "unless the Germans are demoralised by another failure against Russia."

With regard to any major assault on France, the British commanders were divided over where landings might take place—on the Normandy beaches (favored by Mountbatten and the Combined Operations staff) or farther north in the Pas-de-Calais (preferred by Fighter Command, as they could operate more easily from British bases)? Churchill seemed to favor attacking everywhere simultaneously. He sent a minute to his chiefs of staff on June 15, expressing his view that the assault should take the form of at least six heavy disembarkations in the first wave, accompanied by at least half a dozen feints, "which, if luck favours them, may be exploited." He was advocating attacks or diversions along a huge stretch of the Atlantic shoreline, in Norway, Denmark, Holland, Belgium, in the Pas-de-Calais, "where the major Air battle will be fought," on the Cotentin Peninsula, at Brest, St. Nazaire, and the mouth of Gironde. Moreover, there should be at least three waves of assault. Perhaps he was being deliberately provocative, trying to flush out the objections of his chiefs of staff, because he concluded that:

> Unless we are prepared to commit the immense forces comprised in the first three waves to a hostile shore with the certainty that many of our attacks will miscarry, and that if we fail the whole stake will be lost, we ought not to attempt such an extraordinary operation of war under modern conditions.

This essentially remained his view until well into 1943. The cross-Channel operation should only be mounted when the chances of success were overwhelming. When the paper was discussed, later that day, he told the chiefs that success "would depend largely on the magnitude and the violence of the first assault, which should be carried out on the broadest possible front." It fell upon the Commanders of Home Forces General Paget, Admiral Ramsay, Air Marshal Sholto Douglas, and their joint planning staff to investigate what was possible and respond. They pointed out that the scale and tempo of any operation would be limited by the lack of assault craft and shipping, by the difficulty of getting on and off the beaches, by the need to seize ports and airfields, and by the capacity of the ports in Southern England to support the operation. The ports of Le Havre and Cherbourg would need to be seized in order to sustain supplies to the front. The Normandy beaches were identified as the most promising landing grounds, but German air power would need to be engaged over the Calais area, as it was nearer to UK air bases. They had identified the major challenges, all of which would continue to cause headaches for the planners over the course of the next two years, but little detailed planning could be done until the bigger strategic questions had been resolved with the Americans. Future plans were also being overtaken by current events.

Unfortunately, things were only getting worse for the British in the Mediterranean. Churchill endured the humiliation of hearing about the fall of Tobruk (Libya) while in the White House with the president later in June. On his return to Britain, he had to face down a confidence vote in his administration in the House of Commons in which the Labour MP Aneurin Bevan made the stinging rebuke that "the Prime Minister wins Debate after Debate and loses battle after battle."

The discussions about the Second Front continued in Washington in June and London in July. The fifty-one-year-old General Dwight D. "Ike" Eisenhower arrived in the British capital to take up his position as American theater commander. Like his mentor, General Marshall, Ike was a firm advocate for the cross-Channel assault. He was also a good diplomat and a natural team builder.

In keeping with the sentiments expressed in the president's letter and accepting that a major invasion was not possible until 1943, the American military commanders continued to argue for some form of limited operation in 1942 to relieve pressure on the Russians. This was given more urgency by the fall of Sevastopol, the last Russian bastion in Crimea. Harry Butcher noted that "the Red Army is carrying the brunt of the battle. The papers at home and in England are filled with demands for a second front." An operation in France was needed "to serve as life-saver to a drowning ally." He also recognized that the British, having suffered a succession of defeats over a three-year period, were understandably more cautious and realistic, while the fresher Americans were "perhaps inclined to take more chances."

By July 1942, there was mounting confusion on both sides of the Atlantic over the various possibilities and their codenames, which the prime minister and president sought to codify in their transatlantic telegram correspondence. Roosevelt set out their final agreement in his telegram of July 9:

COPY.

(44)

WASHINGTON,
July 9th, 1942.
1002

No. 163.   B.D.

The President

PERSONAL TELEGRAM

TO THE PRIME MINISTER.   SERIAL No. T·976/2.
9. VII. 42

Reference your No. 106 of July 6th.   It is recommended that our code words be clarified as follows:

1.   That the term "Bolero" be used to designate the preparation for and movement of United States forces into the European theatre, preparations for their reception therein and the production, assembly, transport, reception, and storage of equipment and supplies necessary for support of the United States forces in operation against the European continent.

2.   That the term "Sledgehammer" be used to designate an offensive operation of the British and American troops against the European continent in 1942 to be carried out in case of German internal collapse or imminent Russian military collapse which necessitates an emergency attack in order to divert German forces from the Russian front.

3.   That the term "Roundup", or any other name which you may desire, be used to designate an offensive operation against German dominated Europe to be carried out by combined American and British forces in 1943 or later.

THE CHARTWELL TRUST

(Sgd)   ROOSEVELT.

Received by teleprinter 9. 7. 42.

Sent to: Gen. Ismay. ✓

59

Telegram from Roosevelt to Churchill, July 9, 1492. (Churchill Papers, CHAR 20/77/101)

The codename for the full-scale assault would evolve over time. Roundup would become Super Roundup, which would ultimately become Overlord.

But in the short-term the president accepted that Roundup could not be contemplated until after Bolero and the buildup of forces. He also recognized that Sledgehammer (the more limited operation) was only likely to take place in an emergency. But the nature of these operations still needed to be worked out. Plans were drawn up for a limited seizure of the Cotentin Peninsula, followed if successful by the liberation of the Channel Islands.

The British continued to push back, and Churchill was determined to be front and center of the discussions. When General Marshall and Admiral King arrived in July 1942 and met with members of the British General Staff before seeing him, it invoked his fury. Butcher's account has him striding up and down the room at Chequers (the prime minister's official country residence) tearing pages from a book of British war laws and berating Harry Hopkins while asserting in the most vigorous language that "he [Churchill] was the man to see first, that he was the man America should deal with, and that the British Army-Navy chiefs were under his command." Resolving strategy with the Americans and resisting their plans for any immediate lodgment in France was a clear prime ministerial priority.

Logistical arguments were carefully deployed. The obvious weakness in the US concept of Sledgehammer was that it would take time to build up the required American forces in Britain. In 1942, the United States could guarantee only three and a half divisions. Even then, complex questions arose as to how the US troops would cross the Atlantic, land on the beaches, and be supplied once ashore. Escorts, tonnage, and landing craft were going to take time to assemble in the right place and numbers. There were not enough landing craft available for a landing in force, and certainly not of the type to land sufficient quantities of tanks and armored vehicles.

In the meantime, the Americans were expecting the British to provide the majority of the troops, the naval support, and aerial protection for any operation. And, with all their other existing commitments, the British simply did not have the numbers, nor did they have full control of the skies above the continent. Even the strategic value of establishing a limited presence across the Channel was questionable. It was not clear how much support it would give the Russians, as the Germans already had a strong presence in France and might not need to withdraw troops from the east. Ultimately, it was unlikely that any bridgehead could be held for long without the ability to feed in sustained reinforcements.

And then there was the risk of being seen to do nothing or too little. If Sledgehammer was not launched and the Anglo-British forces concentrated instead only on Bolero, building up forces in Britain for the later, larger assault would offer no immediate support to the Russians and would see the Allies sitting idle in the west while the Red Army bore all fighting in the east, something both Churchill and Roosevelt were extremely reluctant to countenance. And time was against them. The window for any operation in France was rapidly closing, as the Atlantic winter weather and high tides meant that any cross-Channel operation was better conducted in spring or summer.

By July, Eisenhower was working on the detail for Sledgehammer with Paget, Douglas, and Ramsay. Their report conceded that "owing to a recent re-estimate of the number of landing craft that will be available this autumn, we do not consider the operation can be undertaken before 15 November." Even then, they were unsure that they would have the necessary British gliders or American glider pilots, could not depend on the support of local resistance groups because of the extreme vigilance and activity of the Gestapo, and were clear that the operation could only be considered in the event of a crack in German morale. From the end of September, they could only rely on short periods of consecutive days of good weather and, without a port, it seemed impossible to maintain the beachheads.

Churchill put his views succinctly in one of his celebrated "Action This Day" telegrams to President Roosevelt on July 14, 1942. Styling himself a "Former Naval Person," in recognition of the fact that their wartime correspondence had begun in 1939 when he was still First Lord of the Admiralty, he wrote:

COPY

ACTION THIS DAY

PRIME MINISTER'S
PERSONAL TELEGRAM

SERIAL No. *T. 999/2*.

FORMER NAVAL PERSON TO PRESIDENT
Absolutely Personal and Secret

No.114.

    I am most anxious for you to know where I stand myself at the present time. I have found no one who regards "SLEDGEHAMMER" as possible. I should like to see you do "GYMNAST" as soon as possible, and that we in concert with the Russians should try for "JUPITER". Meanwhile all preparations for "ROUND-UP" in 1943 should proceed at full blast, thus holding the maximum enemy forces opposite England. All this seems to me as clear as noonday.

      W.S.C.

      14. 7. 42.

Telegram from Churchill to Roosevelt, July 14, 1942. (CHAR 20/77/129)

Gymnast was the initial codename for an operation against French North Africa. It would later be rebranded as Operation Torch. Jupiter was an attack on German forces in Norway. The telegram is an expression of Churchill's desire to take the offensive, but not in France where the Germans were strongest and the risks greatest. It is a position he would continue to hold. In a more detailed telegram to the president, he expanded on some of his reasons: The diversion of shipping necessary for a limited Sledgehammer operation in France would damage

British imports. Even if successful, it would hinder, not help, the larger
Roundup assault and the wider war effort by losing essential landing
craft, disrupting the training of troops, creating a narrow front across
the Channel that would have to be sustained to the detriment of the
larger operation, and by diverting planes away from the bombing of
Germany. He chose not to mention the advantages to Britain of securing
North Africa and the Mediterranean, though he did describe Gymnast
as the best way of relieving pressure on the Russians and as "the true
Second Front of 1942" and "the safest and most fruitful stroke that can
be delivered this autumn."

So, an attack on French North Africa was dangled as the best alternative to Sledgehammer; an invasion of Vichy-held (and nominally neutral)
Morocco and Algeria. This would be an American-led operation bringing the United States into the European theater. After all, US forces
might still be welcomed as liberators, while the British were yet to be
forgiven for their action against the French fleet at anchor in Algeria. If
successful, it would relieve pressure on the British fighting in Egypt and
Libya, open up a new front against Rommel's forces in the desert, facilitate a decisive end to the North African campaign, and free up British
forces for campaigning in France. It would enable the Allies to practice
amphibious operations and landings on a less-well-defended shoreline,
where untried US troops would not face veteran German units. The
operation could also take place relatively quickly with overwhelming
Allied naval and air superiority.

It was these practical considerations that gradually tilted Roosevelt
toward Churchill's preferred strategy. The process was helped by continued British weakness in North Africa. There was a dawning realization by the Americans that they could not allow the British to lose
in the Mediterranean. In any event, the US commanders were also
divided among themselves. The Anglophobe Admiral Ernest J. King,
commander in chief of the US Fleet, continued to demand greater
resources for the Pacific theater, which had an inevitable ripple effect
on any supplies for France.

Then came the ill-fated Dieppe raid of August 1942; the next step
in Churchill's strategy of escalating raids against France. The aim

had been to capture and briefly hold the town of Dieppe on the French shoreline; a complex amphibious tri-service operation on a scale not yet attempted by Mountbatten and his Combined Operations team.

The operation was preceded by a fraught exchange in the Cabinet Room on June 30. Captain John Hughes-Hallett, the naval adviser at Combined Operations, was given the unenviable task of presenting the plans to the prime minister:

> Mr. Churchill suddenly turned to me and asked whether I could guarantee success! The C.I.G.S. [General Brooke, later Lord Alanbrooke] interrupted and told me not to reply. "If he, or any-one else, could guarantee success," he said, "there would indeed be no object in doing the operation. It is just because no-one has the slightest idea what the outcome will be that the operation is necessary." Mr. Churchill then said that this was not a moment at which he wanted to be taught adversity. "In that case," said Alanbrooke, "you must abandon the idea of invading France because no responsible General will be associated with any plan-ning for invasion until we have an operation at least of the size of the Dieppe raid behind us to study and base our plans upon."

In any event, there was much to study. The operation went badly. The Canadian Second Division bore the brunt of the assault. There was a stronger than expected enemy presence, which when coupled with poor communications between the ground troops and their air and naval support, resulted in difficulties in landing tanks and heavy armor and a failure to seize key objectives. The Canadians were pinned down and badly mauled on the beaches. The tanks could not climb the shingle beaches. Losses were high. The town was not taken. The failed operation was a stark reminder of the difficulties of conducting such an amphibious assault and consequently another nail in the coffin of Sledgehammer. Seizing an enemy-held port by frontal assault would not be easy. Brooke saw it as a lesson "to the people who are clamouring for an invasion of France." Churchill also preferred to view it as a lesson and would not "hear of the word 'failure,'" but the lesson was surely that the

Allies were not yet ready for a return to France. In the words of Professor Paul Kennedy, the psychological lesson of Dieppe was that when the Allies did come ashore in France, "they were going to have to be very, very good."

Operation Jubilee—Disaster at Dieppe

"[T]he very last thing they'd (the Germans) ever imagine is that we would be so stupid as to lay on the same operation again." With these words, Vice Admiral Louis Mountbatten, commanding the Combined Operations Headquarters, authorized the planning for Operation Jubilee—an attack on the port of Dieppe—to proceed. It was a successor to Operation Rutter, also a planned attack on Dieppe, called off the month before. Six thousand Allied troops had been briefed in great secrecy aboard their landing ships on July 3, 1942, that their objective was Dieppe. However, with a six-week delay, when Operation Jubilee was launched on August 19 toward the same objective, it is inconceivable that the Germans did not know that Dieppe was the focus of the attack. In Dieppe, both German soldiers and French civilians were on edge. "Tommy *kommt*" (Tommy is coming) was a frequent exchange. They were ready.

The butcher's bill on August 19—3,623 men killed, wounded, or taken prisoner of the 6,086 men who landed, largely from the Canadian Second Infantry Division—confirms the scale of the disaster that was Operation Jubilee. Proportionally, this was one of the highest casualty rates in Western Europe in the Second World War. To this must be added the loss of a Royal Navy destroyer and 33 landing aircraft with a further 550 killed and wounded, and 100 Allied aircraft lost, mostly Spitfires and Hurricanes, with 109 airmen killed, wounded, or captured. For comparison, German losses on land—591 killed or wounded and 48 aircraft downed—were modest. For Winston Churchill in Cairo, recovering from a bruising summit with Stalin in Moscow, the news of the failure of Jubilee was another bitter pill to swallow, less than two months since the fall of Tobruk in North Africa.

The purpose of Operation Jubilee had been to launch an amphibious assault on the German-occupied port of Dieppe, to hold the town and port for a short time and thereby test the feasibility of mounting a direct attack on an enemy-held port, before conducting a fighting withdrawal. Within the plan, there were to be landings on six separate beaches, of which all except one failed. To take a positive from this negative, one of the conclusions drawn after Jubilee was that when the Second Front in Europe would eventually be mounted, the assault must be guarded by the highest level of operational security, be conducted over open beaches, and the logistics must be through ad hoc harbors, the genesis of the improvised Mulberry harbors.

But if there were failings at the operational and tactical levels of war, Jubilee must be seen in the wider strategic context of the overall conduct of the war. Churchill was under huge pressure from both the Americans and the Russians to agree to an early return to France, but the failure of Jubilee proved conclusively that Operation Sledgehammer—a return in force to northern Europe in 1942—would fail and cast severe doubt that Operation Roundup—an invasion in 1943—was also too risky to be contemplated. Although Churchill had hoped for more local success from Jubilee—largely to quell Stalin's complaints about British unwillingness to confront the Germans on land—he next proposed Operation Torch, an Anglo-American assault on the western North Africa coast. This, and the subsequent invasions of Sicily and southern Italy, bought time for a thorough analysis of the failings of Jubilee and for far better preparations to be made for Operation Overlord in 1944.

Having won the strategic argument with the Americans that, although a policy of the defeat of Germany first had primacy, Churchill had also persuaded them that the route to success was via the Mediterranean and only later to return to France. Meanwhile, Stalin would have to be content with diverting

German divisions away from Russia, as the Mediterranean demanded, the round-the-clock bombing of Germany from English airfields, and the supply of weapons delivered by the Artic convoys. These all provided breathing space for the lessons of Jubilee to be analyzed and absorbed.

Intelligence was a major failing. The reconnaissance and knowledge of the German dispositions at Dieppe was poor. Although Tenth Panzer Division was thought to be in reserve around Amiens, this was uncertain. The fighting capability of the defending German 302nd Static Division was unknown. Study of the topography, especially the nature of the beaches, was poor. The shingle beaches led to the bogging in and stranding of many of the tanks and other armored vehicles. Cooperation between the landing and the air forces was inadequate, and the fear of the loss of a capital ship meant that the Royal Navy refused to commit a battleship to onshore bombardment. Given the loss of the HMS *Prince of Wales* and HMS *Repulse* off Singapore the previous year, this was understandable, but the solution for the future was air superiority over the battlefield, not a refusal to commit valuable firepower. In 1942, there was much to learn. Mercifully, by the launch of Operation Overlord in 1944, these lessons had been learned. However, the shadows of Gallipoli, Norway, and now Jubilee did nothing to lesson Churchill's "black dog" (the Victorian term he used for depressive moods).

Hughes-Hallett observed it all from one of the accompanying naval ships. It fell on him to implement some of the lessons learned. His key recommendation was the creation of a permanent assault force, to support further raiding and to commence the detailed training and preparation that would be needed for a return to the continent. As a result, he was ordered to form and command Force J; "J" for "Jubilee," the codename for the Dieppe operation. Establishing his headquarters in Cowes on the Isle of Wight, he began with a handful of assault ships and a few flotillas of landing craft. This was an essential early step in creating the professional force for D-Day.

Churchill learned of the outcome of the Dieppe raid while in the Middle East, shortly before returning from his latest overseas trip. His mission had been twofold: to remove General Claude Auchinleck from his command in North Africa and to meet for the first time with Marshal Stalin in Moscow. These two events were not unconnected. The change in command in Egypt was seen by Churchill as vital for restoring morale and reenergizing the conflict against Rommel. Responsibility passed to General Alexander as the overall theater commander, with General Montgomery—after the sudden death of General "Strafer" Gott—assuming command of the Eighth Army. Victory in the desert remained the immediate British priority. They needed to win the battle they were already fighting before they could focus on other fronts.

This was also the crux of the message that Churchill took to Moscow: namely, that there would be no Second Front in France in 1942, and that the Anglo-American allies had decided to prioritize Operation Torch and attack French North Africa. The British prime minister would later compare taking this news to the Kremlin as like "carrying a large lump of ice to the North Pole."

> *I do not like the job I have to do.*
> *I cannot think my views will go down well.*
> *Can I convince them of our settled view?*
> *Will Stalin use Caucasian oaths and yell?*
> *Or can I bind him with my midnight spell?*
> *I'm really feeling rather in a stew.*
> *It's not so hot a thing to have to sell.*
> *No Second Front in 1942.*

Those lines form part of a poem called the *Ballade of the Second Front,* which was written by General Wavell while sitting on the floor of the Liberator B-24 bomber carrying the British party back from Moscow to Tehran. In it, Wavell gives humorous voice to Churchill's anxieties going into the meeting. Despite an initial warm welcome, described by Churchill as "totalitarian lavishness," the timing of a Second Front in France quickly dominated the discussions, with Stalin using a key meeting in his office in the Kremlin on August 13 to make his views only too clear.

According to Ian Jacob, one of Churchill's military advisers who was brought in to take the minutes:

> Stalin appeared quite at home, and made his remarks in a very low, gentle voice, with an occasional gesture of the right hand, and never looked the Prime Minister in the face.

But what Stalin said in his quiet, measured tones was calculated to cut Churchill to the quick. The Germans were not supermen; the British Army lacked the courage to face them. Roosevelt and Churchill should honor their plans to seize the Cotentin Peninsula now. Ultimately, it took a Churchillian threat to leave Russia early, coupled with promises of a Second Front in 1943 and a private, late-night, eating and drinking session with Stalin (more totalitarian lavishness during which Stalin devoured a suckling pig), to ensure a cordial end to proceedings, but the British left with no doubts as to Soviet wishes.

And those wishes were shared by large sections of the British Parliament, press, and public who also felt that the country needed to do more to support their Soviet allies. From the autumn of 1942, this only intensified against the backdrop of the Battle of Stalingrad, which was featured week after week in newspapers and cinemas as a heroic Russian defense against the German invaders, one that contrasted with British surrender in Libya and Singapore. As Roosevelt had put it back in April, "Your people & mine demand the establishment of a front to draw off pressure on the Russians, & these peoples are wise enough to see that the Russians are today killing more Germans & destroying more equipment than you and I put together." Mrs. Churchill's Red Cross "Aid to Russia" Fund raised its first million pounds for essential supplies and medical equipment from the British people in just three months between October and December 1941. And this in spite of all the domestic shortages. It would go on raising money for the rest of the war, through individual donations, flag days, concerts, and a range of high-profile fundraising activities. Churchill could not ignore the groundswell of support for Russia at home, not least because it was very close to home indeed—with his wife, Clementine, chairing the Fund. He insisted on sending vital supplies to Russia via the dangerous Arctic convoy route to Archangel and Murmansk, he supported the Allied bombing of Germany, and he threw his weight behind Torch, but many—in Russia, America, and Britain—continued to press for more. His friend and erstwhile rival, the media magnet Lord Beaverbrook, resigned from the Cabinet in February 1942 and used his newspapers to lead a campaign calling for a "Second Front Now."

By the end of 1942, Churchill had secured the preferred British strategy of fighting in North Africa rather than France. He had done so in spite of opposition from both his American and Soviet allies and in the teeth of significant criticism and pressure at home. In reality, the adoption of the strategy was a recognition of British weakness and imperial overstretch. Both Roosevelt and Stalin ultimately had no option but to go along with it, as the Americans were not yet strong enough to invade France on their own (and were ultimately reliant on use of the United Kingdom as a forward base in order to do so), while the Russians—for all their hard words—were under attack and had no option but to accept any assistance that their Western allies could offer.

It is easy to see why D-Day gets knocked back to 1943. Neither the British nor the Americans believed a large-scale assault was feasible, and Sledgehammer was seen as too limited and too risky. But it is less obvious why the Allied invasion of France does not happen until 1944. The answer lies partly in the law of unintended consequences. The decision to proceed with Operation Torch, and the operations that flowed from it, further delayed the buildup of forces in the United Kingdom. This was not immediately apparent to Churchill at the time.

November 1942 was a good month for the Anglo-American armies. General Montgomery finally defeated Rommel at the Second Battle of El Alamein, achieving that long-awaited British victory, and began to advance across the Libyan desert from the east. Meanwhile, at the other end of North Africa, General Eisenhower landed in Morocco and

Algeria and deployed eastward. The Germans were now caught in a pincer movement.

This initial success led Churchill to resurvey the big picture. In a note to his chiefs of staff in early December, he felt that the most important new factor was the impending German defeat in Russia, which might reduce 180 German divisions to "little more than brigades" and was likely to prevent the transfer of enemy troops from the eastern to the western theater. It led him to produce an optimistic target schedule for 1943 that predicted the clearing of the North African shoreline by the end of January, the opening of the Mediterranean by March, the assembly of the necessary landing craft for the cross-Channel operation in Britain by June, the completion of preparations for Roundup by July, and "Action," meaning the liberation of France, in August or September.

Unfortunately, it quickly became clear that those American and British pincers in North Africa would take much longer to close. The American-led ground troops in the west faced more initial opposition from Vichy French forces than anticipated, the political situation remained volatile, and their attempts to push toward Tunis were soon bogged down in wet weather and impassable roads. The British Eighth Army was initially able to exploit its victory in Egypt by crossing the Libyan desert, recapturing the port of Tobruk, and advancing as far as the coastal city of Agheila. But thereafter, its advance was stalled by the difficulties of supply over such vast distances, the Germans having left the key port of Benghazi severely damaged. German resistance in Tunisia remained determined and stubborn, and in Rommel the Allies faced a capable commander with a sizable army. Intelligence estimates were that he had fifty thousand Germans and thirty thousand Italians. Even allowing for the fact that they were not all frontline troops and lacked tanks and artillery, this was still a considerable obstacle; one that would take several months to defeat.

Meanwhile, in France, Hitler had responded to events by ending all vestiges of Vichy independence and further strengthening his grip on the country. He was now busy further fortifying the French coastline. In March 1942, Führer Directive 40 recognized that Allied landings were now likely and correctly identified the risk of the British using landing craft, paratroops, and airborne forces to land on the beaches. It called for the defense of the most likely target areas and resulted in the building, between 1942 and 1944, of thousands of concrete gun emplacements, antiaircraft batteries, and command and observation posts along the Atlantic shoreline. All of this would make a cross-Channel assault progressively more difficult. Meanwhile, continuing losses to U-boats in the Battle of the Atlantic were threatening British supply lines, and the war in the Pacific was eating into American shipping quotas. Churchill's schedule quickly looked unrealistic.

It was against this backdrop that Churchill and Roosevelt and their Anglo-American Combined Chiefs of Staff met again to consider their next steps. The conference took place in Anfa, on the outskirts of the Moroccan port city of Casablanca, January 14 to 24, 1943. Symbolically this was an important moment. The American commander in chief, in spite of his disability (he was unable to walk unaided as a result of polio), had traveled across the Atlantic Ocean to meet with the British prime minister in the theater where their troops were now fighting side by side. Harold Macmillan, the British resident minister in Algiers, likened it to the meeting of two great Roman emperors. For both Churchill and Roosevelt, this was an escape from the routine of Washington and Whitehall, and it was also the moment to determine their joint war strategy going forward.

According to Ian Jacob, a key member of the British team, Churchill wanted to have his cake and eat it. He wanted to exploit success in as many theaters as possible, with the cleansing of the North African shoreline to be followed by the capture of Sicily and accompanied by the reconquest of Burma and a moderate invasion of France. He was determined to resist American demands for the primacy of France and prepared his team for a continuation of their strategy of gradual persuasion of the Americans, which he said must be like "the dripping of water on stone." He knew that General Marshall still favored conducting Operation Roundup, the full-scale invasion of France, at the earliest opportunity. The head of the US Army remained convinced that the quickest way to Berlin lay through western France.

The issues were now extensively debated. The Combined Chiefs of Staff gathered in conference once or twice a day to thrash out a joint military strategy, while the president and prime minister used their rather more luxurious villas to host less formal meetings with key advisers concentrating on the big political issues. The recommendations of the chiefs of staff were then discussed and ratified at three plenary sessions attended by Churchill and Roosevelt on January 15, 18, and 23. What emerged was a more or less complete acceptance of the preferred British viewpoint; the large-scale, cross-Channel assault was to be further delayed, subordinated to operations designed to secure the Mediterranean and reduce German strength before undertaking any major operation in France.

By the plenary meeting of January 18, General Alan Brooke reported that, after "days of argument," the Combined Chiefs had agreed on the outline of a document "setting forth the general strategic policy for 1943." The priority was seen as dealing with the U-boat menace. This was to be the first charge on Allied resources as it would "provide security for all our operations." Thereafter, the primacy of the war against Germany was confirmed over and above that against Japan, with the aim of forcing the enemy to withdraw ground and air forces from the Russian front. But this was to be accomplished by operations from North Africa, not the United Kingdom. The next target had been identified as the Italian island of Sicily. It was agreed that the Allies would continue "preparing forces and assembling landing craft in England for a thrust across the Channel" but only "in the event that the German strength in France decreases, either through withdrawal of her troops or because of an internal collapse." The green light was given to specific operations in the Pacific, including the capture of Rabaul and East New Guinea (a province in Papua New Guinea), and plans were laid for an end-of-year offensive in Burma (now Myanmar) and for bridgeheads across the Chindwin River. The maximum combined air offensive was to be conducted against Germany from the United Kingdom, with a view to breaking German morale, and every effort was to be made to induce Turkey to enter the war on the Allied side.

General Brooke could hardly believe his luck. Churchill felt the same. This was an almost wholesale acceptance of their preferred British strategy. It was no doubt helped by the fact that the Americans were not as prepared or united in their views going into the meetings. Admiral King remained determined to see US naval operations in the Pacific, and these continued to draw heavily on American production quotas, especially for shipping and landing craft. The Americans would later complain that they were both outnumbered and outmaneuvered by the British at Casablanca, but the records of the Casablanca meetings reveal many sound reasons why the president, Marshall, and the Americans had little choice but to agree to the joint strategy.

There were certainly lessons to be learned from Operation Torch that suggested further preparations were needed before attacking in France. The landings in Morocco had been hampered by the size of the Atlantic waves. Resistance in Algeria had been heavier than anticipated. And this had been an assault against a less-well-defended shoreline. First contact with the Germans in Tunisia had highlighted the continued difficulty of facing a battle-hardened enemy. Operations in the Pacific could not simply be abandoned and were now competing for resources. The U-boat menace in the Atlantic made it more difficult to bring men and materials across the ocean in the numbers that would be required for a cross-Channel assault, especially while destroyers and escorts were committed to convoy duties, both across the Atlantic and to Russia. There remained huge logistical difficulties. The Americans did not yet have enough divisions available to secure and hold the North African shoreline, fight in the Pacific, and countenance a major invasion of northwestern Europe. There was still a shortage of shipping and landing craft, especially tank-carrying craft. In contrast, a move against Sicily was easier to mount from North Africa, might knock Italy out of the war, and would help the Allies secure the Mediterranean, reopening a faster shipping route from Europe to the Pacific and thereby releasing the necessary shipping for other theaters.

For Roosevelt and Churchill, delay remained another major political consideration. If the Allies simply stopped after securing North Africa and switched to building up forces for an assault on western France, then there would be a considerable gap—while the required forces were assembled in Britain—during which their armies would not be engaging the enemy anywhere in Europe. At Casablanca, they were already concerned at the prospect of even a few months' delay between operations in Tunisia and Sicily. The optimum time for a cross-Channel operation, in terms of weather and tides, was between May and September. Issues of shipping and production meant that the requisite forces and landing craft could not be assembled in the United Kingdom in time for a spring or summer offensive. These factors, when taken together, made a large-scale assault in 1943 almost impossible. Better therefore to use the existing momentum in the Mediterranean and to prepare the ground for a major operation in 1944.

There was also a natural caution, arising from the level of complexity and the associated risk of failure, which led the Allied military planners to build their relationship and refine their tactics in what was believed to be a safer theater of operations. Dennis Wheatley, best known as a writer of thrillers and novels about the occult, was working just a few rooms away from the prime minister in the treasury building as part of wartime intelligence, a member of the London Controlling Section charged with creating elaborate deception plans to protect British operations. As such, he was one of the few people allowed to read all the War Cabinet, Defence Committee, and chiefs of staff minutes. His view, admittedly expressed later with the benefit of hindsight, was that Churchill's perception of Roundup was not as a mighty invasion, but "as the codeword implies, a landing to 'round up' any German units that might still be resisting after the defeat and disintegration of the German Army had been achieved by some other means."

The prime minister's level of support for the cross-Channel operation certainly shifted from one moment to the next, depending on events and with whom he was speaking. Brooke became incensed in May 1943 at what he saw as the prime minister's inconsistency and his maddening desire "to carry out ALL operations simultaneously irrespective of shortages of shipping!" Churchill wanted the flexibility to be able to exploit success when and where it happened, especially given how rare it had been before 1942, and he saw huge risks in putting all the British eggs in one basket. Hence, he was prepared to prod his commanders and to explore all options. It was also in his nature to constantly seek new outlets for action.

But after Casablanca, he was certainly not alone nor at odds with Brooke in advocating for further delay in France. This was the accepted strategy of the British chiefs of staff. In May 1943, at much the same time that Brooke was complaining about Churchill, Eisenhower recalled the British chief of the Imperial General Staff saying that "he would be glad to reconsider the cross-Channel project, even to the extent of eliminating that bold concept from Allied strategy." Brooke's diary from the same month records his exasperation with General Marshall for still wanting to push straight into France, prompting his later reflection that "the Americans still failed to grasp how we were preparing for a re-entry into France through our actions in the Mediterranean." There was an undeniable difference in emphasis between the Allies, though the debate was far more complex than it is sometimes now portrayed.

What Churchill and Roosevelt did agree on at Casablanca was the need to impose unconditional surrender on Germany. This sent a clear signal to their absent Soviet ally, to neutral powers, and to their opponents that that they were going to see things through to the end.

By 1943, the main steps on that long road had been agreed. The Mediterranean would be the immediate priority, but preparations would be stepped up for a larger entry into France in early 1944. It was a compromise, but the fact that the president, Marshall, and Eisenhower all ultimately agreed was a recognition that this provided the surest and safest way to victory at what they believed would be the lowest cost. With hindsight and our knowledge of the success of Overlord, it is a decision that has been and can be challenged, but from the military perspective there were clearly a number of obstacles that had to be overcome before any large-scale, cross-Channel operation could be launched.

This does not mean that Churchill was prepared to abandon operations in France altogether. At the plenary meeting of the Casablanca Conference on January 18, he returned to the idea of a more limited assault, advocating seizing and holding a bridgehead across the Channel. In 1942 he had opposed Operation Sledgehammer, now he told the Combined Chiefs of Staff that looked more favorably on it in 1943 that he thought it should be given a "sharper point," including a commander and a target date. The president agreed and suggested preparing a schedule for the buildup of forces by month. He also suggested there should be a British commander. Churchill replied that the question of command should be determined later, but that they should designate a British commander at this time "who could undertake the planning of the operation." Ultimately, he felt that command of such an operation should be held by an officer of the country furnishing the largest number of troops. In January 1943, it was clear that any limited cross-Channel operation conducted in the short-term would have to be a primarily British affair as there was only one American division in the United Kingdom.

The speed of any American buildup was revisited in the final plenary meeting of January 23. When Churchill expressed disappointment that there would only be four fully equipped American divisions in the United Kingdom by August 15, 1943, he was told by Marshall that the figure would probably be five, and that by the end of the year there might be as many as nineteen. Churchill wondered whether this could be speeded up by using luxury transatlantic liners as troop carriers or by reducing the amount of equipment needed to support the troops, estimated at an initial eight tons per man with a further 1.3 tons per man per month. He also questioned whether savings could be made on vehicles and reserves, stating that, "Fighting men for the beaches were the prime essential." His comments must have raised eyebrows among the military commanders, but here was a theme to which Churchill would return. He remained a product of the Victorian army and was not always capable of grasping the enormous logistical tail required by a modern army.

As 1943 began, the invasion of France had been deferred, not canceled. Principles had been laid down for its command and planning. Many of the challenges identified at Casablanca would now influence its development. For Churchill, it was about seizing the immediate opportunity. There was an obvious advantage in going into Sicily and securing the Mediterranean. France remained a far riskier proposition, and he preferred to hold back, to see the enemy weakened, to build up forces, and to be ready to move across the Channel if and when circumstances changed.

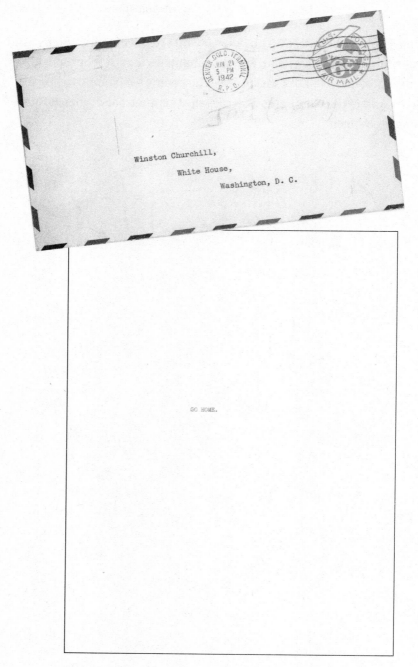

DENVER, COLO. TERMINAL
JUN 21
5 PM
1942
R.P.O.

Winston Churchill,

White House,

Washington, D. C.

GO HOME.

Letter and envelope sent to Churchill and kept by John Martin, June 1942.
(Martin Papers, MART 4)

Chapter 4

Preconditions for Success

*"All right if you won't play with us in the
Mediterranean we won't play with you in the
English Channel."*

1943 WAS THE YEAR THAT MADE D-DAY POSSIBLE. IN JANUARY, AT THE
Casablanca Conference, it still seemed a remote possibility; an operation to be planned for but not necessarily undertaken. Churchill and
Roosevelt had decided to appoint a commander, but as of yet there was
no real plan and no troops to command. As a result, it was agreed not to
appoint a Supreme Commander but, instead, to have someone charged
with producing the detailed planning. General Frederick Morgan was
given the role and designated chief of staff to the (nonexistent) Supreme
Allied Commander (COSSAC). His interview was a "delightful visit for
lunch at Chequers" on April 4 with the prime minister. Churchill duly
reported back that Morgan seemed "a capable and sensible officer."

Morgan was not a battlefield commander. He had served as an artillery officer in the First World War and subsequently in India. He had
fought in the retreat from France in 1940 and thereafter developed a
reputation for operational planning. When the Allies went into North
Africa, he was asked to plan for the occupation of Spanish Morocco;

when they looked to build on their success in Tunisia, he was tasked with considering an invasion of Sardinia. In the event neither plan was needed, Morgan was used to his projects going nowhere and was under no illusions about the strange and uncertain nature of his latest role. His Staff College Report from 1928 noted that he "has a keen but kindly sense of humour which should prove a great asset to him." He was going to need it.

Upon his appointment, General Brooke told him: "Well, there it is. It won't work, but you must bloody well make it."

Morgan later wrote, "There followed months of toil in an atmosphere of persisting doubt and uncertainty. Not until the last moment could I be sure that I had not laboured in vain, had not merely contributed one more project to the vast library of rejects."

Churchill minuted his chiefs of staff on April 18, 1943, regarding the new COSSAC role. At Casablanca he had indicated that he was prepared to revisit Sledgehammer and might be in favor of a limited assault on France within the next year, especially in light of a German defeat on the Eastern Front. Now, he reversed that view, writing: "A German collapse being extremely unlikely and not to be counted upon this year, and neither American reinforcements nor landing-craft being available, we cannot do 'Sledgehammer' in 1943." Instead, General Morgan should work with Fighter Command and Combined Operations to prepare an "amphibious feint" designed to bring about a major air battle and reduce the power of the Luftwaffe. He should deploy "Camouflage and pretence on the most elaborate scale" to keep alive the threat of the invasion and pin the enemy in the west, and only finally should he continue Operation Bolero, the gradual buildup of forces, and the "long-term study" for Roundup, the major cross-Channel assault, while also making "month-to-month arrangements in case of a German collapse." In case there was any doubt about the level of priority Churchill was applying to this new role, the prime minister then specified that "General Morgan's organisation does not require to be very large or numerous." In an earlier minute to Brooke, he had made clear that there was no use proceeding with "the creation of this vast complicated staff when so far only one American division has reached this country and there are no immediate prospects of heavy reinforcements."

Churchill's focus was clearly on the Mediterranean and the forth-coming operation against Sicily. The orders that were then issued to General Morgan by the chiefs of staff were more diplomatically phrased but amounted to much the same. The Allied object was the defeat of the German fighting forces in northwest Europe:

> To this end the Combined Chiefs of Staff will endeavour to assem-ble the strongest possible forces (subject to prior commitment in other theatres) in constant readiness to re-enter the Continent if German resistance is weakened to the required extent in 1943. In the meantime, the Combined Chiefs of Staff must be prepared to order such limited operations as may be practical with the forces and material available.

In particular, Morgan and his team were tasked with preparing three sets of plans. First was the elaborate camouflage and deception scheme designed to extend over the entire summer and keep alive the German expectation of a cross-Channel assault in 1943. This was intended to pin down enemy forces in France, thereby easing pressure on the Russians at the Eastern Front and the British-American armies in the Mediterranean. The need to undertake Churchill's amphibious feint was specified. Second, there was to be a plan for a return to the continent in the event of German disintegration "at any time from now onwards with whatever forces may be available at the time." And third, Morgan was to plan for a full-scale assault against the continent in 1944 "as early as possible."

Morgan was hampered by the fact that his was an administrative headquarters with no operational forces under its direct command and reliant on cooperation with others. The army forces earmarked for the invasion of Europe were the First Canadian and Second British Armies, together forming the Twenty-First Army Group, but these were under the control of General Bernard Paget as commander in chief of Home Forces; a situation mirrored in the American Army where General Jacob

Devers commanded the forces in the United Kingdom being built up for a campaign in France. Air Marshal Trafford Leigh-Mallory would soon assume command for the Allied Expeditionary Air Force, and Admiral Sir Charles James Little was commander in chief, Portsmouth. Cutting across all of this was the role already given to Mountbatten and his Combined Operations Headquarters (COHQ), which effectively gave them an interest in any amphibious operation. This was the strange new world that Hughes-Hallett found himself navigating. In charge of the naval assault force for any operation against France, he was reporting to Combined Operations, while drawing on naval resources from Portsmouth and working with Morgan's new team, for which he was soon acting as the naval chief of staff. In his words, "a good deal of 'Coffee-housing' went on between General Morgan and senior officers at COHQ."

It is from this point, as Morgan's team gets to work in May 1943, that Operation Roundup—the invasion of northern France—is renamed Overlord. But its development still had a long way to go. The last chapter has shown that its planning could not be considered in isolation. It was part of a global war that saw Churchill and Roosevelt struggling to manage limited resources, to balance the competing demands upon them, and to respond to ever changing events. Delay and slow progress were in part the result of prioritizing the war in North Africa and the Mediterranean, but part of the reason for that prioritization was that a number of preconditions had to be met before the Allied liberation of France could be seriously contemplated. These might be summarized as follows:

- A sophisticated level of British and American interservice cooperation
- Control of the seas
- Mastery of the air
- A huge buildup of men and materials
- A greatly weakened and overstretched enemy
- The existence of enough landing craft to get the army safely ashore and keep it supplied

- The development of officers and troops with real combat experience and high morale

It is worth looking at each of these in turn. Could any of these preconditions have been met before the spring of 1944?

A SOPHISTICATED LEVEL OF BRITISH
AND AMERICAN INTERSERVICE COOPERATION

John Martin was Churchill's Principal Private Secretary and accompanied his boss to Washington, DC, in June 1942. The visit was not low key, and the presence of the British prime minister as a guest of the president in the White House was well known. A letter, postmarked from Denver, Colorado, survives in Martin's papers. It was simply addressed to "Winston Churchill, White House, Washington D.C." Once opened, its contents were even more succinct. Just two anonymous typescript words on an otherwise blank sheet of paper. "Go Home." With the benefit of hindsight, much of what has been written about the wartime partnership between Britain and America has focused on its closeness, on the creation of a *special relationship* (a term that was coined by Churchill but not popularized by him until after the war when he delivered his famous Iron Curtain speech at Westminster College, Fulton, Missouri, in 1946) . We tend to forget that these sentiments of brotherhood were far from universally shared on either side of the Atlantic in 1942. Elements of American public opinion were still fiercely isolationist and anti-British, just as elements in Britain were pro-Russian and anti-American.

From the top down, from the prime minister and president, it took time to build close political and military ties and develop the trust and teamwork that underpinned the alliance and made Overlord possible. The Anglo-American and interservice cooperation, planning, and staff work needed to make an assault against Hitler's European fortress was never going to be produced by desk clerks working in offices; it had to be forged and tested in war. There had been some secret British and American staff talks prior to Pearl Harbor. Immediately afterward, a clear partnership framework had been established with the creation of the Combined Chiefs of Staff Committee. This brought together the joint service chiefs of each country (the military heads of their respective army, air, and naval forces) and gave the British chiefs of staff permanent representation in Washington, DC, establishing a constant communication channel with their American counterparts. The big strategic decisions concerning Overlord and D-Day were taken at a series of major conferences throughout 1943, culminating in the Tehran conference in November attended by Marshal Stalin for the Soviet Union. These meetings were often difficult, but they allowed a common strategy to be hammered out. Central to Allied cooperation was the principle, adopted from early 1942, that British forces would serve under an American theater commander, as would American forces serve under a British commander. Whichever country had the largest forces in the theater would have the command. Churchill played a clear role in creating this framework, but it was one thing to establish a structure, another to build trust and allay national suspicions and rivalries.

The International Road to D-Day: A Timeline of the Key Conferences in 1943

The president, prime minister, and their Combined Chiefs of Staff met regularly during 1943 to develop their joint strategy. These meetings all had a bearing on the timing and nature of Overlord.

The year began with the Casablanca Conference (codename Symbol), held between January 14 and 24, 1943, in French Morocco. The immediate priority was to resolve the next political and military steps, coordinating the American and British advances from west and east into Tunisia and dealing with arrangements for the administration of French North Africa. Thereafter, the conference decided that the next Allied objective would be against Sicily. This was recognition that they were not yet strong enough to move against the heavily fortified Atlantic shoreline of France and effectively pushed D-Day back to 1944. The conference recognized that the defeat of the U-boats in the Atlantic and the further bombing of Germany were necessary precursors to a cross-Channel assault. However, the decision was made to appoint a British general to further develop plans for operations against France.

May saw Churchill engage in shuttle diplomacy. In Washington, DC (codename Trident, May 12–25), he met with the president and Combined Chiefs. Thereafter, he flew to Algiers (May 29–June 4), accompanied by Generals Marshall and Brooke, where he was joined by Foreign Secretary Eden and met with Eisenhower and the military commanders about to engage in Operation Husky, the invasion of Sicily. These meetings finalized the arrangements for the assault on Sicily but left open the question of moving into Italy thereafter. The decision was made to postpone the cross-Channel assault until May 1944, as, given other operations, it would not be possible to build up the required forces and equipment prior to that date. Churchill was particularly keen to exploit success in Sicily with attacks against the Italian mainland, while Marshall argued strongly for the primacy of Overlord. Eisenhower was prepared to contemplate some further action in Italy while forces continued to be assembled in the United Kingdom for the assault on France.

The Quebec Conference (codename Quadrant, August 17–24) took place in Canada in the aftermath of the fall of Mussolini and against the backdrop of the successful Allied invasion of Sicily. Churchill and Roosevelt were hosted by the Canadian prime minister, William Lyon Mackenzie King, though he was excluded from the key Allied discussions. Churchill accepted the principle of the primacy of Overlord over the Mediterranean, though he continued to urge operations in Italy, in part as a means of diverting German forces from France. He advocated seizing Sardinia and Corsica. The conference also discussed the plan to simultaneously attack southern France (Operation Anvil) in May 1944 as a further means of occupying the Germans and preventing them from amassing forces against Overlord. Discussion took place concerning the war in the Pacific and future cooperation regarding the atomic weapons that the Allies were developing.

The year ended with the Tehran Conference (codename Eureka, November 28–December 1), which was itself sandwiched between two meetings with Churchill, Roosevelt, and their staffs at Cairo, November 23–26 and December 4–6. Churchill had hoped to use the first Cairo Conference to coordinate European strategy with Roosevelt ahead of the Tehran Conference with Stalin, but in this he was thwarted by Roosevelt's reluctance to engage in bilateral diplomacy before his first meeting with the Soviet leader and by the presence of the Chinese nationalist leader Chiang Kai-shek, which meant that discussions focused largely on the Pacific. At Tehran itself, Churchill had to accept the clear American and Russian decision to prioritize Overlord over operations in Italy. The Soviets agreed to launch their own simultaneous offensive on the Eastern Front (Operation Bagration), while deception measures were discussed, along with plans for the attack on the south of France (Anvil, now given the codename Dragoon). There was also much discussion of the importance of Turkey joining the war on the Allied side, though at the subsequent second Cairo Conference, President Ismet Inönü of Turkey refused to abandon his country's policy of neutrality.

These conferences punctuated the debate on the timing of D-Day, but by the end of 1943 the stage was set for Operation Overlord. Churchill, Roosevelt, and their Combined Chiefs would not meet again until after June 6.

Back at COSSAC, General Morgan and his American deputy General Barker inevitably found themselves at the center of these mutual national suspicions. General Barker "earned for himself the reputation in his own service of being 'sold out to the British,'" while General Morgan's "own efforts at internationality soon caused me to be regarded . . . as 'Sold out to the Yanks.'" Generally, Morgan found that when meeting the British authorities about Overlord, "one had to be conscious of their skepticism towards the whole affair" and "their idea of co-operation was that others should co-operate with them and not vice-versa." There were moments when he felt that "it was not easy to convince oneself of British bona fides." With the Americans, "it was more a matter of keeping bubbling enthusiasm within practical bounds" while managing their reservations about British adventuring in the Mediterranean, the Balkans, and the Aegean. To the British, Eisenhower was just a "politico-military figurehead"; to the Americans, Montgomery was massively overrated.

At the highest levels, Churchill, Eisenhower, and Morgan all sought to combat these national prejudices by bringing people together. Churchill led by example, entertaining British and American commanders at Downing Street and Chequers. He also gave his blessing to a Churchill Club that was created in central London in one of the evacuated houses of Westminster School. Elaborately decorated by Robert Lutyens and managed by Pamela Churchill (later Harriman), the prime minister's daughter-in-law and a consummate hostess and networker, it was open to all American and Dominion officers and other ranks with a university education; running concerts and lectures to expose them to British history, culture, and society. On a more practical level, General Morgan made good use of the restaurant and bar at his Norfolk House headquarters in St. James's Square to bring together British and American team members and visitors. It set the precedent for later developments. Come April 1944, Harry Butcher would report that camaraderie was "helped a lot by the fact that we have American coffee at our desks around eleven each morning and British tea around five."

When Eisenhower was given command of Torch, a British admiral, Andrew Cunningham, was appointed as his naval commander for the operation. After Casablanca, when he became the Allied Supreme Commander in North Africa, Ike had British deputies for all three services—Cunningham for the navy, Tedder for the air, and Alexander for the army. When Cunningham was recalled to London as the new First Sea Lord, he was replaced by another Brit, Admiral Ramsay, architect of the Dunkirk evacuation, who had worked on the initial plans for Roundup and coordinated the naval aspect of the Sicilian campaign. In North Africa and Sicily, US generals Bradley and Patton served alongside British generals Montgomery and Anderson. Alexander would go on to become the theater commander in Italy, but Eisenhower took Montgomery, Ramsay, and Tedder with him when he became the Overlord commander. They may not have always agreed, and elements of personal rivalry and competition undoubtedly remained and sometimes loomed large (with Montgomery and Patton the worst offenders), but they knew each other well and—for the most part—could work together well.

This bond was not forged instantaneously. In 1942. Eisenhower was acutely aware that the

> whole basis of our higher organization was new. Time and again during the summer old army friends warned me that the conception of Allied unity which we took as the foundation of our command scheme was impracticable and impossible; that any commander placed in my position was foredoomed to failure and could become nothing but a scapegoat to carry the odium of defeat for the whole operation.

And there were certainly incidents. During the final stages of the Tunisian campaign in March 1943, the British corps commander, General Sir John Crocker, was highly critical of the performance of an American division when talking to the press, prompting much British and American antagonism and bad blood. However, by June 1943, with North Africa cleared and the Allies poised to invade Sicily, Churchill was praising Eisenhower's leadership, and General Marshall was prepared to argue that the Germans' greatest discomfort now "came not so much from their loss of troops so from the fact that the United States and Great Britain have worked so well as a team." It was in North Africa in 1942–43 that the commanders for Overlord gained their first experience of working together against the common enemy: the same enemy commander in General Erwin Rommel that they would face one and a half years later in Normandy.

The common language no doubt made things easier, but cultural differences remained. When Eisenhower supported a plan for the British to open up their homes to Americans, he was told by Mr. Stevenson, head of the American Red Cross, that it would normally take two or three years before a British family would invite a stranger in. Tensions grew in proportion to the increasing number of American troops in Britain. The racist treatment of African American service personnel by their white American counterparts led to objections from some British citizens. Churchill dodged questions on the issue in the House of Commons in September 1942, and the matter soon ended up before the British War Cabinet on October 13. It was decided that while the UK authorities would do nothing to interfere with segregation within the American Army, they would not allow it to be enforced within British military or civil establishments. Instead, in papers that certainly seem racist today, they suggested explaining the white American viewpoint to British audiences while urging the British to avoid contact with African Americans. The Cabinet emphasis was clearly to avoid conflict with their US allies. This did not stop other quarrels from arising between British and American soldiers, young men with pent-up energy, who routinely fought one another on the streets of the southern port towns in which they were then garrisoned. Dinners and drinks for officers only went so far. The special relationship was real and worked, but like all relationships, it needed time and always had its limits.

CONTROL OF THE SEAS

In his own words, the only thing that ever really frightened Churchill during the war was the U-boat peril: "I was even more anxious about this battle than I had been about the glorious air fight called the Battle of Britain."

Churchill had served twice as First Lord of the Admiralty, the civilian minister with responsibility for the British Navy; first in 1914–1915 at the beginning of the First World War and then again for a similar period at the beginning of the Second World War in 1939–40. While neither tenure had been a universal success, with both marked by friction with his admirals, Churchill remained supremely confident in his own understanding and knowledge of naval matters. By the end of 1942, it was clear to him and to the president that the Battle of the Atlantic would have to take precedence over all other theaters of operation, including any cross-Channel assault.

It was a battle that was expressed in figures—Allied merchant shipping losses in one column, numbers of German U-boats (submarines) sunk in another; production numbers versus losses on both sides. Churchill was self-deprecating about his own mathematical abilities. In his autobiographical memoir *My Early Life*, written in 1930, he wrote:

> I had a feeling once about Mathematics, that I saw it all—Depth beyond depth was revealed to me—the Byss and Abyss. I saw, as one might see the transit of Venus—or even the Lord Mayor's show, a quantity passing through infinity and changing its sign from plus to minus. I saw exactly how it happened and why the tergiversation was inevitable: and how the one step involved all the others. It was like politics. But it was after dinner and I let it go!

Chart showing U-boat activity, February–July 1942.
(Churchill Papers, CHAR 20/135/23)

One way in which Churchill digested the huge amount of information arriving on his desk was to have the complex figures and statistics converted into graphs and charts. Hand-drawn specially for him, these colorful documents presented the realities behind the figures in a highly visual and easily comprehensible manner. The message they were conveying about the loss of Allied merchant shipping in the Atlantic was unmistakable, and Churchill would later write: "How willingly would I have exchanged a full-scale attempt at invasion for this shapeless, measureless peril, expressed in charts, curves and statistics!"

The backdrop to the Casablanca Conference in January 1943 was a crisis in the Atlantic. The Germans now had more than two hundred operational U-boats hunting in wolf packs and concentrating their efforts in the gap that existed mid ocean where their submarines could not be harried by air attack; the Allies lacking the range to reach them from their bases in Newfoundland and Iceland. The preceding year, 1942, had seen the loss of 1,664 Allied merchant ships, nearly eight million tons. Despite the huge production capacity of the United States, the Germans were still sinking ships faster than the Allies could construct them while simultaneously building U-boats faster than they were being lost. Imports were falling and oil supplies, on which the Allied war effort ultimately depended, were dangerously low.

Britain was an island, cut off from most of neighboring mainland Europe by Hitler's occupation, and dependent—in an age before large-scale commercial air freight—on imports by sea for her survival. With traffic through the Mediterranean almost impossible, her main supply routes were now coming across the Atlantic Ocean. If these could not be maintained, then the country might be brought to its knees and forced to negotiate. In any event, a heavily besieged country would not be in a position to act as a forward base for an Allied liberation of France. Not only did the German U-boat campaign threaten the American ability to assemble troops and materials in Britain, it also diverted British and US naval resources into defending the merchant convoys, thereby hampering their ability to take the offensive in the Channel.

It was a battle that the young Christian Oldham watched unfold. Born in 1920, she had felt compelled to do her bit and, as the daughter of an admiral, quickly realized that she had no real option but to join the Wrens (the Women's Royal Naval Service). After basic training, she took an administrative post at the Wrens headquarters near London's Admiralty Arch. Like Joan Bright she worked through the Blitz, stealing moments of pleasure attending concerts and theater performances as the bombs fell. For a time, she was in charge of a degaussing range in East Tilbury, demagnetizing the hulls of merchant ships so that they would not fall prey to magnetic mines. As Christian grew in confidence, she sought more responsibility.

In early 1942, she qualified as an officer. Her job was to oversee the accurate plotting of the movement of ships at sea, and she assumed responsibility for teams of Wrens, first in Plymouth, then Edinburgh, and ultimately Belfast—all vital control centers in the battle for the Atlantic. The work could involve fifteen-hour shifts relaying the latest radar sightings and intelligence information, mapping the progress of the Allied convoys, and recording the sinkings. It left her in no doubt that, "We had to win the Battle of the Atlantic. Losing it would mean losing the war altogether."

Small wonder, at Casablanca, that this threat was recognized by the combined Allied leadership, which stated that "measures to be taken to combat the submarine menace are a first charge on the resources of the United Nations [the preferred US term for all countries fighting the Axis powers] and provide security for all our operations."

It took the first half of 1943 to win the Battle of the Atlantic and establish command of the seas. This was achieved by a combination of resources, tactics, technology, and intelligence. Churchill used the convening power of his office to bring together the relevant authorities in a new Anti-U-boat Committee, which helped coordinate the British response across the armed services and government departments. He ordered the suspension of the Arctic convoys, carrying much needed supplies to Russia, and concentrated all British naval escorts in the Atlantic. Pressure was applied to speed up delivery of Liberator aircraft with very long-range capabilities, thereby helping to close the gaps in air cover. New technology was introduced. Short-wave radar, undetectable by the U-boats, allowed British planes to detect enemy submarines on the surface. New forward-throwing, anti-submarine mortars were introduced. Efforts to bomb U-boat docks and production facilities were largely unsuccessful due to the strength of the concrete pens, but the introduction of new "support groups" of naval ships, independent of the convoys, dedicated to hunting, locating, and destroying U-boats, made a huge impact, especially when accompanied by escort carriers (normally merchant ships converted to carry planes), effectively eliminating all air gaps and allowing aircraft to put up defensive screens around convoys and take the fight directly to the enemy.

What was not apparent at the time, nor allowed to be included in the early histories of the war at sea, was the complementary role played by intelligence. The change in British cyphers helped hide the convoys from the sharp eyes of German codebreakers, while the British breaking of the German naval (codename) Shark settings for U-boat traffic by the team at Bletchley Park is what helped guide the new support groups to their targets. By May 1943, the situation in the Atlantic was transforming.

Not that this was immediately obvious at the time. In Belfast, Christian anxiously plotted the course of ONS-5, a slow convoy of forty-three ships bound for North America, following its tortuous progress through heavy Atlantic seas and then watching in alarm as a huge U-boat wolf pack closed in and began to cause havoc. "Signal after signal came in and the teleprinter buzzed on relentlessly." On this occasion, her professionalism masked a specific personal agony. Her new fiancé, John Lamb, was the first lieutenant on board the destroyer HMS *Oribi*. At one point, his ship rammed U-125. Fortunately, *Oribi* remained afloat and John was unscathed (and would go on to marry Christian). The U-boat went down.

This convoy sailed at a turning point. The Germans were now taking heavy losses, and Admiral Dönitz withdrew his submarines from the Atlantic, an essential prerequisite to Overlord. It still took time to confirm the success and then capitalize on it by building up forces and supplies in Britain, but the Allies were now in a position to divert naval resources to offensive operations against the continent. Yet considerable risks remained. The U-boats, safe in their heavily protected pens on the French coast, might still play a role in trying to prevent any cross-Channel attack. They could also rely on support from the flotillas of small, fast, torpedo-wielding E-boats (a type of gunboat known as S, or Schnellboot to the Germans) operating out of Cherbourg or Le Havre; ships that were capable of both defensive minelaying and attacks on Allied landing craft.

MASTERY OF THE AIR

Mastery of the air was just as important to the success of Overlord as command of the seas. In 1942, the British had pushed back against Sledgehammer, the more limited operation in Brittany or Normandy, on the grounds that their fighter force would be eaten up very quickly by continual engagement with the enemy above the continent. These fears had seemed justified by the strength of the German Luftwaffe over Dieppe during the subsequent raid in August. In any air battle over France, the Germans would enjoy the home advantage of being closer to their bases and thus able to refuel more quickly. Air supremacy was therefore felt to be an important prerequisite to a successful invasion of Europe, particularly one that was intended to push on into Germany. One of Churchill's essential preconditions for Overlord was "that there must be a substantial reduction in the strength of the German fighter aircraft in North-West Europe before the assault took place."

The Allied strategy was built around a policy of attrition and dispersal, accompanied by huge production. The aim was to build up British and American capacity while systematically reducing that of Germany and Italy through sustained bombing of industrial centers, including the synthetic oil plants and ball bearing factories that provided the Luftwaffe with its aviation fuel and vital components. In so doing, Churchill and Roosevelt initially also hoped to demonstrate to Stalin that they were diverting German air forces away from the Eastern Front.

The Allied strategy that emerged from the Casablanca Conference was to intensify the bombing of Germany to destroy enemy morale and production capacity, while maintaining operations in the Mediterranean and the threat of operations against France from Britain. Churchill's orders to General Morgan were that he should prioritize deception operations designed to lure the Luftwaffe from France into a general air battle that would reduce their strength. Some of the resulting deception measures and plans would prove far more successful than others, but it was not over the Channel but rather on the Russian front that the power of the German Air Force was ultimately broken.

Indeed, it is somewhat ironic, given that the Western Allies had hoped to use air power to relieve pressure on the Soviet Union, that the supposedly far inferior Red Air Force now played a key role in reducing German air power. In part, this was by sheer weight of numbers. By the summer of 1943 the Russians were able to mobilize about 10,000 front-line aircraft, while the total German forces in the west and east only numbered 3,551 serviceable combat planes. Both Russian and American production capacity was far greater than that of Germany, while their production centers were out of the range of possible German attacks. The fall of Mussolini and the Italian armistice of September 1943 further increased the pressure on the Luftwaffe, removing the Italian air force, the Regia Aeronautica, from the Mediterranean theater. The Germans were increasingly unable to compete, but it took time to build Allied forces up while grinding the Luftwaffe down. As with the war at sea, 1943 witnessed the decisive shift in the balance of power.

Yet another factor was the relentless bombing of Germany by the Allies. It was a strategy that Churchill had endorsed from the moment he became prime minister, one of the few ways in which he had taken the fight to the enemy. But again, it took time. The year 1942 saw both the arrival of the American Eighth Air Force in Britain and the appointment of the single-minded Air Marshal Arthur Harris as head of British Bomber Command. Harris favored the area bombing of German cities and production centers and introduced larger-scale raids. The Casablanca Conference further increased the tempo, unleashing Operation Pointblank against German military and industrial targets. With the Americans bombing Germany by day and the Royal Air Force at night, the Luftwaffe was forced to divert more and more resources to the defense of the German homeland.

By February 1944, the Allies' own analysis was that the completion of Operation Pointblank was in sight. The American Economic Warfare Division calculated that German single-engine fighter production had been reduced from 950 per month to 250, with twin-engine fighter production down from 225 to 50, and output of crucial ball bearings cut by 40 to 50 percent.

But it was not all about numbers. Allied tactics were also more flexible; allowing air resources to be switched more easily between theaters and operations—playing a strategic role in bombing one moment and a tactical one in supporting ground troops the next. Each theater had an independent air command working alongside the army theater commander. This is not to say that all was peace and harmony. In a future chapter we will look at the intense debate that raged around bombing strategy in the immediate prelude to D-Day, but the international and interservice Allied command structures allowed these issues to be discussed and resolved. Suffice it to say that, by the end of 1943, the Allies had the numbers, the experience, and the confidence in the air to contemplate Overlord.

That grand narrative is reflected in the personal stories of countless individuals, many of them now lost to history. The Allies certainly had a large pool from which to draw. Their bomber and fighter crews came from around the Empire and Commonwealth and across North America. On July 3, 1941, Roland MacKenzie walked into a recruiting office in Calgary and volunteered for the Royal Canadian Air Force. A banker by profession for the last thirteen years, having left school at sixteen, he was described by his interviewing officer as: "29 years old, 5 foot ten, 145 lbs, confident, easy, upright, neat, conservative, clean, slender, of clear speech, quick, deliberate, alert, sincere and reserved." He had no prior flying experience, but he was one of many Canadians who still felt a sufficiently strong connection with Britain to put his life on hold and in danger for the next four years. By September 1942, he had literally graduated with flying colors from the pilot training school in Saskatoon and was soon entrusted with training others, itself an often-dangerous task. Roland was part of the huge expansion in men and materials that made Overlord possible. In June 1943, he was sent to the United Kingdom and began to train on bombers. A poignant manuscript note in his logbook survives: "Through Adversity to the Stars—6 weeks of life in Bomber Command 1 in 3 chance to survive." He was now preparing for the role he would play in supporting D-Day and was only too aware of the risks.

Bomber and fighter crews came from around the Empire and Commonwealth; from Canada to the Caribbean. David Olusoga, in his book *Black and British*, has reminded us that over one hundred men from the West Indies were decorated for their service with the RAF or Royal Canadian Air Force.

HUGE BUILDUP OF MEN AND MATERIALS

The buildup of American and other national forces in Britain had started in the immediate aftermath of Pearl Harbor, but it had initially been small. The American Thirty-fourth Infantry Division had arrived in Northern Ireland in January 1942, followed by the first detachments of the United States Eighth Air Force in Southern England the following month. A year later, there were more than a thousand American aircraft in the country, many engaged in the bombing of Germany. It had taken longer to assemble substantial ground forces. Operation Torch, and the diversion of the American troops to North Africa, had meant that, as late as early 1943, there was only one US Division in the United Kingdom. Nor was it possible simply to transfer large numbers across the Atlantic without putting in place the substantial infrastructure that would be needed to sustain them.

In May 1942, Churchill authorized the creation of a Bolero committee in London to consider the requirements of an increased American presence. This involved taking agricultural land for the building of aerodromes and training areas. The British were already anticipating receiving more than one million American service personnel and having to build in excess of seven hundred aerodromes. With manpower resources already stretched, this was not something that could be achieved immediately, especially while shipping remained under threat in the Atlantic. It took time to build up the Allied forces, just as it took time to wear the enemy down.

A GREATLY WEAKENED AND OVERSTRETCHED ENEMY

Yet perhaps the real turning of the tide was one that Churchill himself chose to largely downplay in his Cold War–era history of *The Second World War*, and that was the smashing of the German army on the Eastern Front in Russia in 1943. It is noticeable that he devotes only six pages to the siege of Stalingrad (now Volgograd) in volume IV and just three pages to the Battle of Kursk in volume V. Yet these huge land battles, fought by enormous armies, far larger than those deployed by the British and Americans in North Africa or the Mediterranean, accounted for the vast majority of German combat losses. By autumn, the Red Army had pushed the Wehrmacht back hundreds of miles on a huge front and had retaken Kiev in the Ukraine.

It is easy to see why Churchill might not want to focus attention on the scale of the Russian success. Much of the original rationale for attacking in France had been to relieve pressure on the Russians. Throughout 1942, he remained acutely conscious that the Russians were still killing more Germans and destroying more equipment than the British and Americans put together. In early 1943, when Moscow was informed of the decision at Casablanca to attack Sicily rather than France, it caused a near breakdown in British relations with the Soviet Union. In March, Stalin denounced Churchill for reneging on repeated promises to establish a Second Front in Western Europe in 1943, writing, "I deem it my duty to warn you in the strongest possible manner how dangerous [it] would be from the viewpoint of our common cause [to] further delay in the opening of the second front in France . . . about which I feel I cannot be silent."

In private, Churchill was prepared to admit that he felt "so very conscious of the poor contribution the British and American armies are making in only engaging perhaps a dozen German divisions during the greater part of this year."

But the nature of the Allied fear about the Soviet Union was also changing. In 1942 their worry had been that the Russians might collapse and that a limited intervention in France might be required as a last-ditch measure to divert German attention and help prop them up. By the middle of 1943, the tables had turned. The sheer scale of Soviet success on the battlefield introduced a new element into Allied planning, namely the fear that Germany might collapse completely, leaving the Soviets in possession of large swathes of the continent. That was not the outcome that Britain had gone to war for in 1939.

The Germans were certainly becoming increasingly stretched. In February 1943, British military intelligence was observing the withdrawal of troops from France to the Russian and North African theaters and concluded that thirty enemy divisions had been lost or capitulated at Stalingrad. Of equal significance was the dilution in quality of the German army, which hitherto had seemed so strong. Divisions were being reformed and sent into battle with untrained troops, a shortfall of numbers, and a lack of equipment, while the transfer of forces from one operational theater to another suggested that their reserves were running low.

Another of Churchill's preconditions for D-Day was "that there should not be more than twelve mobile German divisions in Northern France at the time the operation was launched, and that it must not be possible for the Germans to build up more than fifteen divisions in the Succeeding two months." The numbers were going in the right direction, especially when size and quality of German divisions were taken into account, but in February 1943, British intelligence was still indicating that the Germans had thirty operational divisions in France and the Low Countries. Unfortunately, this number would rise as the Germans began to anticipate the Allied offensive in France.

Should the Allies have gone into France in strength in 1943, as some American commentators clearly felt at the time, and some historians have argued since? It is of course impossible to know what the result would have been, but looked at from Westminster or the White House, it remained a very risky proposition. Until at least halfway through 1943, Germany still threatened Britain's supply lines across the Atlantic, had the ability to mount a significant air defense over France, and might still have been able to transfer large numbers of troops from Russia and the Mediterranean—especially as the price for a cross-Channel assault in 1943 would have been the Allies stopping after their victory in Tunisia and leaving Italy as an enemy power and the Mediterranean as a contested sea. Even then, it was uncertain that they would have been able to build up sufficient forces fast enough to take on a less weakened enemy at an earlier date in France. There would have been a period of inactivity that might have jarred with British and American public opinion at home, simultaneously allowing the Germans to further strengthen their defenses in France, and the result of a repulsed invasion—a Dieppe on a far grander scale—would have had huge repercussions for Allied war strategy. It seems unlikely that Churchill's government would have been able to survive such a catastrophic defeat. Roosevelt, too, would have come under increased political pressure and might have had to refocus American efforts on the Pacific. The morale of the Allies and the countries of the Empire and Commonwealth would have been severely shaken, while that of Germany strengthened, perhaps allowing her to regroup and stabilize on the Eastern Front. All this is, of course, in the realm of counterfactual, but it is the sort of speculation that Churchill, the president, the Combined Chiefs of Staff, and their joint planners were obliged to engage in on a daily basis.

THE EXISTENCE OF ENOUGH LANDING CRAFT
TO GET THE ARMY SAFELY ASHORE AND KEEP IT SUPPLIED

The ability to deliver the troops and their equipment onto the beaches is an often-overlooked factor in the success of D-Day. Britain and the United States had large navies and could get their armies across the Channel but, without the control of large deepwater ports (which were inevitably going to be heavily defended), they had no way of getting them ashore. Planning for D-Day was dependent upon securing the necessary number and variety of landing ships and craft. These were essential for any amphibious operation, and they simply did not exist in any significant numbers at the beginning of the war. A report in April 1939 concluded that Britain would not have the landing craft to put a single brigade ashore for six months and would not be able to contemplate capturing and holding enemy territory for two years. Once the war started, production of such craft accelerated. By the end of 1941, the number under construction in Britain was 348, while the 1942 program planned to deliver 1,168 by May 1943. The Americans also threw themselves into large-scale production.

But it was not just a matter of building the landing craft. You also had to have a small, specialized navy to operate them. As early as October 1941, Mountbatten was talking about the need to train sixteen thousand men.

Churchill, Roosevelt, the Combined Chiefs of Staff, and their planning teams spent huge amounts of time wrestling with the logistics of the landing craft. They were needed for North Africa, Sicily, Italy, and in large numbers in the Pacific. They had to be maintained and moved. They also had to be available in Normandy in sufficient numbers not just for the initial assault, but for the crucial days thereafter when the beachheads needed to be reinforced and supplied from the sea. Such planning had to factor in losses through bad weather or enemy action.

The final Overlord operation would involve a staggering 4,126 landing ships and craft, including 55 large infantry landing ships, 236 tank landing ships, 248 smaller infantry and 837 tank landing craft, 502 assault craft and 464 craft for mechanized equipment, as well as a raft of more specialized vessels. It inevitably took time to assemble, to recruit and train the crews, and develop the procedures and tactics for such an armada.

THE DEVELOPMENT OF OFFICERS AND TROOPS
WITH REAL COMBAT EXPERIENCE AND HIGH MORALE

And then there was the issue of morale. The Allied forces might have had an increasing advantage in terms of quantity and quality of arms, but prior to 1943 they had yet to develop the ability to cultivate the self-belief to use them effectively. Until the Second Battle of El Alamein in November 1942, the British Army had not had a large-scale, decisive victory against the Germans. Small wonder, then, that Churchill wanted to savor and celebrate the moment, ordering the ringing of British church bells and proudly announcing at the annual Lord Mayor's luncheon in London's Mansion House: "We have victory—a remarkable and definite victory. The bright gleam has caught the helmets of our soldiers and warmed and cheered all our hearts." American troops had to suffer their own baptism of fire at the Battle of Kasserine Pass in Tunisia in February 1943, before they too gained in experience and became more battle-hardened.

Churchill, Eisenhower, and Montgomery were all great believers in the value of high morale. Winston would certainly have been aware of Napoleon's dictum that "the moral is to the physical, as three is to one." All three believed that commanders should be seen by their men.

Eisenhower felt that it paid big dividends in terms of morale, which, "given rough equality in other things, is supreme on the battlefield."

While Montgomery felt that "one of the chief factors for success in battle is the human factor."

Churchill maintained that "battles were not won by arithmetical calculations of the strength of the opposing forces." Having put himself center stage in 1940, becoming the main voice and image of the British war effort, he knew that he had a role to play in building and sustaining that confidence. Search the internet and you can find a wonderful period piece of *Pathé News* footage of Churchill visiting the troops in North Africa in June 1943. Dressed eccentrically but distinctively in his zip-up siren suit and a pith helmet, complete with dark glasses, walking cane, and cigar, the prime minister is clearly the star attraction as he travels from unit to unit and from one photo opportunity to another. He is pictured talking to a huge audience in the amphitheater at Carthage, visiting an American unit, driving past cheering troops while flashing his signature V for Victory salute and addressing others from the back of a lorry. It is a role that he clearly relished. This was deliberate leadership from the front by a natural showman who enjoyed the limelight.

Morale is a difficult quality to define, but it depended on having the right training and equipment, on having experience of victory, and confidence in commanders and colleagues.

By the end of 1943, the essential preconditions for Overlord had largely been met. The Allies had secured control of the sea and were increasingly dominant in the air. Germany had lost her European ally and was massively overextended, fighting on several fronts and unable to keep pace with Allied production. The British and Americans had developed and tested their system of combined command. Their troops had fought side by side in North Africa and Sicily and gained valuable experience of planning and executing amphibious landings on enemy-defended shorelines in both. None of this meant that the attack on France was a fait accompli. It was clear to all involved in its planning that this was an operation of an entirely different magnitude.

For a start, the invasions of North Africa and Sicily had confirmed the difficulties inherent in such amphibious operations. In Sicily, in July 1943, the Allies had overwhelming numerical superiority and were facing an already demoralized Italian army and a German force of little more than two divisions, far smaller than that in France. Yet they still encountered difficulties and took significant casualties. The weather once again caused problems, with the initial airborne assault running into high winds. Paratroops were scattered and gliders lost at sea. Problems coordinating the naval and air bombardments with the landings on the beaches resulted in aircraft being lost through "friendly" fire and troops put ashore in the wrong places. Though the beaches were secured, the Germans subsequently held up the advance of Montgomery's troops and ultimately evaded capture and escaped from the island.

Thomas Rodgers, known as TL, from Andalusia, Alabama, was a member of C Company of the 504th Parachute Regiment, part of the United States Eighty-second Airborne Division. Described by one of his comrades as, "Quiet, unobtrusive and retiring," TL was a big man, but one who "smoked little and [perhaps unusually for an American paratrooper] never drank or cursed." He was dropped into Sicily in the darkness of July 10, the second night of the operation, and was lucky to make it safely to the ground. Twenty-three aircraft and some of the descending paratroopers were shot down by their own side. It high-lighted a problem that needed to be fixed and led directly to the creation of a special unit of pathfinders, specially trained volunteers who would parachute behind enemy-held lines ahead of the main force and use lights and radar to guide the others safely in. Characteristically, TL was one of those who stepped forward for this special training. "When asked to accept a dangerous assignment, he would reflect a moment and then answer quietly, 'I'll go.'" Volunteering to be a pathfinder would prove a fateful decision that would lead him to play a key role in Operation Overlord.

In the short-term, however, Sicily had highlighted just how difficult Normandy might be. The northern French shoreline formed the most heavily defended section of Hitler's Atlantic Wall—a huge series of concrete fortifications intended to stretch from the French frontier with Spain all the way up to northern Norway. Plus, there was still the risk of U-boats, E-boats (gunboats), and mines in the Channel. The Luftwaffe was down but not out, and the German army still main-tained a large number of divisions in France (including formidable panzer divisions). Success could not be taken for granted. There were still lessons that needed to be learned. John Selwyn Lloyd, a young staff officer for the Second Army and future British foreign secretary, was just one of those charged with studying these beach landings and developing new techniques for moving troops on and off the shoreline. He visited Sicily in July 1943, testing out landing craft and examining beach obstacles.

The war also had a momentum of its own. Just as North Africa led to Sicily, success in Sicily culminated in the overthrow of Mussolini and to the Anglo-American allies moving belatedly onto the Italian mainland in an unsuccessful attempt to forestall German control of the country. Churchill was certainly a leading advocate of following up on Sicilian success by moving into Italy and stubbornly remained so in spite of the continuing buildup of American forces in Britain for Overlord. Even before the invasion of Sicily, and while protesting that he had no intention of interfering with plans for the cross-Channel operation, he was urging Eisenhower to quickly exploit any opportunity arising out of the fall of the island and expressing his fear that Ike would interpret his mission in too narrow a fashion. By July, he was convinced that the right strategy for 1944 was a maximum effort in Italy, advancing to the line of the river Po and preserving options to seize Vienna or turn against the south of France. Thereafter, he became the biggest advocate for two successive amphibious operations, designed to leapfrog enemy forces on the peninsula The first, with landings at Salerno in September 1943, aimed to seize Naples; the second at Anzio in January 1944 was designed to facilitate the capture of Rome. Both landings were heavily contested, and the Allies faced strong German counterattacks designed to force them back into the sea. The forces at Anzio struggled to break out of the beachheads. In a frank letter to General MacArthur, the American general commanding Allied forces in the southwest Pacific, Churchill admitted that what he had hoped would be a wildcat looked in danger of becoming a "stranded whale."

Far from the soft underbelly of Europe, as described by Churchill, Italy was to prove a hard, mountainous spine, one that was extremely costly in men and materials. Churchill specifically asked that some American paratroops be kept back from France for use in Italy. As a result, TL Rodgers and the 504th would go into Salerno and Anzio and would spend the next few months slowly fighting their way up the peninsula. One of their number would angrily reply with a roll call of battlefields when told that the paratroops had it easy and were the glamor boys of the army: "Sicily, Salerno, Shrapnel Pass, the Plains of Naples, the Volturno, Cassino and sixty-three days on Anzio. Now go goof your gums on a clam, you silly bastard!" But, as time went on and losses mounted, the American military leadership increasingly looked at these operations as pulling resources away from the main battle in France. To Brooke and the British chiefs of staff, Salerno and Anzio were salutary warnings of the difficulties that would be encountered in storming the Normandy beaches.

But it was the natural momentum of war, and the difficulty of disengaging from operations once started, that helped keep the Allies away from the northern French coastline.

As the second half of 1943 unfolded, as American forces began to arrive in Britain in strength, and as the preconditions for a cross-Channel assault were steadily met, Churchill fell into line and supported Overlord as the primary joint operation for 1944. But this did not mean he saw it as the only operation.

He undoubtedly had one eye on the postwar situation. If Britain were to remain an imperial power, which was certainly his hope, then she needed to control the eastern Mediterranean. Winston was wary of instability in the Balkans or Soviet domination in Greece, especially after the Italian surrender, and was furious when Eisenhower refused to divert resources from his Mediterranean command to enable the British to occupy the Greek Dodecanese islands formerly held by Italy and now seized by Germany. Foremost among these was Rhodes. He appealed to Roosevelt in a telegram of October 8, 1943, earnestly praying that his views might receive some consideration at this critical juncture and stressing that "this operation could be fitted in to our plan without detriment either to the advance in Italy of which as you know I have always been an advocate, or of the build-up of Overlord which I am prepared faithfully to support." Notice the revealing contrast between his active promotion of campaigns in the Mediterranean with his passive endorsement of Normandy. Unsurprisingly, it prompted a quick slap-down from the president who had no intention of being diverted into what he viewed as a Greek sideshow, arguing, "Strategically, if we get the Aegean Islands [including Rhodes], I ask myself where do we go from there and vice-versa where would the Germans go if for some time they retain possession of the Islands."

Churchill's telegram to British foreign secretary Anthony Eden, who was visiting Moscow, captures his position. Written on October 29, it confirms that he still wanted the best of both worlds:

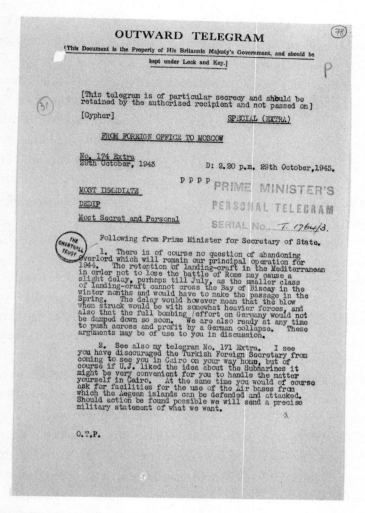

(78)

P

(31)

[This telegram is of particular secrecy and should be
retained by the authorised recipient and not passed on]

[Cypher]   SPECIAL (EXTRA)

FROM FOREIGN OFFICE TO MOSCOW

No. 174 Extra
29th October, 1943   D: 2.20 p.m. 29th October, 1943.

                              p p p p   PRIME MINISTER'S
MOST IMMEDIATE
                              PERSONAL TELEGRAM
DEDIP

Most Secret and Personal   SERIAL No. T. 1764/3.

    Following from Prime Minister for Secretary of State.

    1. There is of course no question of abandoning
Overlord which will remain our principal operation for
1944. The retention of landing-craft in the Mediterranean
in order not to lose the battle of Rome may cause a
slight delay, perhaps till July, as the smaller class
of landing-craft cannot cross the Bay of Biscay in the
winter months and would have to make the passage in the
Spring. The delay would however mean that the blow
when struck would be with somewhat heavier forces, and
also that the full bombing /effort on Germany would not
be damped down so soon. We are also ready at any time
to push across and profit by a German collapse. These
arguments may be of use to you in discussion.

    2. See also my telegram No. 171 Extra. I see
you have discouraged the Turkish Foreign Secretary from
coming to see you in Cairo on your way home, but of
course if U.J. liked the idea about the Submarines it
might be very convenient for you to handle the matter
yourself in Cairo. At the same time you would of course
ask for facilities for the use of the Air bases from
which the Aegean islands can be defended and attacked.
Should action be found possible we will send a precise
military statement of what we want.

O.T.P.

Telegram from Churchill to Eden, October 29, 1943. (Churchill Papers, CHAR 20/122/78)

Churchill was trying to maintain as much equipment as possible, including vital landing craft, in the Italian theater for as long as possible. Rebuffed by Roosevelt, he was also trying to enlist the Soviet Union and Turkey in his plans for an offensive against the Dodecanese islands. The Turks had spent much blood, time, and effort to seize Rhodes from Europeans in the fifteenth and sixteenth centuries; now Churchill wanted them to abandon their neutrality and help the British hold it against the Germans by providing air and naval bases. Perhaps unsurprisingly, they refused.

For Churchill, these Italian and Mediterranean campaigns were also about winning laurels. It was now obvious that the Americans would contribute the largest forces for Overlord and that the commander in France would therefore be American—either Marshall or Eisenhower. Ike got the job in December 1943, and the British general, "Jumbo" Wilson, replaced him as Supreme Commander in the Mediterranean. This left Brooke very disappointed, as Churchill had implied to him that the job might be his.

Yet Churchill still had to fight a rearguard action throughout the autumn to quash American suggestions that the Overlord and Mediterranean theaters be combined into a giant European super command. He clearly feared that the result would be a single, all powerful, American commander in chief, most probably General George Marshall. On the other hand, with Wilson as the Supreme Commander in the Mediterranean and Alexander commanding the Fifteenth Army Group fighting in Italy, Churchill could at least claim that the British were still in charge on one battlefront. The capture of Rome seemed a particularly glittering prize and Churchill was not ready to give up on it.

It was in this spirit that the British prime minister approached the Tehran Conference, the first meeting of the "Big Three"—himself, Roosevelt, and Stalin—held in the Iranian capital in November 1943. En route to see the US president for a pre-meeting in Cairo, he fumed about the "evils of Americans." He was clearly very animated, and Brooke was worried about the line his boss might take in the conference, with Churchill inclined to say to the president, "all right if you won't play with us in the Mediterranean we won't play with you in the English Channel," and being prepared to let the United States direct its main effort to the Pacific. His mood cannot have been made any easier by poor health, exacerbated by the strain of travel. It was no doubt further tested by Roosevelt's refusal to discuss the European strategy with him at their pre-meeting in Egypt. The presence of Chiang Kai-shek, the Chinese

Casey Villa,
CAIRO.

~~XXXXXXXXXX~~
~~XXXXXXXX~~

November 26, 1943.

My darling,

Sarah assures me that she has kept you up
to date with her accounts of our journey. We came
through the whole way safely and uneventfully on the
RENOWN, but many guardian angels were employed on the
sea and in the air to ward off evil. I have completely
recovered from my cold, ~~but~~ it has left behind a nasty
cough which occurs in the morning when I awake but
does not bother me during the daytime.

We have now been five days here and so far
have only really tackled the Chinese end of the business.
However, a good deal has gone on behind the scenes in
the sense of bringing the British and Americans nearer
together on the great and grim issues with which we are
confronted. Tomorrow at first screech of cock we
start for CAIRO THREE and we shall stay there I hope
three or four nights. U.J. meets us on the evening
of the 28th. It has not been possible to come to

6.

I have not yet succeeded in gripping affairs
as I hope and mean to out here, but I have a feeling
things will go the way I want. Tomorrow we start so
very early that I am now going to sleep for an hour
before dining with the Embassy in Cairo.

Tender love my darling Clemmie
How I wish you were out here
to see the variegated show.

Your ever loving

W

First and last page from Churchill's letter to Clementine Churchill, November 26, 1943.
(Baroness Spencer-Churchill Papers, CSCT 2/32/42 & 47)

nationalist leader, meant that their Cairo discussions focused primarily on the war in East Asia and the Pacific.

On November 26, Winston sent a long letter to Clementine from Cairo. Key passages are revealing of his frustrations:

> We have now been five days here and so far have only really tackled the Chinese end of the business. However a good deal has gone on behind the scenes in the sense of bringing the British and Americans nearer together on the great and grim issues with which we are confronted. Tomorrow at first screech of cock we start for CAIRO THREE [Tehran] and we shall stay there I hope three of four nights. U.J. [Uncle Joe, Churchill's nickname for Stalin] meets us on the evening of the 28ᵗʰ. It has not been possible to come to grips with our main problems without knowing what are his views and wishes. . . .
>
> Let me know how public opinion is going on different things. Of course I know it is said in London that I was frustrated in my conduct of the war in the Mediterranean during the last two months. It is not for me to challenge this. I cannot pretend to have an adequate defence of what actually occurred. I have been fighting with my hands tied behind my back, but now I hope to get better arrangements and procure the necessary decisions for future blows on a good scale. . . .
>
> I have not yet succeeded in gripping affairs as I hope and mean to out here, but I have a feeling things will go the way I want. Tomorrow we start so very early that I am now going to sleep for an hour before dining with the Embassy in Cairo.
>
> Tender love my darling Clemmie. How I wish you were out here w[ith] me to see the variegated show.

At Tehran, Churchill was to be disappointed. Roosevelt went out of his way to establish a bilateral relationship with Stalin, and Uncle Joe's views and wishes on Overlord were in harmony with the president's. The Russian and American leaders were now united in their clear desire for a cross-Channel assault in the late spring of 1944. This would be supported by a simultaneous Soviet offensive on the Eastern Front and by an Allied invasion of southern France, drawing on troops from Italy. In breach of the security principle that codenames should have no discernible connection with their operation, the attack in the south was to be codenamed Anvil, presumably because it would be the anvil on which the hammer of Overlord would break the enemy. Churchill tried to stress the importance of continuing to fight in Italy and the Balkans, arguing that in the short-term such operations would continue to draw forces from the Russian front and that later they would divert German forces from Overlord. Success in the Mediterranean might yet bring Turkey into the war on the Allied side. Ultimately, however, the die was cast. A date of May 1944 was set for the invasion of France (Brooke's diary indicates by June 1, 1944) and the primacy, Churchill called it "tyranny," of Overlord was established.

Prior to the "Big Three" meeting with Roosevelt and Stalin, Churchill's old friend Field Marshal Jan Smuts, the prime minister of South Africa, had advised him to secure the Italian flank before embarking on these new operations in France. Churchill had replied, "I hope you will realize that British loyalty to Overlord is keystone of arch of Anglo-American co-operation. Personally I think enough forces exist for both hands to be played and I believe this to be the right strategy."

But the reality was that his hands were increasingly tied. Negotiations with Turkey had failed. Progress in Italy was slow, and more resources would now be siphoned off for France, including for operations against the south of the country. The Balkans were a dead end, Italy a secondary theater. Regardless of Churchill's doubts, the way home now lay firmly through France to Berlin.

His response, according to his long-standing friend Violet Bonham Carter was to ruefully remark:

There I sat with the great Russian bear on one side of me with paws outstretched, and, on the other side, the great American buffalo, and between the two sat the poor little English donkey, who was the only one, the only one of the three, who knew the right way home.

In the context of the convoluted path that the western Allies trod to be poised to invade Western Europe in June 1944, many steps were taken. Under Montgomery, Stan Hollis fought with his Sixth Green Howards comrades from El Alamein through the western desert to Tunisia, eventually linking up with the first US troops to see combat after their landings in November 1942 in French Morocco and Algeria. With North Africa cleared of all Axis forces, Stan Hollis was part of Montgomery's next strategic move in the Allied invasion of Sicily beginning on July 9, 1943. While Stan was fighting, and nearly dying, at Primosole Bridge on the Plain of Catania, General Montgomery could be said to be consolidating his understanding of how to fight and win on the mid-twentieth-century battlefield. He had observed and learned in the closing months of the First World War that the skillful coordination of armor, infantry, artillery, and airpower with sufficient and massive stocks of ammunition could break well-defended positions and restore maneuverability to the battlefield. He eventually achieved this at El Alamein—albeit at some considerable human cost—in the invasion of Sicily, and the subsequent invasion of Italy, before being withdrawn on December 23, 1943, to prepare for the invasion of Europe.

On arrival back in London, Montgomery found himself once more under the overall command of General Dwight D. Eisenhower, but responsible for developing the plans for what became Operation Overlord, the invasion of Europe. He inherited the aftermath of the disastrous assault on the port of Dieppe, Operation Jubilee, in which almost a thousand Canadian soldiers had been killed and nearly two thousand taken prisoner in demonstrating that capturing a well-defended port on the French coast was somewhere between very dangerous and impossible. He resolved that the future invasion was to be across the beaches. His old adversary Erwin Rommel, now in command of the western defenses in France, had come to much the same conclusion. Construction of the Atlantic Wall, largely by forced labor, was accelerated. The stage was being set for the final showdown between the western Allies and Germany on the coast of France. But where? And when? Stan Hollis, now withdrawn with his Sixth Green Howards battalion from Italy to prepare for the battle for Europe, wondered much the same.

TOP SECRET

SHAEF/18231/Ops

25 March 1944

Dear *Prime Minister*

I do not know whether the suggestion I am going to make is practicable or whether it will be repugnant to you personally.

The large scale exercise which it is necessary to carry out about 3rd - 5th May, will seriously detract from the degree of surprise that Plan 'FORTITUDE' is designed to achieve, if the enemy should interpret it in the true sense, as our final rehearsal. Accordingly everything possible must be done to convince the enemy that this exercise is the first, and that Operation 'OVERLORD' is the second of a series of exercises which must be carried out before D day.

I, therefore, submit for your considered opinion the proposal that when you next address the Nation you include a statement somewhat in the following terms: "It will be necessary to hold a series of exercises during the next few months which, being unprecedented in scale, will call for many restrictions on the public. These must be borne with patience and it is the duty of every citizen to refrain from speculation." I consider that such an address, framed in your own words, would greatly assist in concealing from the enemy the date of 'OVERLORD'.

It is intended that after your statement a similar warning will be given to the DUTCH, BELGIAN and FRENCH peoples through the medium of the BBC, primarily with the object of preventing untimely uprising in their countries.

Faithfully,

Dwight D Eisenhower

The Right Honourable Winston Churchill,
"Chequers".

TOP SECRET

Letter from Eisenhower to Churchill, March 25, 1944.
(Churchill Papers, CHAR 9/204B/175)

Chapter 5

Bodyguard of Lies

"In wartime... truth is so precious that she should always be attended by a bodyguard of lies."

THE LATE AFTERNOON OF NOVEMBER 30, 1943, FOUND WINSTON Churchill celebrating his sixty-ninth birthday in the unlikely surroundings of the Russian Legation in Tehran, the capital city of Iran. Here, he was taking part in a plenary meeting of the first "Big Three" conference with President Roosevelt and Marshal Stalin. The British prime minister and the American president were accompanied by their leading political and military advisers—Hopkins, Harriman, Marshall, King, Eden, Dill, Brooke, Cunningham, Portal, and Ismay were all present. Stalin was there with Molotov, his minister of Foreign Affairs, and the Soviet military hero Marshal Kliment Voroshilov. Agreement had already been reached on launching Operation Overlord in May 1944. Whatever the precise date, the British and Americans were now committed to a cross-Channel operation within the next six months "on the largest scale that would be permitted by the landing craft available at that time."

Toward the end of the meeting, the conversation turned to the difficulties of hiding the preparations for such an offensive from the enemy. Churchill referred to the number of depots for equipment being constructed in Southern England and the changing appearance of the coastline.

He asked Stalin about making arrangements for a combined cover plan, prompting the Russian leader to describe how on "such occasions, the Soviets had achieved success by the construction of false tanks, airplanes and airfields" in sectors where no operations were planned, knowing that they would be picked up by German intelligence. This had sometimes been done on a huge scale and been accompanied by the deliberate use of radio signals to lure the enemy into attacking the wrong targets.

In response, Churchill observed that, "In wartime . . . truth is so precious that she should always be attended by a bodyguard of lies." The full quote appears in his war memoirs; the contemporary minutes simply record him saying "truth deserves a bodyguard of lies."

As Churchill conversed with Stalin in Tehran, he knew that deception was but one part of the intelligence armory that would be crucial to success on D-Day. To deceive the enemy, it was essential to know what they were thinking and planning. To measure success, it was imperative to see their responses to Allied actions in real time. And at all times it was essential to guard against enemy espionage and make sure that the Allied plans were adequately protected. Put simply, intelligence and deception were two sides of the same coin, and Churchill knew that one of the key prerequisites for deception planning was to try to discover through intelligence what the enemy thought you were going to do. If successful, one could then construct a deception plan to reinforce the enemy's (wrong) convictions about your future intentions. Of course, the enemy would be trying to do the same thing.

The area of intelligence and counterintelligence, deception and espionage, is one in which Churchill had a long-standing interest. He relished hearing about covert missions and successful spying operations, and by 1944 he already had a long history of personal involvement with the security services. Indeed, as Warren Dockter has pointed out, his very first military adventure in Cuba, between November and December 1895, around the time of his twenty-first birthday, had been officially sanctioned by the War Office precisely because it had a clear intelligence value. Churchill and his friend and fellow officer Reginald Barnes used their army leave to take the role of British military observers, accompanying a Spanish column engaged in suppressing a Cuban national uprising. But they had also been charged with gathering information on Spanish weaponry and tactics. Before departure, the two young subalterns had been summoned to a meeting with General Chapman, the army's director of military intelligence, who furnished them with "maps and much valuable information" and requested that they "collect information and statistics on various points," including the effect of the new Mauser bullet being used by the Spanish.

Young Churchill had seen for himself the value of military intelligence as a war correspondent and then soldier in the Second Boer War. And once in Parliament, as the newly elected MP for Oldham, he called for the reorganization and additional funding of the intelligence division of the army, which he described as being starved "for want of both money and brains."

As Home Secretary in the Edwardian era, he had strengthened the creation of the new home security and foreign intelligence services (which would become MI5 and MI6), supporting the clandestine examination of mail and the introduction of a register of resident aliens. As First Lord of the Admiralty in 1914–1915, he had supported the signals interception, codebreaking, and analysis work of the Navy's Room 40, the precursor to Bletchley Park. In the 1920s, he had used his intelligence community contacts to inform his campaign against communism, before switching his focus in the following decade to Nazi Germany, and on becoming prime minister in 1940 he had insisted on seeing as much raw intelligence as possible, setting up his own statistical unit within the Admiralty and then Downing Street to help him make his own interpretations and analysis.

Information flowed into Churchill's office from a huge range of civilian and military channels. His own daughter Sarah was a section officer in the Photographic Interpretation Unit of the Royal Air Force Intelligence Branch at Medmenham, where she sometimes worked twelve-hour overnight shifts looking at aerial reconnaissance photos in support of European and North African operations; later writing, "Puzzling and tedious as it often was, there were moments of terrific excitement and discovery." Human intelligence was collected from interrogated prisoners and from the network of agents overseas operated by the Secret Intelligence Service (SIS, also known as MI6). German radio traffic was intercepted and analyzed to identify the location of enemy units. But

Churchill quite rightly attached the greatest significance to the special signals intelligence work of the Government Code and Cypher School at Bletchley Park, codenamed Ultra. Hidden in plain sight in the heart of the Buckinghamshire countryside, a team of codebreakers and analysts was engaged in breaking encoded enemy communications, including the fiendishly complex Enigma cipher machines used by the Germans to protect their most secret diplomatic and military messages.

By the end of 1943, Churchill was sitting like a spider at the heart of his own worldwide intelligence web. MI5, the Home Intelligence Service, was responsible for rounding up German spies and had been successful in turning almost all of them into double agents. This was coordinated through the Twenty Committee, so named because the Roman numerals for twenty were XX, a double cross. The Special Operations Executive (SOE) was smuggling agents into occupied countries to support sabotage and guerrilla operations. The Political Warfare Executive (PWE) was disseminating covert propaganda to undermine enemy morale and encourage resistance. Deception plans to protect military operations were being devised and coordinated by the London Controlling Section (LCS), a clandestine military operation that worked alongside the Joint Planning Staff. These organizations had all been developed or expanded during the war and now enjoyed levels of manpower, resource, funding, and power that would have been inconceivable in peacetime.

Coordinating this complex structure of overlapping and sometimes rival secret organizations was not easy. The Joint Intelligence Committee reported directly to the prime minister and the chiefs of staff. But Churchill also had his own liaison officer to the security services, in the form of his trusted aide Desmond Morton. Morton, like many of those involved in wartime intelligence, had served with distinction in the First World War, acquiring a bullet that remained lodged somewhere dangerously near his heart, and was the sort of buccaneering personality whose company the prime minister particularly appreciated. Meanwhile, Sir Stewart Menzies, the head of SIS and known as "C," supplied Churchill with his daily diet of selected raw intelligence derived from Bletchley Park. Access to this material was understandably extremely tightly controlled. It was brought to Churchill in a special locked buff box for his eyes only and for which he kept the key. His Private Secretary, Jock Colville, made the mistake of recording this secret in his diary in October 1940, only to realize his mistake and cross the whole page through.

When the leading codebreakers asked for more resources in October 1941, Churchill immediately issued an order that their requests should be met "on extreme priority." The work of Bletchley Park did not become public knowledge until 1974. This meant that its role was not evident in early histories of the Second World War, including Churchill's own memoirs and the British official histories of the conflict. Yet it under-pinned all intelligence activities. The following letter is a rare wartime example of Churchill mentioning the establishment at Bletchley and shows his continued patronage of the organization:

(201)

October 16, 1943.

Personal and Confidential.

My dear Postmaster-General,

I am glad to learn from the Director of the establishment at Bletchley of the very valuable assistance which your Department is affording him, particularly with regard to satisfying the vast communication needs and in the provision of certain highly technical and delicate machinery.

You are at liberty to convey, confidentially, my appreciation of this invaluable contribution to the war effort to those officials who are directly engaged in assisting this organization.

Yours very sincerely,

Captain the Rt. Hon. Harry F.C. Crookshank, M.P.

Letter from Churchill to Postmaster-General, October 16, 1943.
(Churchill Papers, CHAR 20/94B/201)

The British prime minister made a point of meeting with many of those involved in clandestine war work, and clearly enjoyed hearing firsthand the details of secret operations. No previous occupant of 10 Downing Street had ever been as informed on intelligence issues. But this created its own problems. Churchill had to adjudicate on competing demands and rivalries between the different organizations, and to decide what could be revealed, when, and to whom. He regularly bombarded his commanders in the field with "most secret" or Boniface information derived from his secret intelligence sources but had to be careful not to do so in a way that endangered agents or compromised the material derived from the breaking of the German codes. A principle was established that no Allied operation could be undertaken in response to Ultra information if to do so might reveal to the Germans that their codes had been broken; there must always be some plausible alternative cover story for how the information had been obtained. This might take the form of a plane being hastily dispatched to overfly a newly revealed enemy location.

The following is an example of Churchill using the Boniface information to inform his commander in the field. In this case, the recipient is Montgomery in Tunisia in the closing stages of the North African campaign in March 1943:

Scrambled to C.'s office 4 p.m.
28.3.43.

CLEAR THE LINE. PRIME MINISTER'S

PERSONAL TELEGRAM

SERIAL No. T·391|3

PRIME MINISTER TO GENERAL MONTGOMERY.
 Personal and Secret.

(To be transmitted through 'C').

1.   Bravo: I was sure of it.   Now the question is
the cop.

2.   Presume you know all Boniface, viz: Firstly,
164th Division has lost nearly all its vehicles and heavy
weapons.   Secondly, 21st and 15th Panzers are regathering
on heights south-east of El Hamma.   Thirdly, Italian
Commander-in-Chief (quote) of Mareth garrisons (unquote)
asked 15th Panzer Division to provide a battle group to
cover his last retreat at Zouitinat, a point about 13
miles south-east of El Hamma and 13 miles south-west of
Gabes.   You should have received all this through other
channels, but to make sure I repeat it.

            God bless you.

                    W.S.C.

                    28.3.43

Telegram from Churchill to Montgomery, March 28, 1943.
(Churchill Papers, CHAR 20/108/121)

Good intelligence underpinned the success of Overlord but some
of the ingredients for that success had only just come to fruition by
late 1943. It was only in the spring that a deal has been reached in
Washington, DC, for full Anglo-American collaboration on codebreaking and signals intelligence. Meanwhile, as we have seen, the

breaking of the German naval Shark settings for U-boat traffic by the Bletchley codebreakers in March had been vital in winning the Battle of the Atlantic, enabling the location of enemy submarines to be accurately determined, and thereby making the passage of men and materials across the ocean much safer. The subsequent cracking of the strategic ciphers between Berlin and the German army commanders in France gave a further advantage prior to D-Day, allowing the Allies to know the disposition and planned movements of many enemy units.

By the time of the Tehran Conference, the British had rounded up the German agents in Britain, had developed a comprehensive network of double agents to feed back misinformation, were listening in real time to German communications, and had established a network of guerrilla groups and agents within occupied France, ready to undertake sabotage operations.

It was a world with which Joan Bright had become very familiar. Her calm efficiency and engaging manner had brought her to the notice of General "Pug" Ismay, Churchill's military adviser and chief of staff, and she had been brought upstairs to the "principal" floor within Whitehall, where she was running a Special Information Centre for the British military commanders and maintaining the registry for the chiefs of staff. In her words:

> I was given a carpet, a long polished table, wall maps, an easy chair and some official secrets.

In fact, she was now one of the best-informed people in Britain: a keeper of the official secrets. As such she was also one of a very few who were aware of the final piece in the intelligence jigsaw—the deception planning that would provide Churchill's bodyguard of lies.

Even as Churchill joked with Stalin at Tehran, he already knew better than most that the British were well versed in such deception operations. In April 1942, when first considering American plans for an assault against the continent, he had prefigured his "bodyguard of lies" quote by telling Hopkins and Marshall that "the true objectives could . . . be obscured in a cloud of rumours." In fact, the British were already masters of the dark arts.

When fighting superior numbers of Italians in North Africa in 1940, General Wavell had created a special "A" Force to trick the Italians in the desert. It was led by Lieutenant Colonel Dudley Clarke. Dennis Wheatley, who regarded Clarke as the "Father of Deception," described him as small and fair-haired but with a strange quietness about his movements and an uncanny habit of suddenly appearing in a room without anyone having noticed him enter it. He built up a formidable network of secret agents and undertook deception operations throughout the huge Mediterranean theater, including the Middle East and Africa. Subsequently, as commander-in-chief India, Wavell employed Major Peter Fleming, the brother of the James Bond creator, Ian Fleming (who was himself working in naval intelligence), to head up his deception section in the subcontinent. So successful were these overseas operations that they led in October 1941 to the creation of the London Controlling Section (LCS) with a mandate to coordinate Allied deception worldwide and to lead deception planning in the European theater.

Wavell wrote to Churchill urging that the unit be strengthened. It began to assume a greater prominence from June 1942, partly because the Allies were now finally in a position to contemplate more offensive operations in Europe, which would require deception plans, but also because of the appointment of Lieutenant Colonel John Bevan as the Controlling Officer. Bevan had distinguished himself in the First World War, but he was far from a standard career soldier. In 1918, he had been given the task of establishing the German Order of Battle for their spring offensive. This work had brought him to the attention of Churchill, then minister of munitions. Thereafter, Bevan had spent the interwar period running the family firm of stockbrokers and was well connected in military and political circles, being the brother-in-law of General Alexander. He quickly developed a good personal relationship with General Brooke, thereby ensuring that LCS's voice was heard by the chiefs of staff at the very summit of Allied decision-making.

Bevan surrounded himself with other well-connected, intelligent, slightly unorthodox, and creative individuals like the author

PRIME MINISTER'S
PERSONAL TELEGRAM

SERIAL No. _T. 759/2_

COPY

IZ 354
TOO 1230/21
TOR 1415Z/21

MOST SECRET.

MOST IMMEDIATE.

From: Armindia.

To: Air Ministry.

12461/C   21.5.42.

Private for Prime Minister from General Wavell.

      I have always had considerable belief in deceiving
and disturbing enemy by false information. C in C Mideast
instituted special Branch Staff under selected officer charged
with deception enemy and it has had considerable success. I
have similar branch in India and am already involved in
several deception plans. These however can have local and
ephemeral effect only, unless part of general deception plan
on wide scale. IHQS can only be provided from place where
main strategical policy is decided and Principal Intelligence
Centre is located. Coherent and long term planning of
deception must be centred there. Fully appreciate value of
work done by I S S B and Controlling Officer but have
impression the approach is defensive rather than aggressive and
confined mainly to cover plans for particular operations.
May I suggest for your personal consideration that policy
of bold imaginative deception worked between London,
Washington and Commanders in the field by only officers with
special qualifications might shew good dividend, particularly
in case of Japanese.

TOO 1230/21

(Circulation)

Col. Jacob.

Telegram from General Wavell to Churchill, May 21, 1942.
(Churchill Papers, CHAR 20/75/68)

Dennis Wheatley, whose scarlet-lined Royal Air Force greatcoat and cane must have made him look like a creation from one of his own horror novels, or Bevan's deputy, Major Ronald Wingate, a double first from Balliol (meaning that he graduated from Balliol College, University of Oxford, with top honors in two subjects), who had served as a political officer in Aden during the First World War, before spending much of his career in India and becoming governor of Baluchistan. The section was strategically located within the Treasury buildings, close to Churchill's own offices, and not far from where Joan Bright was working with General Ismay and the chiefs of staff. This meant that LCS was well placed to work with the wartime planning staffs and the other intelligence agencies. Indeed, in its early days, the unit lacked its own secretarial assistance, and Dennis Wheatley was obliged to turn to Joan Bright for help with typing out one top-secret deception plan. Of course, the central location was also ideal for conducting clandestine business over alcohol-fueled dinners in the privacy of London's Pall Mall Clubland.

LCS's first experience was gained in protecting Operation Torch, the landings in Morocco and Algeria. There was a very real fear among the Allied planners that the buildup of forces in Britain or in the tiny British enclave of Gibraltar would be seen by enemy agents from Spain and that they would be targeted by Luftwaffe bombers or U-boats as they assembled for the assault on the beaches. The initial LCS cover story for the buildup in Britain was that forces were being assembled for a possible attack against Norway or France. This was not easy. For the story to be convincing, there had to be troops available and equipped for such operations in the United Kingdom, and those troops had to believe that they might be about to be sent across the North Sea or the Channel. With all available resources being diverted to support Torch and finding equipment for fighting in North Africa, it was obviously going to be difficult to persuade the authorities to provide Arctic clothing and supplies. As Wheatley put it, "nearly everyone we approached scarcely bothered to conceal the fact that he thought this new-fangled deception racket a lot of nonsense."

More successful were the cover plans for the converging of the Allied forces in North Africa. Information was put out that they were going to reinforce Malta or invade the south of France or attack Italy or Greece. This information was fed to the enemy by double agents, through diplomatic channels, by misleading the troops involved and by planting false intelligence. The aim was to create uncertainty and at the very least contribute to enemy caution. The fact that German air and submarine forces were held back farther east of the actual objectives suggests that it enjoyed some success. These were all lessons that were learned and applied for D-Day. Similar measures were applied the following spring when the Allies made their next major move into Sicily.

One particular deception—Operation Mincemeat—has since gained a particular notoriety. In a plot that would later become the subject of a bestselling book and successful film, the aptly named *The Man Who Never Was* (remade in 2022 as the film *Operation Mincemeat*), the body of a Welsh drifter was given the identity of a British staff officer and dropped into the Mediterranean off the coast of Spain. The false plans carried by the corpse suggested that the British were going to attack in the eastern Mediterranean or Sardinia rather than in North Africa. When the body was recovered, the false dispatches were passed to the Germans. Even if they did not swallow them "rod, line and sinker" (as Wheatley certainly believed), enough uncertainty was caused to prevent them from moving more troops to the west. The brainchild of a flight-lieutenant in MI5 (the home intelligence service) but carried out largely by a team from within MI6 (the overseas intelligence service) and supported by Bevan's LCS, Mincemeat demonstrates the complex interdepartmental nature of these operations. It is also a good example of creating a credible plan, as the Allies had indeed debated attacking Sardinia. Indeed, some on the British planning staff continued to believe that it would have been a less costly operation than Sicily and more effective in reasserting control of the Mediterranean. Churchill received a personal briefing about Mincemeat from Bevan.

After the appointment of General Morgan, Colonel Bevan and his team worked with COSSAC to maintain the pressure on the Germans in France through several further, if ultimately less successful, deceptions involving supposed operations against Norway or the French shoreline. As specified by Churchill in his directive to Morgan, these were designed to keep the enemy in France occupied and unsettled, to draw Luftwaffe forces out into combat, and, most important, to prevent the reinforcement of Italy. This led inevitably to further codenames as a succession of interrelated deception operations were concocted to keep the Germans guessing. Under the overall designation of Operation Cockade, there was Tindall, the notional sailing of five divisions from Scotland against the city of Stavangar in Norway, that would then be called off to release forces for Operation Starkey, a feigned attack with fourteen British and Canadian divisions on Boulogne, supposedly to be followed almost immediately by Operation Wadham, an assault by two American Army divisions on Brittany, both of which would also be called off at the last minute.

In his memoirs, General Morgan was open about the difficulties faced in mounting these deceptions. It was not always possible to get the resources to make them convincing. Perhaps unsurprisingly, the Admiralty refused to loan him their obsolete battleships to impersonate an invasion fleet, nor would the Royal Air Force Fighter Command allow enemy reconnaissance aircraft access to British airspace in order to overfly and photograph his dummy aeroplanes and airfields.

Yet these fake operations were undertaken with increasing scale and sophistication, involving real troop and ship movements, supported by actual air attacks on enemy positions. Operation Starkey was the largest. It took place in late August and early September 1943; a feint against the French coast around Calais by a genuine naval force, designed to test the German response and draw the Luftwaffe into a real air battle with the RAF. A huge force was assembled in the waters between Gravesend and Southampton, comprising 100 major and 260 minor landing craft, plus a further 175 dummy landing craft and 95 coastal vessels. There was a special fleet of 20 oceangoing ships, designed to test the sailing of a convoy through the channel—something that had not been attempted since the fall of France. This was a naval force three times larger than that used in the raid on Dieppe.

A full-scale movement exercise was undertaken by the army to create the impression that several divisions were being concentrated in the south of England. Commandos launched a number of raids on the

French coast. The Twenty Committee used its network of double agents to feed false intelligence to the Germans, suggesting that an assault was imminent. Three days were spent minesweeping and clearing a path for the force in the Channel. Antiaircraft units were installed on the ships, and tanks were loaded into landing craft at Dover. German airfields in the Pas-de-Calais region were heavily bombed.

Churchill followed the progress with great interest, sending a good-luck telegram as the operation launched. For him, its primary importance was almost certainly as a diversion for the Allied landings at Salerno in Italy, pulling German air forces away from the Mediterranean.

Hughes-Hallett, now a commodore, was responsible for the naval planning. On September 8, the ships sailed from their anchorages around the Solent toward Dover, before turning toward Boulogne and the beaches around Fécamp. Hughes-Hallett was on board the destroyer HMS *Albrighton* as the fake force sailed out into the Channel, maintaining close contact by means of a scrambled VHF link with Air Marshal Leigh-Mallory, who was providing fighter cover and standing ready with his forces should the German Air Force respond to this bait. A smoke screen was provided from coastal and landing craft, while radio jamming was provided by mobile units driving along the cliffs of the British South Coast. The ships got to within ten miles of the French coast before turning back. All ships were safely back in port by September 9.

Starkey failed to bring about the hoped-for air battle. Intercepted radio traffic indicated that the Germans suspected it was a feint and held back their forces. The operation was regarded as a failure by those who planned it. Yet there were some positives. The ships were able to sail down the Channel largely unopposed. The enemy coastal batteries around Calais did open fire, but without result. In so doing, they revealed their location and were exposed to attack by American bombers. Overall, the operation contributed to the general German uncertainty about Allied intentions, and reinforced the view that Calais was where the Allied attack would ultimately come. It also proved a most valuable training exercise for navy and army testing the interservice and international cooperation that would be vital for successful landings and confirming that the United States Air Force and the RAF could work well together. It highlighted the difficulty of assembling landing craft in sufficient numbers and led to loading procedures being refined and improved. Most important, perhaps, it provided valuable lessons for the bigger deception that would accompany Overlord itself.

Churchill's quote about "bodyguard of lies" was seen by the members of LCS, who had access to all the War Cabinet papers. John Bevan's response was to pay homage and give their deception operation for Overlord the codename of Operation Bodyguard, which would once again seem to breach basic security protocol by being too revealing of its purpose. All the techniques developed by the unit since 1942 now came into play and on a much grander scale. By early 1944, it was clear to the Germans that Allied forces were being assembled in huge numbers in Britain and that an invasion of the continent must soon be attempted. Suggestions that these troops were going to the Mediterranean or Pacific would no longer be convincing. The decision had been made to land on the Normandy beaches. Now it was vital to trick the enemy into believing that the Allies were planning to land elsewhere in northern Europe, and—once the landings had taken place—to convince them that Normandy was just a feint and that the main assault was still to come at a different location. If this could be done, then the Germans might hold back some of their forces for a few weeks, buying the Allies vital time to establish, secure, and reinforce their bridgehead.

The plan, developed by Bevan and the LCS, and refined by Lieutenant Colonel David Strangeways, who was brought from Italy by Montgomery, did this by playing on existing German fears. It was clear that Rommel had identified the Pas-de-Calais region as a likely invasion site. It was the closest point to Britain, and therefore easy for the Allies to reinforce by sea and protect by air. A successful landing and breakout would open the road to Paris. To reinforce this impression, an illusion on an enormous scale was needed. Nothing less than an entire fake army group would suffice. Thus, while the real invasion forces were assembling in the south of the country, a fictional First United States Army Group (FUSAG) was being created in Kent and Essex on either side of the Thames Estuary. This was done by taking real army units, known to be in England, and generating fake radio traffic that indicated they were now being assembled and trained in the east of the country (even though in most cases they were not). The signals were accompanied by the presence of dummy landing craft, the appearance of troops and vehicles with fake insignia, and by false intelligence from a range of double-cross agents. There was even a notional commander in chief in the person of General George Patton, recently disgraced after an incident in Sicily when he had slapped two soldiers suffering from battle fatigue. Patton was known to be feared by the Germans who correctly assumed that he would ultimately play a role in any French campaign. This part of the overall Bodyguard plan was intended both to deceive the Germans and to hide and protect the real invasion buildup. It was known as Fortitude South. But it was not the whole plan.

Fortitude North was the simultaneous attempt to use further deception measures to keep the Germans guessing in Scandinavia. Hitler was known to fear that the Allies might attack in Norway. Again, this was seen as a credible threat. The British were holding troops in Scotland, they had attacked Narvik in 1940, and had been encouraging guerilla operations within Norway ever since. Geoffrey Pyke, working for Mountbatten and Combined Operations, had spent time working on new vehicles mounted on skis to traverse ice and snow. Indeed, Churchill had repeatedly pressed his chiefs of staff to mount just such an attack, while previous deception operations, such as Tindall, had deliberately seeded this possibility. Now the Allies were able to play on these fears by creating a notional British Fourth Army under the command of Lieutenant General Sir Andrew Thorne, who was the genuine commander of British forces in Scotland. The Allies falsely suggested Thorne would lead an assault against Stavangar, in conjunction with a simultaneous Soviet attack against Norway. The usual range of deception tactics were deployed to reinforce this impression: troop exercises, fake wireless traffic, and dummy equipment. But they were also accompanied by a novel diplomatic initiative. The British authorities now began to imply to the government in neutral Sweden that they might be about to liberate neighboring Norway. As part of this exercise, an entirely fictional scenario was put to Sweden that it might want to offer humanitarian assistance to Norway and help police the country in the event of a German collapse following an Allied attack. It was correctly assumed that the news would leak back to Berlin from pro-German elements in the Swedish government.

There is not space here to do justice to the full complexity of the deceivers' plans. A huge range of channels were utilized to suggest that the Allies were facing delays in assembling their forces or were waiting on a Soviet offensive or on further results of their bombing campaign. There was even a suggestion that there might be an attack in the Bay of Biscay. Just before D-Day, the actor Clifton James, a double for Montgomery, put on an incredible public performance in Gibraltar, playing the British general in front of enemy agents to convince the Germans that an attack in France could not be imminent while one of the senior commanders was in the Mediterranean. The idea was to keep the enemy guessing. There is an irony here. In 1942, Churchill had advocated attacking occupied Europe at multiple locations on the Atlantic shoreline from Norway to the mouth of the Gironde, utilizing at least half a dozen feints, "which, if luck favours them, may be exploited." This had never seemed feasible and would have divided Allied resources— Eisenhower and Montgomery were clear that the actual military blow needed to be concentrated for maximum impact—but it was of course possible to create multiple diversions and threats. The enemy was to be kept confused and guessing.

Operation Bodyguard was now in place on a scale and level of sophistication that were only possible in 1944 after years of experimentation, practice, and building of networks. Deception had proved its value and was now a fully integrated part of the planning process. Churchill was not directly involved in developing these decoy operations, but he loved this type of subterfuge and acted as a consistent patron and advocate for the work.

Suggestions that he announce a fake summit with Roosevelt came to nothing, but there was one small role for the prime minister. On March 26, he broadcast to the British nation, and in his final remarks he warned his audience that "in order to deceive and baffle the enemy as well as to exercise the forces there will be many false alarms, many feints and many dress rehearsals." These lines were put in at the request of Eisenhower, who had sent a "Top Secret" message to Churchill the previous day, keen to convince the Germans that his planned major dress rehearsal on the South Coast on May 3–5 was just one of a series of such exercises, and in the hope that Overlord itself might be initially seen as just such a feint.

Churchill knew, of course, that the deception plan was inevitably the shadow of the actual plan, and that both had to work. The early signs were positive. As preparations began in earnest, the German military remained spread along the French coast. They knew the blow was coming, but not where or when the hammer would fall.

Chapter 6

Mulberries and Gooseberries

"Gentlemen, I am hardening on this operation."

IN MILITARY PLANNING, ESPECIALLY AT THE OPERATIONAL—THE campaign—level war, there is a very close relationship between the commander, the staff, the plan, and the outcome. This is essential because the plan and its outcome are the personal responsibility of the commander. The staff deal with much of the detail, but the essence of the plan—the operational idea—belongs to the commander. The buck starts and stops with the boss.

Although General Dwight D. Eisenhower, Ike, was to be in overall command in Europe, General Bernard Montgomery was to be the land forces commander for the assault phase, and it was he who was responsible for delivering the overall success of Operation Overlord and the Normandy campaign. This, in turn, led to the defeat of the Germans in the west in 1944–1945 and contained the Red Army's further expansion into Europe. In the final analysis, it was the boots on the ground of the land forces that determined the successful outcome, enabled, of course, by the inestimable contributions of the naval and air forces, in support. Bernard Montgomery was the architect of the foundation of that success, Operation Overlord.

Piers for Use on Beaches

CONDITIONS OF BEACH

Average gradient is 1 in 200 and beaches are open to the south west.

CONDITIONS OF TIDE

2. Range of spring tides is 30 feet and the strength of the tide parallel to the beach is 4 knots at springs.

SCAFFOLDING PIERS

3. A pier to be of use for unloading ships of 20 foot draught would have to be 1 mile in length and 40 foot in height at the seaward end. The present type of scaffolding pier does not exceed 20 foot in height. It is doubtful whether a pier of these large dimensions could be made with scaffolding, but in any case the amount of material required would be prohibitive.

PONTOON PIERS

4. A pontoon pier would have to be similar in length. All floating piers suffer from the disadvantage of having to be securely moored with heavy anchors. Even then they are most vulnerable and will not stand up to a gale of wind. The strength of the tide is so great that the moorings will have to be very large. If large pontoons were moored, 20 yards apart, at least 200 anchors would be required. The sea-ward end of a floating pier must be particularly well moored and the mooring chains form an obstacle to ships coming alongside. Owing to the poor ratio between the weight of a floating pontoons and the weight they can carry, and to their vulnerability to sea wind and tide, they are not favoured in comparison with scaffolding piers on open beaches.

Minute on *"Piers for Use on Beaches,"* annotated by Churchill, May 26, 1942.
(Churchill Additional Papers, WCHL 13/4)

As we have seen, by 1944, the planning for the return to northwestern France had passed through many hands and changes of codename. Mountbatten and his Combined Operations team had been charged with making the initial preparations but were confined by lack of resources. Things then changed with the arrival of the Americans. Plans for a large-scale attack (codenamed Roundup) had been developed in 1942 by Eisenhower and the British commanders of Home Forces—Paget, Douglas, and Ramsay.

The Allied sequence of conferences had resolved at the Trident or Third Washington Conference in DC in May 1943 that the western Allies would open the Second Front in Europe in 1944. Ike—the consummate convener of Allied cooperation—had been appointed commander of the Supreme Headquarters Allied Expeditionary Force, while Monty—the war fighter—was to be commander of Twenty-first Army Group charged with delivering the success of the overall plan. However, in 1943, both Ike and Monty had been heavily engaged in operations in North Africa, Sicily, and Italy. To get planning for the reentry in Europe underway, and to plan for a number of other potential contingencies in Europe, Lieutenant General Frederick Morgan had been appointed as chief of staff to the (unnamed) Supreme Allied Commander (COSSAC). As we have seen, his was an ultimately thankless job but nevertheless he had produced a draft plan for Operation Overlord.

Morgan's initial plan was for a three-divisional assault aimed on a narrow front directly at Caen in Normandy, the other main option of an attack on the Pas-de-Calais having been argued out (the coast was felt to be too heavily defended and more difficult to land on). When Eisenhower was shown the COSSAC plan in Algiers in October 1943, he was appalled and expressed his doubts at wanting to be the overall commander. "Not enough wallop in the initial attack" was his much-quoted comment. Ike was not alone in his criticism of the draft plan. Churchill and Chief of the Imperial General Staff Brooke had little faith in the COSSAC plan, perhaps explaining at least part of their lack of initial enthusiasm for Overlord.

Ike asked to see Monty in Algiers on December 27 to discuss Overlord. At this meeting, both men agreed that the COSSAC plan needed strengthening and that the price to pay for this was potentially a month's delay from May to June 1944. The two generals then met again in Marrakesh, where Churchill was recovering from a near-death experience.

By December 1943, the British prime minister was running on empty. Completely exhausted after the Allied conferences in Tehran and Cairo, he traveled to Tunisia to see Eisenhower. It was one journey too many, and he collapsed with pneumonia. The attack was life threatening. The crisis occurred on December 14, when his doctor, Lord Moran, recorded:

> He was very breathless and anxious-looking. I felt his pulse: it was racing and very irregular. The bases of his lungs were congested, and the edge of his liver could be felt below the ribs. . . . As I sat by his bedside listening to his quick breathing, I knew that we were at last right up against things. It was four hours before the heart resumed its normal rhythm, and I was relieved to count a regular pulse of 120.

Moran called for medical backup. A team of experts was hastily assembled. Digitalis, used to treat heart conditions, was administered. Sulfadiazine, an antibacterial drug, was used to fight the pneumonia. The War Cabinet was informed, and Clementine Churchill flew in from Britain. Meanwhile, Churchill spoke of being prepared to die in Carthage, telling his daughter Sarah, who was traveling with him, "Don't worry, it doesn't matter if I die now, the plans for victory have been laid, it is only a matter of time." A recent study of this episode by two eminently qualified medical consultants, Allister Vale and John Scadding, concluded that fear of his death was not an exaggeration, and that the overall mortality from pneumonia of this type in the early 1940s was higher than 40 percent for someone his age with a related heart condition.

With the benefit of the best care available, sustained by the presence of his wife and daughter, and protected by a detachment of the Coldstream Guards, Churchill pulled through. After Christmas, he left for a period of recovery in Marrakesh (Morocco), a favorite haunt from his prewar days. He took with him the plans for Overlord, and it was from his convalescent bed that he began to engage with the detail of an operation that was now just six months away.

On New Year's Eve, Eisenhower and Montgomery both flew to Morocco. Churchill rang in the changes by celebrating with the newly appointed Overlord commanders. Ike had just relinquished his position as Supreme Commander in the Mediterranean theater and was returning to the United States for a brief period of rest before taking up his new role. Montgomery was heading straight for Britain.

A well-timed German strike on Churchill's villa in Marrakesh could have ruined the Allies' new year and seriously disrupted the liberation of France. Instead, Montgomery recalled an amusing dinner with Mrs. Churchill and Lord Beaverbrook. Churchill was well enough to engage in some intensive lobbying of the two generals. He bombarded Eisenhower with demands and questions regarding the pending Allied landings at Anzio in Italy and took the opportunity to share with Montgomery the plan for Overlord. This was the first time Monty had seen it in full, and Churchill was keen to get his first impressions.

Not one to join the prime minister's post-midnight celebrations, the famously austere Montgomery retired to bed early and used the time to write down his first reactions. His main point was that the initial landing was on too narrow a front and confined to too small an area. This would lead to confusion getting on and off the beaches. There needed to be clearer and greater separation between the British and American landing areas. According to Montgomery, Churchill received this information in bed the following morning, though Winston's recollection of their conversation was more colorful. In his version, the key exchange happened later in the day:

> When he [Montgomery] arrived at Marrakesh we had a two hours' drive out to our picnic at the foot of the Atlas. I had given him early in the morning the plan prepared over so many months by General Morgan and the Anglo-American Joint Staffs in London. After he had read it in summary he said at once "This will not do. I must have more in the initial punch."

As Montgomery was not yet acting in an official capacity and had not yet had the opportunity to consult Air Marshal Tedder or Admiral Ramsay, who were commanding the air and naval forces for the Normandy landings, he asked for his paper back. Churchill replied that he would keep it for his personal information. Instead, he made immediate use of it, firing off a multipage telegram to the chiefs of staff via General Ismay on January 2 in which he cited Montgomery's "very serious criticism that the proposal to move so many divisions in over the same narrow strip of beaches would be quite impracticable and would lead to inextricable confusion." On the first page of his telegram, Churchill also emphasized the need to replace words like *assault* or *invasion* with *enter* and *liberation.* He was at pains to get the tone as well as the detail of the operation correct. The word *invasion* was to be reserved for Germany. It was an important distinction. Back in London, Brooke—about to be appointed a field marshal—noted that the prime minister "is now becoming very active again!" He was not the only one. Montgomery quickly got to work on reshaping the plan.

From the moment that Churchill showed Montgomery the plan, matters began to change. Montgomery knew that if he was to take charge, he needed to craft the plan, own the plan, and then ensure its success. To Montgomery, the initial landings of three divisions, through which another thirteen would pass by D+12 (June 18), under the COSSAC plan, would replicate the chaos and confusion that characterized the Salerno landings in southern Italy in September 1943 and, as it turned out, would do so again at Anzio in January 1944. For Montgomery, the campaign plan required:

- The initial landings to be made on the widest possible front
- Corps to develop their own operations, within the overall plan, from their own beaches with no other corps landing on those beaches
- British and American armies to be kept separate
- Operations to be developed such that a good port be secured so that the British and American forces have their own port

With these general thoughts expressed, the scene was set for three extraordinary days of conference in London when Montgomery was formally briefed by the COSSAC staff on their plan. At 09:00 on January 3, Monty convened his first Overlord conference. Perhaps sensing the inadequacies of his plan, Morgan allowed his two senior planners to conduct the briefing, explaining as best they could how they had reached their decisions. When complete, Monty announced a twenty-minute break in proceedings before he would give his views. When he took to the floor, he expressed his complete disagreement with the COSSAC proposals. He wanted a focus on a very wide bridgehead, perhaps as far west as St. Malo and as far east as Dieppe. He certainly did not want just a narrow axis toward Caen. He wanted more troops in the initial assault. He gave the planners twenty-four hours to think again.

The next day the conference reassembled. Monty challenged all the figures that had led to the three-division plan, insisting instead that five divisions should make the initial landings. He accepted that attacking on the west side of the Cotentin Peninsula was an ambition too far but insisted a landing must be made on the east side—on what became Utah Beach. He questioned the proposed command-and-control structure. Under the COSSAC plan, the initial assault would be commanded by US First Army for the first week with one American, one British, and one Canadian Corps under command. Then the British and Canadian troops would go under command of First Canadian Army with the British commander of Twenty-first Army Group assuming overall command. While Morgan may have thought that this multinational mishmash might have appealed to Eisenhower, to Monty it was a recipe for confusion and disaster.

By the third day of the conference, the main issues were settled. It was to be a five-division assault, and more landing craft must be found. The bridgehead would be fifty miles wide. Airborne troops would not focus on the early capture of Caen but on the flanks from the Orne River in the east to the southern end of the Cotentin Peninsula in the west, especially to facilitate an early capture of the port of Cherbourg from the land side. It also became clear at that stage that Monty was skeptical about using an artificial harbor, codenamed Mulberry (for which see below). However, all present at the conference were transformed by the decisiveness and energy that Monty now injected into the planning process. As Eisenhower's representative in London and as the land forces commander, all concerned recognized Montgomery's authority. From January 6, 1944, five months before D-Day itself, there began to grow a sense of optimism in Twenty-first Army Group, in sharp contrast to the defeatist atmosphere that had characterized the COSSAC organization. Monty made it quite clear that there would be no more "bellyaching."

Operation Overlord:
The Landing Beaches and the Landing Zones

Once Supreme Commander General Dwight Eisenhower had approved the Land Forces Commander General Bernard Montgomery's revised plan for an assault on a wider frontage than the original COSSAC plan had proposed, the detailed selection of the landing beaches and landing zones could be confirmed. Where possible, and consistent with one of Monty's principles, each beach should be assaulted by the leading formation of each separate corps axis of advance, thus reducing the likelihood of logistic confusion. The airborne forces would protect the flanks of the beach assaults.

From west to east, the assault beaches were confirmed as:

- **Utah.** Between Saint Martin-de-Varreville and Pouppeville on the east coast of the Cotentin Peninsula, Utah Beach was to be assaulted by Eighth and Twenty-second Infantry Regiments of the US Fourth Infantry Division, the leading formation of the US VII Corps under the command of Major General J. Lawton "Lightning Joe" Collins.
- **Pointe du Hoc.** This was not a landing beach, but the US Second Ranger Battalion was tasked to scale the cliffs of

Pointe du Hoc and capture the battery of heavy guns that could be brought to bear on Utah or Omaha Beaches.

- **Omaha.** Between Vierville-sur-Mer and Colleville-sur-Mer, Omaha Beach was to be assaulted by Sixteenth Infantry Regiment of the US First Infantry Division (the Big Red One) and by 116th Infantry Regiment of Twenty-ninth Infantry Division, which was placed under command of the US First Infantry Division for the initial assault. First Infantry Division was the leading formation of the US V Corps under command of Major General Leonard T. "Gee" Gerow.

- **Gold.** Between Arromanches-les-Bains and La Rivière, Gold Beach was to be assaulted by Sixty-ninth Brigade (including Stan Hollis's Sixth Green Howards) and 231st Brigade of the British Fiftieth (Tyne-Tees) Division, the leading formation of the British XXX Corps under the command of Lieutenant General Gerald Bucknall. The Forty-seventh Commando Royal Marines was also to land on the western end of Gold Beach.

- **Juno.** Between La Rivière and Saint Aubin-sur-Mer, Juno Beach was to be assaulted by Seventh Brigade and Eighth Brigade of the Canadian Third Infantry Division, one of the two leading formations of the British First Corps under command of Lieutenant General John Crocker.

- **Sword.** Between Saint Aubin-sur-Mer and the Orne River, Sword Beach was to be assaulted by Eighth Brigade of the British Third Infantry Division, by Forty-first Commando and Forty-eighth Commando Royal Marines of the Fourth Special Service Brigade in the west and by Fourth Commando Royal Marines of First Special Service Brigade in the east. Third Infantry Division was the second leading formation of the British First Corps.

With the proposed landings on both Juno and Sword Beaches, the British First Corps had the most units under command of any major formation on D-Day. This had been the major focus of the former COSSAC plan, and perhaps remained so, with the hope of capturing Caen on the first day.

The flank protection for the beach assault forces would be provided by:

- **In the West.** The US Eighty-second and 101st Airborne Divisions, centered on Sainte-Mère-Église. Their mission was to protect the western flank of Utah Beach and offer the opportunity for US forces to seize the port of Cherbourg as early in the campaign as possible.
- **In the East.** The British Sixth Airborne Division was tasked to capture and hold the crossings over the Orne River and Orne Canal to prevent German counterattack forces threatening the eastern flank of the amphibious operation. They were also tasked to capture the battery of heavy guns at Merville that could threaten the eastern end of Sword Beach.

The analysis of the landings on all the beaches and landing zones will be described in chapter 10.

From the descriptions of Montgomery's galvanizing actions during the first week of January, it would be wrong to ignore the role of Eisenhower in this initial planning. Despite originally preferring the more congenial General Harold Alexander to be commander of the Twenty-first Army Group, rather than Monty, Eisenhower understood that this was a British decision, and when CIGS Brooke persuaded Churchill that Monty was the correct choice, Eisenhower accepted the decision. He may have felt challenged by Monty.

Indeed, Churchill may have initially thought the same. After all, Brooke was frequently challenging him at home. Did he need another awkward general? But Brooke knew that Monty, for all his bombastic and self-enhancing habits, was a fighter and a winner. From his First World War experiences, Monty had learned the importance of identifying the risks in battle and mitigating them with thorough preparation and planning, including the building up of adequate logistic stocks. He liked a "tidy battlefield."

Montgomery outlined the revised plan to Eisenhower on January 21. The price of the enlarged landing force and the wider bridgehead was indeed to be a month's delay. The other issue that was finally settled was that Morgan's command and control plans were rejected—Monty would command all land forces on the ground from the start of Overlord until Eisenhower formally activated the US Twelfth Army Group under General Omar Bradley. He did this on August 1, 1944, assuming overall command himself, as the Normandy campaign was coming to a close. From that moment, the British and Churchill's influence on the conduct of operations in the west would begin to wane.

With control of the military operation passing to Montgomery, who was reporting to Eisenhower, Churchill's ability to influence the military strategy effectively disappeared. Instead, he threw himself into overseeing the delivery of the practical elements that were needed to support the operation's success.

A key problem facing Montgomery and his planning staff was how to sustain the beachheads in the absence of a port. Since 1942, the Normandy beaches had been consistently identified as the best landing grounds for the Allied forces. They were sheltered from the Atlantic swell and were less well defended than the shoreline around the Pas-de-Calais, while still remaining within range of Allied air cover. But crucially, they lacked a deepwater anchorage by which the necessary supplies could be brought in to maintain the troops in a rapidly expanding theater. Cherbourg, at the tip of the Cotentin Peninsula, was expected to be taken quickly but it would not be large enough on its own to sustain an army of more than one million men, while it might take several weeks to capture Le Havre.

The answer to this problem had emerged over the course of the previous two years and had proved to be rather fruity. It lay in the creation of Mulberries, artificial harbors to allow for the unloading and protection from the weather of larger ships, and Gooseberries, man-made breakwaters at shallower depths, to ensure calmer waters for smaller vessels and the all-important landing craft. The walls of these artificial harbors were to be created from a number of specialized concrete and steel elements. Churchill was fascinated by the potential of science and technology and took a keen interest in these details.

A good idea often has many parents, and it is certainly true that the design, creation, and operation of these D-Day ports involved an enormous number of specialist teams. Churchill could claim a role as their godfather. As he was later very keen to point out, his paper on future naval policy for Lloyd George in 1917 had foreseen some of these very developments. In it, he had proposed the creation of an artificial base on the shallow sandbanks of the Horn Reef, off the Danish coast, which could be created from:

A sufficient number of flat-bottomed barges or caissons made, not of steel but of concrete. . . . They would float when empty of water and could thus be towed across to the site of the artificial island. . . . By this means a torpedo and weather-proof harbour, like an atoll, would be created in the open sea, with regular pens for the destroyers and submarines, and alighting platforms for aeroplanes.

Churchill was clearly not the only one to be thinking along these lines, either in 1917 or later, and there is no suggestion he circulated or published his First World War naval policy paper after becoming prime minister in 1940. It fell upon those charged with delivering the return to France to reach the same conclusions when faced with a similar problem. The solution came in stages, but Churchill was there to provide support and patronage at every step. First came the idea for the construction in situ of a temporary pontoon pier, to allow unloading of ships onto the beaches. It was promoted by Mountbatten at Combined Operations and developed by the leading military engineer, Colonel Bruce White. The problems were formidable. Any structures would need to be able to cope with rising Channel tides of up to thirty feet and four knots in strength, as well as battering from Atlantic storms. If floating pontoons were used, then they would have to be very securely moored.

The concept was approved by the prime minister at the end of May 1942. He used his red pen to annotate the paper with his response:

> They must float up & down on the tide. The anchor problem must be mastered. The ships must have a side-flap cut in them, and a drawbridge long enough to overreach the moorings of the piers. Let me have the best solution worked out. Don't argue the matter. The difficulties will argue for themselves.

This document was subsequently reproduced as a facsimile in his war memoirs and framed and hung on his study wall at Chartwell. It was the start of a concerted campaign by the prime minister to get action on the issue. On September 26 he sent a minute to the chiefs of staff and the minister of production, expressing his belief that

> we ought to have three or four miles of this pier tackle. It could of course be used in many places in short sections. Pray do not hastily turn this aside.

Delivery fell to Mountbatten, as chief of Combined Operations. By the end of October, he was wrestling with the logistics, reporting back that a major operation on the French beaches would require a sustained lift of 10,000 to 12,000 tons of supplies every day and that four piers would be needed to handle 50 percent of the total. Three potential designs were being investigated. Churchill kept the matter on the agenda of the Chiefs of Staff Committee, insisting on regular progress reports and sending repeated missives to Mountbatten encouraging him to "press on." Inevitably, the prime minister sought the advice of his science adviser Lord Cherwell, who in turn brought in Brigadier Millis Jefferis of MDI, the head of a specialist weapons research unit established with prime ministerial patronage and often referred to as "Churchill's Toyshop." He wanted the best brains working on the problem and was not prepared to let the matter drop.

By March 1943, he was back on the attack. He wanted to know if the piers could be used to save on landing craft in Operation Husky, the invasion of Sicily, complaining that:

> This matter is being much neglected. Dilatory experiments with varying types and patterns have resulted in our having nothing. It is now nearly six months since I urged the construction of several miles of piers. Was Brigadier Jefferis consulted?

Churchill insisted on writing to General Eisenhower, pointing out that "the conditions are incomparably more favorable to the use of quickly constructed piers in the 'Husky' area than in the English Channel." This, in spite of the fact that Mountbatten had already reported to him that there were enough landing craft to maintain the required forces in Sicily where they were only contemplating supplies through the beaches for one month for one and a half divisions; a tiny fraction of the scale of what would be needed in Normandy. Meanwhile, the trials continued.

The issue was also on the agenda of General Morgan as part of his Overlord planning. But the difficulties remained. The pontoon piers might allow for unloading directly onto the beaches, but they would need protecting against the sustained rough seas that would be expected by autumn. Without some protection that could be put in place very quickly, it was also feared that the smaller landing craft used for the initial assault could suffer very heavy casualties in rough seas. This called for the creation of complete self-contained harbors and barriers on a huge scale and threatened to derail the entire operation. It was at this point that Hughes-Hallett, the naval commodore commanding the assault force, had his moment of revelation:

> On Sunday, June 20, I went with Brian Egerton and Richard Fenning, as was our custom, to attend the morning service at the Abbey, and throughout most of the service I turned the whole

matter over and over again in my mind. During the singing of the Anthem, it suddenly came to me in a flash that we must, and could, create an artificial area of sheltered water on a Napoleonic scale by sinking a host of block-ships so as to create vast break-waters within perhaps 12 hours of the original landing.

Given his religious location, he could put this down to divine inspiration. The use of blockships enabled the nucleus of the Mulberry harbor to be established quickly, as they could sail themselves into position before scuttling. The site could then be strengthened by the addition of all the other elements—the huge concrete blocks and steel structures that would take longer to assemble. It allowed planning for the harbors to proceed at full speed. It was agreed at the first Quebec Conference that there should be two Mulberries, one American off Omaha Beach and one British at Arromanches. Hughes-Hallett worried that the American port was being constructed purely for political reasons, having been told by an American colleague that "our Army boys . . . are determined to have a port of their own." When he warned that it was a technical impossibility because there was no convenient shoal of water on which to sink the blockships and caissons off the American beaches, he was told "but they have set their hearts on an artificial harbour of their own—almost as if it were a status symbol—they will have their way whatever you or I say, so we might as well string along with them." We will return to the fate of the American port. Its British counterpart would later become unofficially known as Port Winston (Churchill declining the official designation of "Port Churchill").

It was a fitting name. Churchill grasped the need for these artificial harbors and now took it upon himself to oversee their delivery in time for D-Day in June. Having recovered from his North African illness and aware that the date for Overlord was now set, he threw himself into the preparations. Given the competing demands for wartime production, he was worried that targets were not being met and that some of the innovations he favored were not being pursued.

The result was a call for immediate action. Upon returning from Morocco in January 1944, he fired off a minute to Cherwell, Ismay,

and General Laycock, Mountbatten's successor as head of Combined
Operations, expressing his concern at "the continued failures on the
Synthetic Harbour business." He then took the chair at a late-night
meeting in the Cabinet War Rooms on Monday, January 24, using the
convening power of his office to bring together the key military and
political departments for a conference at which "everything connected
with the Synthetic Harbours and with the piers and landing stages
should be considered." It was a case of "Action this day."

The ministers in charge of Production, War Transport, and Supply
were brought together with some of the senior military commanders
for Overlord. Bruce White, the designer of the artificial piers, now a
brigadier, was present. Eisenhower was represented by his chief of staff,
General Walter Bedell Smith. Cherwell was there to support Churchill
on the technical issues.

The prime minister kicked things off by stating that he was "disturbed by recent reports about the 'Mulberry' position and feared
some of the projects were lagging behind schedule." There followed
a frank discussion. The Admiralty made clear that, in addition to the
two Mulberry harbors, which might take three or four weeks to establish, another five Gooseberry breakwaters would be required to provide immediate protection for shipping in the shallower water off the
beaches. Rear Admiral Tennant of the Allied Expeditionary Naval Force
confirmed that, without them, casualties to landing craft might be as
high as 20 to 30 percent per day if the water was not reasonably calm on
the landing beaches. The prime minister was playing his role as a prod-
ding stick and demanding action. What was the latest progress on the
different elements required for building these harbors and how could
their construction and delivery "be pressed forward with the utmost
energy"? Were there enough tugs to tow them across the Channel? How
many blockships would be needed and where would they come from?
What could the Americans provide?

Those present were left in no doubt about the urgency of the issue
and what was at stake. The scale of what was being contemplated was
immense. The creation of the two Mulberries and five Gooseberries
required twenty-five thousand feet of blockships plus the towing of

(3)

Copy No. 49

C.O.S. (44) 53 (0)

20TH JANUARY, 1944

WAR CABINET

CHIEFS OF STAFF COMMITTEE

MERCHANT SHIPPING REQUIRED FOR MULBERRIES

Memorandum by the First Sea Lord

At Quadrant[+] the Combined Chiefs of Staff were informed that the provision of Artificial Harbours was necessary to the success of OVERLORD. After QUADRANT the Combined Chiefs of Staff were informed[x]

    (i) that two harbours were required

        (a) An American Harbour assigned to American Forces

        (b) A British Harbour assigned to British and Canadian Forces.

    (ii) that sunken ships should be used as possible components for the shallow water Breakwater to the full extent of their availability.

(W.S.C.)

2. On the 9th October the Chiefs of Staff[/] took note that an American Mulberry and a British Mulberry would be required for OVERLORD and on the 12th January[/] that, in addition to two Mulberries, shelters would be required for landing craft which have been given the name "Gooseberries".

3. As instructed[/] the Admiralty has examined the operational requirement for the composition of the Breakwater in conjunction with S.A.C. and the War Office. It has been established that the most satisfactory solution will be a combination of Bombardon and Phoenix in water of over 2 fathoms and blockships in water of under 2 fathoms.

      + C.C.S. 307, C.C.S. 108th Mtg. and C.O.S.(Q) 8
      x C.C.S. 117th Mtg and C.C.S. 307/2
      / C.O.S.(43) 243rd Mtg. (0)
      / C.O.S.(44) 9th Mtg. (0) and C.O.S.(44) 17 (0)
      / C.O.S.(44) 1st Mtg. (0) and
        C.O.S.(43) 776 (0) 2nd Revise

--1--

Paper prepared for Chiefs of Staff, outlining requirements for constructing artificial harbors, January 20, 1944. (Churchill Acquired Papers, 2/3/62/13) nearly one million tons of material across one hundred miles of open sea. Those assembled were given just seven days to report back. When they reconvened in the same place at the same time, 22:00 hours in the Cabinet War Rooms, on the following Monday, it was clear that the prime ministerial prod had worked. The latest production estimates for the steel pierheads and floating roadways (Whales), for the reinforced concrete caissons (Phoenixes), and the huge interlocking steel crosses (Bombardons) were reported, and the prime minister expressed himself satisfied that "a very substantial part of the requirement would be met in adequate time." The number of tugs remained a potential bottleneck, but priority would be given to shipping extra numbers from the United States.

Mulberries and Gooseberries: A Layman's Guide

The artificial harbors used to support Overlord were the products of a huge construction program carried out around the United Kingdom and involving enormous quantities of steel and concrete. This was the Allied equivalent to Hitler's heavily fortified Atlantic Wall. The two Mulberry harbors comprised the following main elements:

- Blockships—old merchant and naval ships that could sail across the Channel and then scuttle themselves to form part of the harbor wall. They provided an initial breakwater while other elements were being towed across the Channel and assembled.
- Bombardons—huge cruciform steel constructions, each weighing a thousand tons and spanning two hundred feet in length, designed to form interlocking structures and create foundations for Mulberry harbors.

- Gooseberries—artificial breakwaters assembled close
  to the beaches to provide protection from rough seas for
  landing craft and smaller ships.
- Lilos—pipelines of compressed air that, when released,
  would create a breakwater through a curtain of rising
  air. These did not prove technically feasible and were not
  developed.
- Phoenixes—large hollow concrete units, each weighing
  thousands of tons and spanning two hundred feet in
  length, that could be maneuvered into place by tugs
  and then sunk to form part of the Mulberry harbor or
  Gooseberry breakwater.
- Tentacles—plans for floating artificial runways that could
  be used to provide constant air cover over the beaches. In
  the end these were not used as it was possible to maintain
  air cover from the United Kingdom.
- Whales—Pontoon pierhead and floating roadways
  designed to off-load supplies from the deepwater
  Mulberry harbor.

The meeting of January 24 also acknowledged some failures. Not all
the bright schemes of the scientists and engineers had come to fruition.
It was announced that plans to create barriers against the waves using
pipes discharging a constant stream of air bubbles, or inflated airbags
carrying curtains of concrete (codename Lilo), had been abandoned.
There was more of a discussion about the viability of the temporary air-
strips (Tentacle). Churchill described himself as "very disturbed" that
the one existing prototype in America was being broken up for other
uses. He saw a potential win in using these structures to guarantee
the vital air mastery over the beaches, but reluctantly gave way when
Air Marshal Leigh-Mallory, the air commander in chief for the Allied
Expeditionary Force, confirmed that "our" fighters would have sufficient range from the United Kingdom to maintain complete cover over

the beaches, while the artificial airfield would take at least forty-eight hours to erect, by which time the Royal Air Force expected to have constructed two airfields onshore.

Of course, if things had developed slightly differently, they might have been discussing using an aircraft carrier made of ice! While this sounds preposterous, it was a genuine idea from the fertile mind of Geoffrey Pyke. He had been studying the molecular qualities of pure ice and had discovered that if small particles of some other substance, like wood pulp, were suspended in water and then frozen, the resulting material had an incredible tensile strength. Moreover, it could not be easily melted and was very easily repaired. In September 1942, he sent a memorandum of more than two hundred pages to Mountbatten explaining how this new material would win the war and change the world. It opened with a Pykeism, a quote from *The Scandal of Father Brown* by G. K. Chesterton: "Father Brown laid down his cigar and said carefully: 'It isn't that they can't see the solution. It is that they can't see the problem.'"

The paper proposed an incredible number of uses for the new material, which became known as Pykrete, suggesting that it could effectively win the war on its own, but the one that grabbed the attention of Admiral Mountbatten was the possibility of unsinkable ship bergs that could be used to carry aircraft around the globe. Extensive tests were carried out. The codename suggested by Pyke was Habbakuk, a misspelling of Habakkuk, a minor prophet from the Hebrew scriptures (Pyke was Jewish).

Mountbatten clearly relished demonstrating the properties of the reinforced ice. He is supposed to have won over the prime minister by dropping a block into Churchill's hot bath to show it did not melt. At the Quebec Conference in August 1943, he called for a block to be brought into a meeting of the Combined Chiefs of Staff and then proceeded to open fire on it with his revolver. Brooke watched in horror as "the bullet rebounded out of the block and buzzed round our legs like an angry bee." Those waiting outside thought that their chiefs had reached such a level of disagreement that they had started shooting one another, causing Churchill to note dryly in his later war memoirs, "But who in war will not have his laugh amid the skulls?—and here was one."

In the end, the ice carriers proved too difficult and perhaps too revolutionary to develop, especially at a time when resources were stretched, and more conventional weapons were needed in such huge numbers. But as late as June 1943, Churchill still harbored hopes that something might be brought on stream in time to "play a decisive part against the war in Japan" or that the Pykrete be used for static platforms—"seadromes"—to help with the invasion of France. It was not to be.

Another related problem for D-Day was how to deliver the Allied forces onto the beaches in the face of obstacles and heavy defending fire. The beaches were protected by several layers of defense. These began with sunken obstacles, submerged at high tide, including jagged steel structures and wooden stakes with mounted mines designed to knock out landing craft or vehicles coming ashore. Once on the beach, the assault troops faced barbed wire, further obstructions, and land mines, while being subjected to a sweeping crossfire from overlooking gun emplacements, pillboxes, and strongholds. To get off the beach, they needed to break through the concrete seawall. Bombardment from the air and sea would be vital in softening these defenses, but it would not eliminate them. Success was dependent upon having sufficient mobile heavy armor to provide close support for the infantry along with specialist teams to clear a path off the beach as quickly as possible. The Dieppe raid had shown the difficulty of landing tanks on an enemy-held shore and provided a horrible illustration of the vulnerability of infantry if trapped on the beach. This was a nightmare scenario for Churchill, and it is not surprising therefore that he took a keen interest in developing solutions.

Churchill's association with the development of the tank takes us back—once again—to the First World War. As First Lord of the Admiralty in 1914–1915, he had refused to restrict himself to purely naval matters and had embraced the development of new technologies that might help break the trench stalemate on the Western Front. The same motivation that led him to advocate for the Dardanelles Campaign had also caused him to support the development of the Royal Naval Air Service (even taking flying lessons himself) and to sponsor early research into heavily fortified "land ships" that would allow British troops to retake the offensive. In a memorandum to Prime Minister Asquith, written in January 1915, he outlined the problem as the "getting across of 100 or 200 yards of open space and wire entanglements" and suggested that the solution would be

> to fit up a number of steam tractors with small, armoured shelters, in which men and machine guns could be placed, which would be bullet proof. . . . The caterpillar system would enable trenches to be crossed quite easily, and the weight of the machine would destroy all wire entanglements.

In the same paper, he had gone on to call for the production of large shields and for the use of smoke screens to provide cover for attacking troops. Once again, then, by the time of the Second World War, he was already familiar with the challenge faced by the D-Day planners and willing to support technical innovation. This led him to identify a kindred spirit in Major General Percy Cleghorn Stanley Hobart.

Hobart was one of the pioneers of modern tank warfare: A passionate believer in a mobile, mechanized army, he was an uncompromising figure who spent most of his career at odds with the military establishment. The historian and strategist Basil Liddell Hart compared him to Guderian or Rommel, who developed the German panzer forces and principles of blitzkrieg warfare, while noting that "in the British way, he [Hobart] was never given such opportunity of command in war as they obtained." He was first brought to Churchill's attention by the author and independent MP Alan Herbert, who wrote to Winston in October 1936, referring to Hobart as "top dog, I think (or very nearly so) of Tanks" who "has a lot of interesting things he wants to say to someone who like you knows about Defence." Hobart was then commanding the First Tank Brigade, while Churchill was conducting his campaign for British rearmament and opposing the appeasement of Hitler. It is clear that they met and that Hobart warned Churchill of the need for more tanks. At that time, like many others, Churchill had not appreciated the full extent to which armored forces might transform modern warfare. Once installed as prime minister, and faced with the success of the German panzer forces in Western Europe in 1940, he realized that he needed to play catch-up and massively scale up British tank numbers.

By this time Hobart had been forcibly retired from the army. He had been sent to Egypt to form a mobile force for desert warfare (what would later become the Seventh Armored Division, famous under Montgomery for its victories in North Africa as the "Desert Rats") but had fallen out with his commander in chief who described him as "unduly optimistic" about the capacities of the Royal Armored Corps. During the summer of 1940, he was living in Chipping Campden in the Cotswolds, brooding on his dismissal and playing a role in the local defense volunteers known as the Home Guard. Fortunately, he still had friends in high places, who brought his predicament to the ear of the prime minister. Following a meeting at Chequers in October, Churchill was adamant that Hobart was exactly the sort of tank commander he now needed, sending a minute to General Dill, then chief of the Imperial General Staff (head of the army), confirming that Hobart should be given command of one of the new tank divisions.

Hobart assumed responsibility for raising and training the Eleventh Armored Division, but by September 1942 his abrasive personality, strong views on tank warfare, ill health, and age (at fifty-seven he was considered too old to command the division in combat) were continuing to cause friction, and Churchill had to step in and save his career for a second time, writing to the secretary of state for war, describing Hobart as:

> A man of quite exceptional mental attainments with great strength of character, and although he does not work easily with others, it is a great pity we have not more of his like in the Service. I have been shocked at the persecution to which he has been subjected. . . . The High Commands of the Army are not a club.

The timing was fortunate. General Alan Brooke was now chief of the Imperial General Staff and prepared to support Hobart, while preparation for the invasion of France, though subordinate in the short-term to the war in the Mediterranean, was firmly back on the agenda. It was clear that heavy armor was going to be needed to clear the beaches, and General Hobart seemed the man most experienced to deliver it. He was given command of the new and innovative Seventy-ninth Division—a name continued in today's army for the unit charged with original thinking—and, moreover, the freedom, with the patronage of Churchill and Brooke, to develop a force that was capable of leading the assault onto the Normandy beaches.

As foreseen by Churchill in 1915, the tank had already been adapted to clear obstacles, and tanks with specially mounted flails had been used to clear minefields at the Battle of El Alamein, but Hobart was able to take their modification to another level. Every likely German obstacle was studied, and solutions put in place. Special hull-like screens were developed allowing tanks to sail onto the beaches, there were bomb-firing tanks that could blast open concrete fortifications, track-laying tanks that could lay down a route over areas of soft sand, tanks with bridges that could overcome obstacles, and others with flamethrowers or wire cutters. Crucial to Hobart's thinking was that these specialist tanks should also be able to fire and fight, thereby allowing them both to defend themselves and to play an offensive role beyond the clearing of obstacles.

Hobart was not working in isolation on innovation for the landings. Combined Operations and MDI were also involved in developing new weaponry and equipment. The prime minister's scientific adviser, Lord Cherwell, maintained a watch on it all, and his support for particular projects was often vital in getting the prime minister's attention. Meanwhile, Churchill loved nothing more than escaping London to watch the latest demonstration. Not every innovation worked or proved useful. Tanks carrying bright lighting for night attack were not needed once it had been decided to attack in daylight (and were of course themselves potential targets for enemy fire). A proposal for a cliff-bridging device that would take the tanks and mechanized transport direct from the ships and place them on top of the cliffs was felt to be "technically feasible" but not "tactically applicable" to the Normandy coastline. A vital innovation installed soon after the landings was the laying of a pipeline under the ocean (Pluto), which ultimately provided a constant source of fuel from the Isle of Wight across to Normandy.

The tactics mattered, too. To land tanks on the beaches ahead of infantry in rolling seas required an incredible amount of coordination. The production in sufficient numbers of landing craft, especially the larger tank-landing craft, was a bottleneck and source of serious concern right up until early 1944. Their use also required the development of special operational procedures. Tank-landing craft were heavier and traveled more slowly than lighter troop-carrying craft. This meant that all craft had to be carefully assembled at sea off the beaches with their release toward shore carefully timed by the responsible naval officers. Once on the beaches, the assault had to be directed so that the specialist teams and tanks could work together to clear the obstacles and minefields quickly and efficiently; otherwise the constant flow of troops onto the beaches would quickly become backed up and provide easy targets for enemy fire. Once a beach had been seized, beachmasters, specially trained naval officers, were needed to direct traffic on and off the landing sites.

This all required considerable training. The prime minister continued to maintain a watch over it all. He spent time visiting British and American forces, including US paratroops near Winchester, telling them that they had a "great part to play," and that they were the "most modern expression of war." The morning of March 31, 1944, found him in Yorkshire where he visited the Guards Armored Division and watched a lorry being driven through water. Elsewhere, others were making their preparations.

Hughes-Hallett, as the naval assault force commander, had worked hard on growing his command. By the end of 1943, Force J numbered fifteen thousand officers and men and was capable of landing a full division of troops on the various beaches. Hughes-Hallett had twenty-eight assault ships, two hundred tank-landing craft, and a much larger number of infantry-landing craft, motor gunboats, steam gunboats, motor launches, and support craft under his direct control, while other British and American naval resources were being assembled elsewhere around the English shoreline. He had also developed, trialed, and trained his force in procedures for assembling, transporting, and launching the assault. His reward was command of the heavy cruiser HMS *Jamaica*, which—probably much to his regret—did not participate in D-Day.

Roland MacKenzie's journey took him first to Scotland. Arriving in July 1943, he undertook training at Banff and Edzell, familiarizing himself with the tactics and equipment in use in the European theater. Then to Staffordshire to join his crew and to undertake intensive operational training ahead of combat sorties. By January 1944, he was graded "above average" and considered ready.

TL Rodgers and the 504th Parachute Infantry Regiment arrived in Liverpool and transferred to Camp Stoughton in Leicestershire. As his unit began to familiarize themselves with local women and beer, inflicting scabies and pregnancies on the local population, it fell to teetotaller TL to look after them. In the words of one of their own, much of the unit behaved like "uncouth barbarians," so TL and twenty-four others volunteered for detached service as pathfinders in Normandy. His parting words to his friend Ross Carter (who later wrote *Those Devils in Baggy Pants*) were, "I'll be as careful as I can Ross, but I may not be careful enough this time."

Christian Oldham (now married as Mrs. Christian Lamb) was also doing her bit. Recruited in February 1944 for a piece of top-secret work, she now found herself alone in a tiny room in a central Whitehall basement surrounded by detailed maps of the Normandy coastline. Her job was to painstakingly "delineate everything that could be seen on every compass bearing from each landing position, visible from the bridge of an approaching Landing Craft for identifiable confirmation." She was only in her early twenties and privy to one of the greatest secrets of the war. She knew the actual landing beaches. Sometimes she would see Churchill on the stairs. For him, those same secrets made this a time of particular worry.

That's because, while the specialist equipment and training were vital for success on D-Day, the real headache was the sheer scale of the ordinary resources that had to be assembled—the men, their rifles, uniforms, and basic kit. The logistical challenge of gathering the troops in

Southern England and supplying them for a long and growing campaign in Europe was a daunting one. Eisenhower was working on the assumption that, "A reinforced division, in active operations, consumes from 600 to 700 tons of supplies per day." When fighting in a fixed position, it would expend ammunition, when moving it would require petrol. Always, it would need food. Within weeks of the assault, there would be thirty-six divisions on the continent. All would require medical services, administration, engineering support, entertainment, and welfare.

Churchill struggled with the sheer size of the modern army and feared that the logistical tail was too long, threatening the army's freedom of movement. His historical idols, great commanders like Alexander the Great and Napoleon, had exploited success on the battlefield by being able to move quickly, but they lived in a simpler age when armies could live off the land. Notwithstanding that, Churchill feared being bogged down and facing another prolonged and bloody trench war stalemate. In this his views were similar to those of Hobart and Liddell Hart, who favored a fast-moving, mechanized campaign.

As the military plan evolved, Churchill was kept informed through regular meetings with Eisenhower. With progress in Italy slower than expected due to the difficulties encountered by the Allies in breaking out of the Anzio beachhead, the decision was made not to proceed with Operation Anvil, the landings in the south of France, until after the Normandy assault. It was a decision that Churchill welcomed. He knew Anvil would pull further resources away from Italy. Montgomery wanted Anvil canceled altogether, but Eisenhower felt that it still had a vital role to play in opening up another route for bringing Allied men and supplies into France. The issue would resurface again after D-Day and provoke a major row between the Supreme Commander and the British prime minister. But, for now, Churchill seemed broadly accepting of the reworked Overlord plan. Jock Colville, his Private Secretary, noted in his diary for April 4 that, "The prospect of the 2nd Front worries him, though he says he is 'hardening to it.'"

Three days later on Good Friday, Churchill addressed a gathering of all the military leaders at St. Paul's School, Montgomery's headquarters, writing afterward to Roosevelt that "I do not agree with the loose talk which has been going on both sides of the Atlantic about the unduly heavy casualties which we will sustain. In my view it is the Germans who will suffer very heavy casualties when our band of brothers gets among them."

Seating plan for OVERLORD conference at St. Paul's school, May 15, 1944.
(Churchill Papers, CHUR 4/335/42)

He was back at St. Paul's on May 15 to attend the final conference on D-Day preparations. The chiefs of staff and all the main military commanders were present. Churchill spoke after the king. Harry Butcher was not present but, from speaking to those who were, he gathered that "the Prime Minister let go with a slow-starting but fast-ending stemwinder. He preached bravery, ingenuity, and persistence as human qualities of greater value than equipment." Eisenhower described it as "one of his [Churchill's] typical fighting speeches," but pointed out that the Americans were struck "with peculiar force" by one of his expressions.

Churchill had repeated his earlier remark to Colville, telling the gathering: "Gentlemen, I am hardening toward this enterprise." To General Ismay, this simply meant that the more his boss thought about it, the more certain he was of its success. But to Eisenhower—and Americans then and since—this meant that:

Although he had long doubted its feasibility and had previously advocated its further postponement in favour of operations elsewhere, he had finally, at this late date, come to believe with the rest of us that this was the true course of action in order to achieve the victory.

Writing later, Churchill was so adamant that he used this phrase "in the sense of wishing to strike if humanly possible, even if the limiting conditions we laid down are not exactly fulfilled." However good his speech, he had unwittingly provided ammunition for those seeking evidence that he was a latecomer to this party.

In the final months before D-Day, Churchill had time to brood on the impending operation. The apparent imbalance between frontline fighting forces and the huge numbers of vehicles and other personnel required to support them was one that he repeatedly returned to. On May 17, he summoned Brooke to his bedside and berated him on the fact that the invasion plan comprised "1000 clerks of the 3rd echelon" and "catered for one lorry for every 5 men." Two days later he dined with Montgomery and his staff. Churchill's recollection of this meeting differs from Monty's, but it seems that the prime minister had wanted to speak with the general's staff to interrogate them in detail on some of the numbers. According to Montgomery, he took Churchill aside, told him it was too late for any changes; he had made the final decision, and he would not let him argue with his staff who had done "a terrific job preparing the invasion." Moreover, if Churchill thought Montgomery's plan was wrong, "that can only mean you have lost confidence in me." There was an awkward silence, but then tears came into Churchill's eyes. After composing himself, he moved into the next room and, addressing Monty's team, "With a twinkle in his eye he said: 'I wasn't allowed to have any discussion with you gentlemen.'" This was a joust, a sparring session between these two great wartime leaders. Churchill's moods could change quickly and his frustration gave way to a recognition of the burden Montgomery was bearing and an understanding of the need to back him in front of his team.

In his memoirs, Churchill confirmed this story but disputed that Montgomery had threatened to resign. He also refused to let the matter of numbers go, writing:

> I may add however that I still consider that the proportion of transport vehicles to fighting men in the early phase of the cross-Channel invasion was too high and that the operation suffered both in risk and execution from this fact.

Churchill may not have developed the D-Day plan, but he was aware of the main problems and used his powers of patronage to advance and support those working to overcome them. Once he focused on the June date, with six months to go, he homed in on the detail, though some of his interventions were clearly more welcome to the commanders than others. He was particularly interested in the military aspects, having studied them since the First World War, but he could not escape the fact that the operation would have huge consequences for the civilian population—parts of the country were about to go into lockdown. Churchill may have been hardening on the enterprise, but the truth was that he still had plenty to worry about.

Churchill where he loved to be: Surrounded by the Allied commanders in North Africa, 1943. From left to right: Foreign Secretary Anthony Eden, General Sir Alan Brooke, Air Chief Marshal Tedder, Winston Churchill, Admital Cunningham, General Alexander, General Marshall, General Eisenhower, and General Montgomery. (Crown)

The next best thing to being at the front: Churchill's Map Room. (Broadwater Collection)

Raising morale: Churchill talking to US paratroops, March 23, 1944.
(Keystone Press/Alamy Stock Photo)

Watching invasion training in Yorkshire, March 1944. (Broadwater Collection)

With Monty in France, July 1944. (Broadwater Collection)

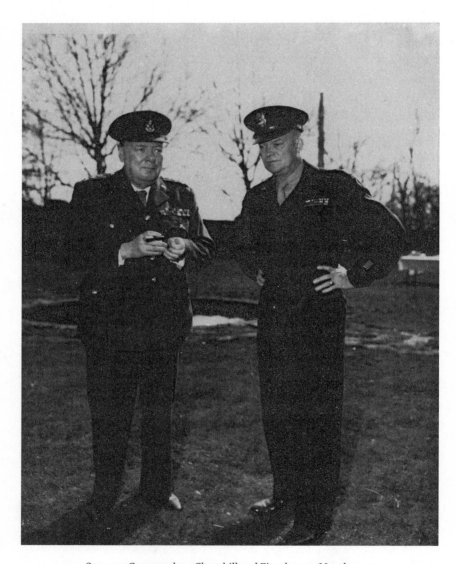

Supreme Commanders: Churchill and Eisenhower, March 1945.

Mastery of the seas and skies. (Crown)

Ready to go ashore, June 1944. (Crown)

Breaking Hitler's Atlantic Wall, June 1944. (Crown)

Flak and obstacles on the beaches, June 1944. (Crown)

Storming ashore, June 1944. (Crown)

General O'Connor, Churchill, Smuts, Montgomery, and Brooke looking for Germans. They may have been in the bushes! June 12, 1944. (Crown)

Churchill talking to British and Canadian troops in Normandy, July 22, 1944. (Crown)

De Gaulle speaking in France, 1944. (Crown)

Commandos on the beach, June 7, 1944. The scene experienced by Tony Hugill. (Crown)

Joan Bright at the Yalta Conference, February 1945. (Lunghi Family)

ABOVE LEFT *Roland MacKenzie DFC.* (MacKenzie Family)
ABOVE RIGHT *Christian Oldham (later Lamb) as a young Wren.* (Lamb Family)

TL Rodgers with his fellow pathfinders, June 1944.
(Public domain, photographer unknown)

Company Sergeant Major Stanley Hollis on parade, wearing medal ribbon including Victoria Cross and two wound stripes on sleeves, c. late 1944–1945. (The Green Howards Trust)

These are maps taken from The Second World War *by Winston S. Churchill*

MAP TO ILLUSTRATE THE MEDITERRANEAN CAMPAIGNS, 1942

Map to illustrate the Mediterranean Campaigns, 1942. (Broadwater Collection)

Normandy, 1944. (Broadwater Collection)

NORTH-WEST EUROPE

Northwest Europe. (Estate of Winston S. Churchill)

Part 2

Execution and Aftermath

COPY

FROZEN No. 1087.

TOO 041220Z.
TOR 041620z.

IMMEDIATE

From:- Sextant.

To:- Air Ministry.

FROZEN No. 1087.   4th January, 1944.

Prime Minister to General Ismay.

Your minute of January 1 about security arrangements for OVERLORD.

1.. I do not think it will be possible to conceal from the enemy that large preparations are being made along our coasts. It may, however, be possible to prevent his guessing when, where or in what strength our forces will be used.

2. I am not in favour of such sweeping restrictions as you now propose, particularly the visitors ban, nor of so early a date as February 1. We must beware of handing out irksome for irksome's sake. The question may be brought before the War Cabinet, but Sir Edward Bridges is to make the members acquainted with this expression of my opinion.

3. I entirely agree with para 5 of your minute. In this connection see a disgraceful article in the Sunday Times of January 2 by Scrutator, para. 1. in which a specific month is clearly indicated. No doubt many of these considerations are present in the minds of military correspondents and others, but none the less harm may be done. In this case I read in the local news that the Sunday Times "has stated that the operation will not take place until the month mentioned" and this no doubt is sent all over the world. You should ask the Minister of Information to consider whether any action can be taken against the Sunday Times and also that the strictest injunctions must be given to all the newspapers, and especially to their military correspondents, against discussing and speculation upon the prospects and possibilities of OVERLORD.

T.O.O. 041220z.

Telegram from Churchill to Ismay, January 4, 1944.
(Churchill Papers, CHAR 20/179/34)

Chapter 7

Lockdown

*"We must beware of handing out
irksome for irksome's sake."*

CHURCHILL WAS WORRIED. BRITAIN WAS NOW AN ARMED CAMP.
However good the deception plan, it was impossible to hide the scale of
the Overlord preparations. By the beginning of 1944, it was clear that
huge forces were being assembled throughout the United Kingdom with
the intention of crossing the Channel.

By June 1944, there would be more than 1.6 million US servicemen
and -women in the country. They were joining Canadian naval, air, and
army units, as well as other forces; some drawn from the British Empire
and Commonwealth, some from occupied European countries.

The whole length of the British south and east coasts was now covered in bases and training grounds. Airfields had sprung up all over
the countryside. This at least helped to confuse the enemy as to exactly
where the blow would fall, as it kept open possibilities for an attack from
Scotland into Scandinavia, or from the east of England toward Belgium
or the Pas-de-Calais, but the longer the wait, the greater the risk of a
security breach.

Concerned by mounting speculation in the newspapers about the nature and timing of the return to France, Churchill wrote to Eisenhower on January 28 informing him that a notice had been issued to the press

> telling them that there must be no attempt to forecast dates even by month or season; that discussion must be avoided of the desirability or likelihood of landings on particular places, sections of coastline or territory; and above all that there must be no estimates of the scale on which attacks would be conducted either in men or material.

The prime minister was particularly anxious that Eisenhower apply the same "stringent attitude" to those press correspondents accredited to his headquarters. The fear was that reporters might gather and exchange small pieces of information and so build up and publish an accurate picture of planned events. Eisenhower's natural instincts were to trust correspondents and to build positive relationships with them, but it was agreed that discretion would be used and that no reporters would be accredited to his headquarters until just before the operation.

Such speculation was not surprising, especially in the British papers. The large military presence on UK soil imposed an ever-increasing strain on the British people and their already creaking infrastructure and economy. By 1944, the civilian population had endured four years of wartime curfews, rationing, and blackouts. The fact that victory was now in sight only made additional restrictions to freedom of speech or movement harder to bear. Yet, this is what the military now demanded in order to protect the security of their operation.

Churchill was caught in the middle. As prime minister and minister of defense, it fell upon him to steer the difficult course between helping the military operation and preserving civil liberties and a semblance of normal life. It was not just the military implications of the Overlord plan that he began to ponder while recovering in Marrakesh. On January 4, in a minute to General Ismay, he expressed his reservations about the proposed restrictions on the home front and of "handing out irksome for irksome's sake."

Once back in London, he proposed a weekly meeting, to be held in Downing Street at 18:00 hours every Wednesday (a slot that had previously been used for his now redundant Anti-U-boat Committee) in order to deal with the civil rather than the military questions. Membership was limited to those ministers most directly concerned. And so the Overlord Preparations Committee came into being.

The first meeting took place on February 2. Participants heard from Minister of Production Oliver Lyttelton about the potential impact of Overlord on the inland transportation system. There was a fear that the wholesale movement of troops and materials would impose a huge additional strain on the railways that might bring everything to a halt. Additional operational traffic was estimated at 900,000 tons, but that would also require the carriage of an extra 400,000 tons of coal to keep the trains moving, while 9,000 extra men would be required to help with the faster loading of a greater number of wagons. Normal "coastwise" traffic would need to be cut to make way for the special military requirements. More use would need to be made of roads and canals. Supplies to troops abroad would be impacted, and Lyttelton recommended that the civilian population at home should be exposed to a publicity campaign "to bring home to every inhabitant in these Islands the absolute necessity of economizing in transport in every form."

By spring, the ability to meet such production targets was being further hit by industrial unrest. The miners of Yorkshire were on strike, as were apprentices from the shipyards in Tyneside, the Clyde, and Yorkshire (protesting against enforced conscription into the mines). If unresolved, this had the potential to become what Churchill called "a situation of utmost gravity" and to require "exceptional measures."

It was a grim picture, and one that was only going to get more difficult. General Morgan, who was now working for Eisenhower on the Overlord preparations, had written to the chiefs of staff stating that the ban on visitors to coastal towns in the south and east was vital to the success of the operation and needed to be in place by March 15. It was suggested that the prime minister should announce it. Several arguments were being made in support of the military position. The ban would reduce the nonresident population, making it easier to detect enemy agents. The leakage of vital information was felt to be more likely through visitors than residents. The strain on transport would be reduced. Enemy bombing would cause less disruption if visitors were absent, while the introduction of these measures would show the public and the United States Army the seriousness with which the British government was taking the operation. The issue pitched the military against the civilian authorities, in the form of the Home Office (responsible for domestic law and order), the Ministry for Home Security, and the Scottish Office, who were not convinced that a sufficient case had been made. They questioned whether the absence of nonresidents would really make it easier to detect enemy agents or reduce the danger of security breaches and felt that the police would only be able to partially enforce the ban through snap checks. They did, however, support giving the police in these areas greater discretionary powers to arrest persons without identity cards, and to close places of public gathering, control refugee movements, and introduce stricter censorship of communications.

Both sides were looking to the prime minister to adjudicate. At this stage, he remained unconvinced by the military case. In a minute to General Ismay and Edward Bridges, the Cabinet Secretary, ahead of the next Overlord meeting, Churchill made it clear that he was "not in favour of the sweeping recommendations now proposed." He was in no mood to be bossed around on his home soil by the Americans, writing, "We do not wish to knock our people about in order to impress the United States." The matter should be considered on security grounds alone, and here he remained skeptical. The idea that the absence of visitors would relieve the roads from panic congestion caused by enemy bombing seemed "rather an echo from 1940" and he thought it just as likely that security breaches would come from residents as visitors.

In particular I deprecate the wholesale character of these orders. Let me have on one sheet of paper a list of the kind of things that you do not wish visitors, as apart from residents, to see and where they are primarily located. I propose shortly to go and make a tour myself of some of these districts.

At the meeting on February 9, it was decided that further information was needed before a decision about the ban could be made, but the police were given their extra powers. On balance, the Overlord Preparations Committee took the view, supported by Churchill, that disruption of civilian life should be minimized for as long as possible, but it was already clear that the emphasis was shifting in support of the military as the days counted down to D-Day, though there was also a security argument for delay, as the announcement of any ban would indicate to the enemy that major operations were afoot.

A very similar debate took place around the question of introducing a travel ban between the United Kingdom and Ireland. The Irish Free State, comprising the counties of southern Ireland or Eire, had won its independence from Britain in 1922 and—much to Churchill's annoyance—had opted for neutrality during the Second World War. Meanwhile, the six counties of Northern Ireland had remained part of the United Kingdom, and the border between north and south had remained open. When Christian Oldham had been based in Belfast in 1943, she and her fellow Wrens escaped British wartime austerity and rationing by undertaking regular raiding parties to Dublin in order to eat as much food as possible and to buy clothes, which they smuggled back past the customs inspectors. As women in their twenties, they were not deemed a security risk, but both the Germans and the Japanese maintained a diplomatic presence in Dublin and travel between the United Kingdom and Ireland provided an obvious channel for the escape of information about the buildup and movement of troops for D-Day.

Once again the arguments were finely balanced. Eisenhower, backed by the British chiefs of staff, regarded the closure of the border as "vital to the success" of his operation and wanted it imposed as quickly as possible, certainly no later than March 15. In contrast, the civil ministries wanted it as late as possible and were concerned about its impact on Irish labor. They estimated that about 100,000 Irish workers were employed in the United Kingdom, many on vital war work, and they knew that they needed more to help meet the construction and transportation deadlines for D-Day. They feared that a ban—or the fear of a ban—would lead many to lay down their tools and go home. To mitigate this, it was suggested that any restrictions be imposed with only twenty-four hours' notice and emphasized as temporary.

The committee resolved to press ahead with the preparations. Roosevelt unsuccessfully urged the Irish government to break off diplomatic relations with the Axis powers, which then provided the perfect cover for the British action. The ban was subsequently announced on March 12, going into effect the following day. Defending it in the House of Commons on March 14, Churchill was keen to link it to Dublin's continued refusal to withdraw Axis representation and to separate his criticism of Irish government policy from his praise for

> the large number of Irishmen who are fighting so bravely in our armed forces and the deeds of personal heroism by which they have kept alive the martial honour of the Irish race.

He was adamant that "No-one I think, can reproach us with precipitancy. No nation in the world would have been so patient." On the advice of his colleagues in the War Cabinet, his statement had been altered to make it clear that this action had not been taken unilaterally, but rather at the instigation of the United States and in response to the need to protect American forces. Some of his more inflammatory language had also been removed to make sure that the emphasis remained on security rather than Churchill's ongoing objections to reopening discussions about the partition of Ireland (with which there might be considerable American sympathy). This did not prevent the Scottish communist MP Willie Gallacher from linking the issues in the House of Commons:

> MR. GALLACHER: I would not like to say anything that would make more difficult a very difficult situation, but I would like to ask if it is not possible, in any further approaches to Eire, to suggest that the question of partition will be a subject for discussion when peace is being decided.

THE PRIME MINISTER: I could hardly think of a more
ill-conceived approach to the unity of Ireland.

Churchill was braced for opposition to this measure, especially from
Ireland and the United States. On March 19, he sent a preemptive telegram to Roosevelt confirming his intention to stop Irish ships and aeroplanes heading for foreign countries. He was at pains to emphasize that
these measures were not being taken out of spite, but rather to preserve
the lives of British and American soldiers and to stop "our plans being
betrayed by emissaries sent by sea or air from the German minister in
Dublin." Churchill was clear that he had no intention of stopping trade
between Britain and Ireland, but neither did he want to make things
easy for Éamon de Valera, the Irish *taoiseach* (head of government). He
was firmly against giving too much reassurance to Dublin about the
measures, suggesting that "there is not much sense in a doctor telling a
patient that the procedure he has just prescribed for his nerve troubles
is only coloured water," and arguing that "we should let fear work its
healthy process."

One door may have been closed against security breaches, but there
were still many others by which information might leave the United
Kingdom. Foreign diplomats based in the country, including those of
neutral powers, had the right to send communications through uncensored diplomatic channels, often called the "diplomatic bag." Should
that be suspended? What about ships and aircraft leaving the country?
Could these be stopped? If so, for how long, without further damaging
the economy?

Churchill's son-in-law, the conservative politician Duncan
Sandys, was one of the authors of a comprehensive report on *Security
Preparations for Overlord*, which sought to address these issues and
identify the measures that might be taken prior to the military operation. The report advocated sweeping restrictions on communications.
All neutral governments should be denied the use of their diplomatic
bags and secret cyphers (encoded telegrams). Their communications
ought to be censored and their representatives forbidden from leaving the country. The report recognized that Ireland was a weak link

between Britain and the outside world and recommended that all mail to Northern Ireland should be censored.

More generally, the report suggested various measures for further tightening, censorship of mail, and controlling the export of local newspapers, which might reveal the precise location of military bases (while recognizing that the national papers had an important propaganda role, although there was a danger that enemy agents would use the small ads columns to convey messages). Greater controls were proposed for shipping, including the exclusion of fishing vessels from the English south coast, while the number of Allied nationals entering the United Kingdom should be kept to a minimum. The tiny British enclave at Gibraltar, bordering Franco's Spain, was identified as a specific weak spot, where the Security Service might play a role in vetting crews sailing to and from Britain.

Crucially, the report supported the idea of a visitors ban, advocating the introduction of restrictions in a coastal belt from the Wash (the estuary in East Anglia separating Norfolk and Lincolnshire) to Cornwall and including the area in Scotland adjacent to the Firth of Forth. Still, Churchill resisted. At the Overlord Preparations Committee meeting on March 1, he remained "most reluctant to impose additional inconveniences on the public unless he was sure that there would be a real gain in security" and the subcommittee on security was instructed to see if the ban could be limited to certain parts of the coast without denying all access. While this may have been popular with any holidaymakers, there was an obvious flaw in the logic and, a week later, the subcommittee pointed out that a more precise definition of the areas to be excluded from any ban would "pin-point the places where preparations were concentrated and give clues to the enemy as to the direction of the assault." When this was reported back to the Overlord Preparations Committee on March 8, the issue was referred upward. It came before the War Cabinet two days later, where Churchill grudgingly conceded and agreed to its imposition. He still doubted whether the ban would improve security, but "it was most important to give the Forces who were to be engaged in 'Overlord' the assurance that everything possible was being done for the success of the operation." By then, he knew that Eisenhower had written to the chiefs of staff pressing for the ban. After more than a month of prevarication, it was introduced and went into effect on April 1.

The issue of limiting diplomatic communications was particularly sensitive. It went against a long-standing convention in international relations that protected the right of diplomats to communicate freely with their home governments. To be effective, it was felt necessary to apply it to Allies as well as neutrals. The only exceptions were to be the United States and the Soviet Union, where a diplomatic row could not be risked. De Gaulle and his French Committee of National Liberation were to be included. There was a justified fear of reprisals by impacted countries, which might respond by censoring the communications of British representatives abroad. While it was felt this could be circumvented by British diplomats using the secure facilities of their American allies, there was also an unexpected security objection. On March 7, Cabinet Secretary Edward Bridges sent a deliberately brief note to Churchill suggesting that he meet the next day—before the Overlord Preparations Committee—with Foreign Secretary Anthony Eden, Lord President of the Council Clement Attlee, "C" (the head of the Secret Intelligence Service MI6, Stewart Menzies), and perhaps the chiefs of staff to deal "with the points of special secrecy which are vital to consideration of the ban on diplomatic communications." Churchill's briefing notes for the ensuing Overlord Preparations Committee meeting give a further glimpse of the intelligence community lobbying behind the scenes, noting that the Foreign Office and MI6 were suggesting that a ban on uncensored diplomatic communications would be against

> our interests because it would leave us in the dark as to what information was leaking out of the country and reaching the enemy. (The extent of our knowledge of what leaks through diplomatic channels will be explained orally); and because a good deal of wrong information—including our cover plan material —reaches the enemy through diplomatic communications.

Here was proof that Britain was not only illicitly intercepting supposedly secure diplomatic communications by neutral powers to gain intelligence but was also actively using these channels as part of the Overlord deception plan. Unsurprisingly, the matter was referred by the Overlord Preparations Committee to the War Cabinet, which decided against imposing the ban at the current time. It was finally introduced at midnight on April 17. Churchill sent the following telegram to President Roosevelt:

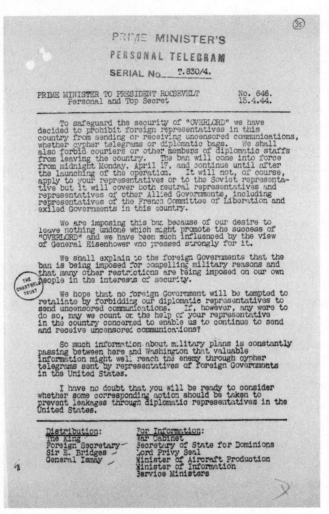

PRIME MINISTER'S PERSONAL TELEGRAM

SERIAL No. T.830/4.

PRIME MINISTER TO PRESIDENT ROOSEVELT   No. 646.
          Personal and Top Secret   15.4.44.

To safeguard the security of "OVERLORD" we have decided to prohibit foreign representatives in this country from sending or receiving uncensored communications, whether cypher telegrams or diplomatic bags. We shall also forbid couriers or other members of diplomatic staffs from leaving the country. The ban will come into force from midnight Monday, April 17, and continue until after the launching of the operation. It will not, of course, apply to your representatives or to the Soviet representative but it will cover both neutral representatives and representatives of other Allied Governments, including representatives of the French Committee of Liberation and exiled Governments in this country.

We are imposing this ban because of our desire to leave nothing undone which might promote the success of "OVERLORD" and we have been much influenced by the view of General Eisenhower who pressed strongly for it.

We shall explain to the foreign Governments that the ban is being imposed for compelling military reasons and that many other restrictions are being imposed on our own people in the interests of security.

We hope that no foreign Government will be tempted to retaliate by forbidding our diplomatic representatives to send uncensored communications. If, however, any were to do so, may we count on the help of your representative in the country concerned to enable us to continue to send and receive uncensored communications?

So much information about military plans is constantly passing between here and Washington that valuable information might well reach the enemy through cypher telegrams sent by representatives of foreign Governments in the United States.

I have no doubt that you will be ready to consider whether some corresponding action should be taken to prevent leakages through diplomatic representatives in the United States.

Distribution: For Information:
The King   War Cabinet
Foreign Secretary   Secretary of State for Dominions
Sir E. Bridges   Lord Privy Seal
General Ismay   Minister of Aircraft Production
                               Minister of Information
                               Service Ministers

Telegram from Churchill to Roosevelt, April 15, 1944.
(Churchill Papers, CHAR 20/162/35)

Gradually, inexorably, the screw was being tightened. The Overlord Preparations Committee meeting of March 15 approved many of the measures outlined in the earlier security report: confirming 100 per-cent censorship of mail to Eire, foreign countries, and Gibraltar, and introducing full censorship for Northern Ireland. It also allowed "artifi-cial" delays to the overseas post, guaranteeing a month's delay between the sending and receipt of most letters to foreign countries. The export of local newspapers was restricted to the Empire and United States and banned to foreign countries, Gibraltar, Eire, and Northern Ireland. Overseas telegrams were subject to paraphrase and delay. Air services to Ireland were heavily restricted and those remaining were run from airports outside the Overlord area, while air services between Aberdeen and Sweden were suspended. Fishing vessels were excluded from the south coast ports, and departures of all ships were controlled in an attempt to delay their arrival at foreign ports. Immigration controls were further tightened and even Allied nationals hoping to enlist were now kept to a minimum.

The increase in security occurred in an atmosphere of increasing tension, one that was undoubtedly made worse by security lapses. For obvious reasons, few people were aware of them, but Churchill certainly was, and they clearly contributed to his worries in the run-up to D-Day.

On March 23, the Americans feared that Overlord had been com-promised. A package containing essential facts about the operation had been intercepted in Chicago, en route to a private address in a part of the city with a high German population. On investigation, it emerged that it had been sent in error by a US soldier who had absentmindedly written his sister's address on the envelope rather than that of the intended War Department recipient. The error was compounded by the fact that the plans were poorly packaged and so had been opened and seen by a number of unauthorized persons; all of which took time to ascertain.

At around the same time, the British were wrestling with a very different type of security breach. On March 10, Duncan Sandys lunched at London's exclusive Park Lane Hotel with Captain Basil Liddell Hart, the eminent historian and military strategist who had been influential in developing theories of modern mechanized warfare. After enjoying their meal, they retired to Captain Hart's private sitting room within the hotel, where, according to Sandys, "In the course of a general conversation about military matters of a non-secret character he mentioned that he had strong doubts about the wisdom of our plan for the invasion of the continent." This set Sandy's ears twitching. Though well connected in military circles, Captain Liddell Hart had no official reason to know about the Overlord plans. Yet in the course of his subsequent remarks, he stated that the plan was to land on the coast of Normandy, on beaches he had known well as a child, possibly mentioned Caen, and "said that Montgomery had made a number of minor improvements to the plan since he had taken over." Sandys "formed the impression that Captain Liddell Hart was in possession of precise information about future military operations." Alarmed, he informed General Ismay and Anthony Eden.

Ismay brought the matter to the prime minister's attention, who ordered an investigation. Churchill decided not to tell Eisenhower at this stage, as he wanted to find out exactly who had been talking to Liddell Hart and whether it was just British officers who were implicated.

Ismay quickly established that Liddell Hart had also met with Sir Stafford Cripps, the Labour politician and minister for aircraft production, at a weekend country house party on March 4, where he had told Cripps "that it was pretty clear that we would not undertake operations against Europe outside fighter cover, that this limited the point of attack to the North of France, whereas his opinion was that we would do better to strike in the bay of Biscay." He then handed Cripps a paper, which Cripps subsequently forwarded to Deputy Prime Minister Clement Attlee, titled "Some Reflections on the Problem of Invading the Continent." Written at the end of January, the paper speculated on a likely assault in northern France and suggested that tactics would be governed by "the time and space conventions of the past"; the danger was that success in getting ashore would only achieve the formation of "a shallow and narrow bridgehead, expanded so slowly that the Germans will be allowed time to concentrate against it."

There was much here to annoy Churchill: the attack on British tactics, the lobbying of senior members of his government (of both main political parties), and the suggestion that Liddell Hart may have been getting insider information on the forthcoming landings. There was also surely a fear, tied into Churchill's own reservations, that Captain Liddell Hart might be right. There was certainly enough for an interview, and Liddell Hart was summoned to an uncomfortable meeting with General Ismay and Brigadier Jacob at quarter past five on the evening of March 19. He admitted having given copies of his paper to Lord Beaverbrook, Stafford Cripps, Duncan Sandys, and to two or three American generals, including Patton and Gerow, but denied receiving classified information about the plan and said that "the Generals had talked to him as a responsible person fairly freely on the general conception."

Churchill was furious and wanted to press the matter to a prosecution, telling Ismay that, "If this man were kept worrying about the matter for some weeks it would be a lesson to him, even if we did not carry through to the end." But the grounds for such a course of action were not really there. Churchill briefed Eisenhower and was incensed to learn that Liddell Hart had still been visiting American headquarters. It led to a final angry outburst to Ismay on the matter:

> I think he should be frightened out of his wits, and have his name put on the gate of all the Armed Forces in this country. We are to blame as it is one of our black sheep and you should reconsider the letter to General Eisenhower from this point of view, making it clear that it is our fault.

Liddell Hart, who was not in good health, was encouraged to return to his home in Westmoreland for a prolonged period (where the security services kept an eye on him).

Ironically, years later in 1969, Liddell Hart would get the last word by contributing an essay to a controversial book titled *Churchill: Four Faces and the Man*. In his essay on Churchill, "The Military Strategist," he would conclude that "from the time the Normandy landing was achieved," Churchill ceased "to have any important influence on the course of the war—or on its sequel." These are themes to which we will return in our final chapter. But in the spring of 1944, Churchill had heard enough from Liddell Hart.

At the end of May, with D-Day imminent, Churchill took a similarly dim view of the presence in Britain of Mr. James Loy Maloney, the editor of the *Chicago Tribune*, well known as a fierce critic of British policy in the American press. Mr. Maloney had been blocked from leaving the country. Brendan Bracken, the minister for information, was incensed that Maloney had been allowed into the United Kingdom in the first place at a time when most travel was restricted, including for diplomats, writing that he would "rather see an invitation issued to Himmler to come to England than to Maloney." The episode occurred just as Eisenhower was asking for the diplomatic travel ban to be extended for a period after D-Day. It prompted a testy response from Churchill to Ike on May 31:

> You probably have no idea of the enormous inconvenience and friction which this system [the diplomatic travel ban] has caused. The Free French Committee is only one instance; but in every case the Foreign Office is gravely hampered. . . .
>
> I must confess that I had not realised that unofficial Americans would be free to go and come between here and the United States during all the time we are putting this ban on all the Embassies. Among those recently put to us was the case of the Editor of the "Chicago Tribune."
>
> Here is a real foe, serving in a paper which announced that the Americans had broken the Japanese cypher, and a paper which the President has described as "United States Fifth Column."

Add to this the lapse of a senior American officer while under the influence and the strange (and apparently entirely coincidental) appearance of several Overlord code words in the *Daily Telegraph* crossword, and you can see why this was a nervous time. Ordinary soldiers making accidental errors; experts making guesses about plans that were too close to the truth. And all the time, constant speculation in the press. No one was immune. Even the reliable Joan Bright later confessed to an anxious moment when she suddenly realized she had just left a briefcase containing official papers in a post office. Thankfully, when she hastily returned, it was still there.

The longer the wait for operations to start, the greater the risk of more incidents. Churchill liked being at the center of momentous events and making decisions, but this was a different kind of pressure—a prolonged period of waiting for the decisive moment to arrive. It was taking a toll on his health.

Churchill was sixty-nine years old and still recovering from the pneumonia that had nearly killed him before Christmas. He had been prime minister for nearly four years and perhaps inevitably the strain was starting to show. There was no stroke or heart attack, but those around him were aware that things were not quite right.

His daughter Mary was with him at the beginning of February. They went together to watch the play *There Shall Be No Night*, set in Finland between 1938 and 1940:

The first scene was 1938—back to Munich. In the interval I said "It takes one back a bit—we've come such a long way since then." Papa said "I knew what would happen then—and I don't now— that is the difference."

The last few times I've seen Papa I've been struck with his anxious preoccupation with the future—his uncertainty. I know he foresees so much more trouble and grief and struggling ahead of us than we can imagine.

Alexander Cadogan, the country's senior diplomat as undersecretary of state, had watched Churchill operate at close quarters since the outbreak of war, attending Cabinet meetings and traveling with the prime minister. But in the spring of 1944, several of his diary entries record his concerns about Churchill's physical and mental health.

Mon 20 March—P.M. looked flushed and was very woolly. Hope he's not unwell.

Tue 21 March—P.M. this morning confessed he was tired—he's almost done in.

Wed 19 April—P.M., I fear, is breaking down. He rambles without a pause, and we really got nowhere by 7.40. . . . I really am fussed about the P.M. He is not the man he was 12 months ago, and I really don't know whether he can carry on.

On May 7, with the Overlord operation only a month away, Churchill made a rare admission of weakness to General Brooke. After watching a film at Chequers, they retired to a little study where Churchill sat by the fire, drank some soup, and—looking very old and tired—said that he was no longer the man he had been:

He said he could still always sleep well, eat well and especially drink well! but that he no longer jumped out of bed the way he used to, and felt as if he would be quite content to spend the whole day in bed. I have never yet heard him admit that he was beginning to fail.

Harry Butcher noticed that Churchill's broadcast of March 26 "lacked his usual inspirational vigour," while Jock Colville considered it indifferent. The language used certainly hints at weariness and frustration. Churchill opened by thanking his audience for all the kindness with which they had treated him "in spite of my many shortcomings," and he admitted that "our progress has not been as rapid or decisive as we had hoped," mentioning the delays to the advance in Italy and referring to his disappointment over Allied failure to dominate the Aegean Islands. An earlier draft even contained a deleted passage in which he had complained about what a full-time job it was "keeping things sweet between us and all the other powers, great and small." Although he concluded with the confident assertion that "Britain can take it. She has never flinched or failed," this was not quite "fight on the beaches."

At times, his anger surfaced. Eisenhower recounted how the prime minister launched into an impassioned tirade against a British staff officer who inadvertently referred to British soldiers as "bodies" in his presentation, and "he said it was inhuman to talk of soldiers in such cold-blooded fashion, and that it sounded as if they were merely freight—or, worse, corpses!"

There is no suggestion that Churchill was like this all the time. There were clearly lighter moments. Joan Bright loved to tell the story of how General Leslie Hollis was on duty for Churchill's office one Saturday morning when Overlord was being planned. The three British chiefs of staff—Brooke, Cunningham, and Portal—had all gone fishing in the country and, faced with a potentially quiet day, General Ismay had gone home. Inevitably, the phone rang. It was Churchill, from Chequers— could the chief of the Imperial General Staff come down and see him as there were one or two things he would like to discuss. Hollis had to explain that he was out of London. The prime minister then asked about the chief of the Air Staff and, with sinking heart, Hollis had to give the same answer. He knew what was coming next. Churchill asked for the First Sea Lord. Same answer.

So there was a pregnant silence . . . "and what might they all be doing?" And Hollis, after a lot of thought, he said "Prime Minister they are fishing." "Fishing" he said, and the wires fused, "fishing" and then there was a long thing about there was this great war going on with one of the greatest build-ups going on for the greatest invasion in history, they go fishing! And he went on saying "fishing" and "fishing" and then he asked if he could see General Ismay and was told that he was in the country. So in desperation the Prime Minister said "Well Hollis" he said "perhaps you could come down."

A wonderful story, probably embellished with the retelling, and one that also appears in Hollis's own memoirs. It captures the spirit of Churchill's restlessness at this time. He was keen to maintain an overview of the preparations. As winter 1943 merged into summer 1944, the intensity of personal, unit, and formation preparation for the invasion of Europe intensified. The success of the largest multinational amphibious operation ever conceived would only be achieved by rigorous training and realistic rehearsal of all the naval, land, and air force units assigned to the Overlord order of battle. The armed camp that was Southern England was the setting for some of the final exercises before the operation was launched. Slapton Sands on the south coast of Devon was identified as similar in topography to Utah Beach on the Cotentin Peninsula where the US Fourth Infantry Division was to make its assault.

With the surrounding villages evacuated and some three thousand local residents required to leave their homes, training on Slapton Sands began in late 1943, but on April 27 and 28, 1944, disaster struck twice. Exercise Tiger was scheduled to last from April 22–28, culminating in practice landings by thirty thousand American troops from the Fourth Infantry Division. To add realism, the rehearsal landings were to be conducted with naval gunfire support screaming from sea to shore over the heads of the young troops as part of their battle inoculation, as they assaulted the beach. The first of the landings was scheduled for 07:30 hours on April 27; however, a number of the landing craft had been delayed by difficult sea conditions and the US naval commander ordered a delay to H-Hour for the exercise until 08:30 hours. The naval gunfire support was due to be provided by the British HMS *Hawkins*. Unfortunately, there were communication failures between the British and American exercising troops. Although the exercise plan had included a thirty-minute pause between the end of the shelling of the beach and the assault landings, the new timings were not received by all units. The tragic result was that US soldiers began landing on Slapton Sands while the British warship was still bringing down lethal fire on to the beach. It is not known to this day how many Americans lost their lives that morning but worse was to follow.

The final phase of Exercise Tiger was to be an even larger landing on Slapton Sands the following morning. It remains remarkable after the initial tragedy that the exercise was not paused, but nevertheless it went ahead. Although operational security and deception were overriding considerations in the preparations for D-Day, information about

Exercise Tiger became known to the German Kreigsmarine. Although most German capital ships had been either sunk or neutralized, flotillas of torpedo-armed E-boats (known as S, or Schnellboot to the Germans) were based in Cherbourg and the Channel Islands. As the exercising fleet of tank and infantry landing craft formed up and sailed out of Lyme Bay on the night of April 27 and 28 toward Slapton Sands, nine German E-boats tracked them and got ready to pounce. Convoy T-4 should have been protected by two British warships, but one of them, HMS *Scimitar*, had suffered collision damage and was withdrawn from the exercise. Although British radar picked up the approach of the E-boats, it was assumed that they were part of the exercise. The remaining escort ship, HMS *Azalea*, took no action. "We sailed along in fatal ignorance," wrote Lieutenant Eugene E. Eckstam, a medical officer aboard the first of two Landing Ship Tanks (LSTs) to be attacked.

Shortly after 01:30 hours on April 28, the Kreigsmarine S-boats launched their attack. Over the next chaotic hour, two of the LSTs were sunk with huge loss of life. Other vessels were badly damaged. Vehicles and men had been embarked with full loads of live ammunition and fuel to simulate the real landings, but this merely added to the intensity of the fires on the stricken ships. Extraordinarily, the soldiers had not been trained how to wear their life jackets properly. Many drowned as their life jackets, incorrectly tied around their waist, caused them to turn upside down in the water. At a sea temperature of only forty-two degrees Fahrenheit, many more were to die of hypothermia before they could be rescued. The confusion of the night was further exacerbated by the exercise being conducted in radio silence and the subsequent realization that the British escort ships and the American landing craft were on different radio frequencies.

With dawn came the appalling knowledge that there had been a major tragedy. In total some 749 US soldiers and sailors lost their lives that night, two LSTs were sunk and two others badly damaged. Although the E-boats escaped with no casualties, Supreme Headquarters Allied Expeditionary Force ordered RAF Lancaster bombers with 12,000-pound "Tallboy" bombs to eliminate the E-boat bases in early June.

Other lessons were learned from the Convoy T-4 tragedy. Ships were to zigzag, not steam in straight lines, radio frequencies were to be common across the fleet, rescue boats would be among the landing craft to pluck struggling soldiers from the sea, and all ranks were to be trained in how to wear their life jackets properly. After the disasters of April 27 and 28, the supreme irony was that Fourth Infantry Division landed successfully on Utah Beach on June 6, 1944, with the loss of only 197 soldiers killed or wounded. Their success had come from the awful price paid during Exercise Tiger, the truth about which was suppressed at the time as classified information. Later, the losses during Exercise Tiger were not reported by SHAEF until August 1944 and then absorbed within the reported casualties of the actual D-Day landings. There is now a memorial on Utah Beach commemorating the 946 American servicemen known to have died in the two tragedies off the coast of Slapton Sands during Exercise Tiger. Their sacrifice was not in vain. Rehearsal was essential to ultimate success, but such losses did nothing to lessen Churchill's anxiety about the actual landings. Here was an illustration of why preparation, deception, security, and lockdown were so important.

Despite this, the prime minister allowed his twenty-nine-year-old Private Secretary, Jock Colville, to rejoin the Royal Air Force and undertake a short period of operational flying around D-Day. He admired bravery and remembered his own youthful military adventures with fondness and nostalgia. In granting permission, he spoke of his own desire to see action, telling Colville that he [Churchill] "would be among the first on the bridgehead . . . if he possibly could—and what fun it would be to get there before Monty." An idea had been sown to which he would return. But even releasing his Private Secretary carried risk. Colville had been photographed alongside the prime minister. If shot down and captured, he knew many secrets, including the likely date and place for Overlord. It was agreed that he would not fly over France until after D-Day. When Colville joined his squadron, he found that speculation about the date for the operation was rife and also dangerously accurate. When his new colleagues correctly guessed the likely date and place of the assault, he "could only hope the Germans were less intelligent in their deductions."

It was in Churchill's character to show his emotions, and in the months leading up to D-Day the dominant ones were increasing impatience and frustration. He was able to oversee and to influence the civil preparations, but he longed to play a bigger role in the military operations. Eisenhower kept Churchill informed but also at arm's length, working from his headquarters outside London at Bushy Park, near Hampton Court Palace, and through the Combined Chiefs of Staff. The British prime minister was not yet ready to give up all influence. The political could not always be so easily disentangled from the military. Questions remained over the control and use of air power. The stage was set for one last prime ministerial foray into the strategy for Overlord.

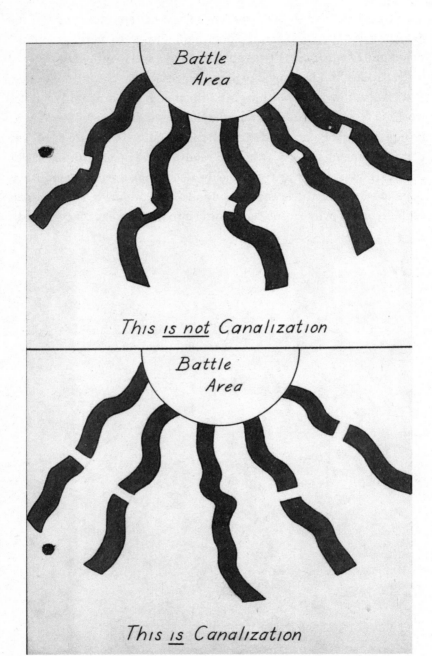

Diagram from papers of Air Vice Marshal Bufton illustrating the type of damage to railway lines needed to disrupt the enemy, c. 1944. (Bufton Papers, BUFT 3/44 part 3)

Chapter 8

Bombing Civilians

*"There was a limit to the slaughter
and the resulting anger and resentment
which it would arouse among Frenchmen
beyond which we could not go."*

IT WAS NOT JUST LOCKDOWN WITH WHICH CHURCHILL WAS WRESTLING. He was also brooding on the nature that the Allied offensive would take. Air superiority over France had been one of the preconditions for Overlord, and by early 1944 the Allies had huge air forces assembled in Britain. But this does not mean that there was full agreement on how to deploy them.

The command structure was complicated. Eisenhower's deputy commander was British Air Chief Marshal Arthur Tedder, and their Allied Expeditionary Force had its own air force, which was under the command of Air Marshal Trafford Leigh-Mallory. This comprised fighter aircraft, light and medium bombers that could be used in support of the ground troops, and specialist reconnaissance, transport, and glider towing craft.

Control of the American heavy bombers, part of the United States Eighth Army Air Force, lay with Lieutenant General James Doolittle. He reported to Lieutenant General Carl Spaatz, as commander of the US Strategic Forces in Europe, who in turn reported to Eisenhower as the overall American theater commander. Yet, the British heavy bombers were controlled separately by Bomber Command, run by Air Marshal Arthur Harris, reporting to Chief of the Air Staff Charles Portal. Royal Air Force Coastal Command was also independent, under Air Chief Marshal Sholto Douglas. Above it all sat the Combined Chiefs of Staff, Churchill, and his Defence Committee, the War Cabinet, and Roosevelt, as American commander in chief. This would not have been a problem if they had all agreed on a clear strategy for use of air power, but they did not.

Types of Air Power

Tactical air power involves the use of air forces in support of units on the ground or at sea. Tactical forces can be called upon to provide fighter protection in the air above the battlefield and to bomb enemy positions, fortifications, vehicles, or vessels threatening Allied troops. They also provide specialist functions like photographic reconnaissance and air transport, bringing troops and supplies to the battlefield. The aircraft protecting the D-Day assault on June 6 were operating tactically.

Operational air power involves the use of air forces to obtain specific operational objectives, such as the preliminary bombardment of a shoreline or the destruction of specific targets. The famous Dambusters Raid by 617 Squadron RAF against the Möhne and Edersee dams in Germany on the night of May 16, 1943, is an example of operational air power.

Strategic air power involves the large-scale use of air power, bypassing the battlefield on the ground, to obtain a specific strategic or political aim. Operation Pointblank, the combined Allied bomber offensive aimed at crippling German fighter production and conducted over a sustained period between summer 1943 and spring 1944, is an example of strategic air power.

In 1944, the Allied Expeditionary Force had its own tactical air force under Leigh-Mallory that was also capable of conducting operations essential to the success of Overlord. The US Eighth Army Air Force and British Bomber Command were operating as independent strategic forces, engaged in a wholesale bombing campaign against Germany in northwestern Europe, but were now called upon to offer operational and even tactical support for the operation.

Eisenhower believed that all Allied air forces operating in the Western European theater should be subordinated to his command for the period immediately preceding and following the D-Day operation, arguing that "when a battle needs the last ounce of available force, the commander must not be in the position of depending upon request and negotiation to get it." Spaatz and Harris argued that the best use of their strategic heavy bomber forces was to continue what they were doing already, and that their ongoing, large-scale bombing of German cities and industry would cripple the German economy and destroy the enemy's morale, thereby weakening resistance to Overlord. Spaatz, in particular, felt strongly that hitting German oil supplies was the best way to bring the enemy to a standstill. They did not believe that it was right to use the huge—but often inaccurate—destructive power of their forces in support of ground troops or on specific military objectives, such as railways, roads, and bridges, that might be pinpointed more accurately by smaller aircraft or sabotage. Harris was characteristically blunt:

> [T]he only efficient support which Bomber Command can give to Overlord is the intensification of attacks on suitable industrial centres in Germany as and when the opportunity offers. If we attempt to substitute for this process attacks on gun emplacements, beach defences, communications or dumps in occupied territory we shall commit the irremediable error of diverting our best weapons from the military function, for which it has been equipped and trained, to tasks which it cannot effectively carry out. Though this might give a specious appearance of

"supporting" the Army, in reality it would be the gravest disser-
vice we could do them. It would lead directly to disaster.

Eisenhower was not to be moved. He maintained that he needed
an all-out bombing offensive against German fortifications and infrastructure to support an assault on this scale and that the bombers were
needed as far more than "a mere adjunct to the Tactical Air Command."
He got his way. Bomber Command and the Eighth Army Air Force were
brought under his overall control for the period immediately surrounding Overlord.

For Churchill this raised several questions: Was it right to divert
so many resources from the bombing of Germany? What was the best
way of using the bomber forces to support operations in France? And
what would be the impact on the French population of a bombing
campaign on the scale now proposed by Eisenhower? Churchill had
expressed concerns as early as November 1943 that the Germans
"will gain a very sensible relief from Air Attack in consequence of the
opening of Overlord" but had also recognized that it would be very
difficult to resist a claim from the commander in chief "to control
all the strategic bomber forces during the actual period of Overlord
as they are an integral and vital part of his operation." In practice,
control was always going to pass to Eisenhower for the period around
D-Day; a question of when, not if. But this did not mean the prime
minister lost interest in how the bomber forces would be deployed.

Churchill had already enjoyed a long relationship with the development and use of air power. As secretary of state for war and air in
the immediate aftermath of the First World War, he had presided
over the early growth of the Royal Air Force, and as the minister in
charge of the colonies, he had sought to harness that new power for
political ends, using planes instead of troops to police the deserts of
Mesopotamia and Transjordan (Iraq and Jordan). During the 1930s, he
had argued passionately for rearmament and in particular the development of a modern bomber force. On becoming prime minister in 1940,
one of his first actions had been to sanction bombing raids against the
enemy, and he had continued to advocate these as a means of taking the

offensive, wearing Germany down in an attempt to break her economic capacity; destroying her morale and easing pressure on the Russian and Mediterranean fronts. His celebrated speech at the height of the Battle of Britain praising the bravery of the fighter pilots—"Never in the field of human conflict has so much been owed by so many to so few"—had gone on to pay tribute to the bomber crews:

> [B]ut we must never forget that all the time, night after night, month after month, our bomber squadrons travel far into Germany, find their targets in the darkness by the highest navigational skill, aim their attacks, often under the heaviest fire, often with serious loss, with deliberate careful discrimination, and inflict shattering blows upon the whole of the technical and war-making structure of the Nazi power.

At the Casablanca Conference, he had supported the directive intensifying the Combined Air Offensive against Germany, and he had consistently presented the ever-increasing raids against German cities as a means of offering support to the Soviets. He supported Operation Pointblank, the strategic campaign to bomb Germany by night and day in order to cripple the country's military, industrial, and economic system.

He saw the bombing campaign as both a prerequisite and an accompaniment to Overlord. Having watched Britain endure the Blitz, he had few qualms about the impact of the bombs on the German civilian population and was influenced by his scientific adviser, Lord Cherwell, who argued that it would help to break the spirit of the German people. Understandably, however, he was not so keen on breaking the spirit of the French people. Indeed, ever since 1940, he had actively encouraged their resistance and continued to believe that they could and would play an important role in their own liberation, rising up against their Nazi occupiers. But could he expect them to do so while suffering from an escalating Allied bombing campaign?

Britain and her allies had been bombing German targets in France since 1940, and the scale and intensity of these actions had gradually increased as more resources had become available. Richard Overy, in his excellent book *The Bombing War*, has documented the process. In July 1940, the War Cabinet had agreed that any military target could be bombed in the occupied parts of France, extended a year later to the bombing of factories—albeit only in daylight to ensure better accuracy and so minimize civilian casualties. Then, in early 1942, the rules were relaxed again, and Churchill consented to the general bombing of European targets. Shortly afterward, a huge bombing raid, the largest yet undertaken by the Allies, dropped 419 tons of bombs on the Renault motor works and surrounding workers' housing on the outskirts of Paris, killing almost four hundred people. Thereafter, Britain's desperate situation in the Battle of the Atlantic led to devastating raids on the port city of Lorient in early 1943, with Allied bombs destroying almost everything—except their target, the seemingly indestructible concrete U-boat pens.

By the beginning of 1944, there were already signs of growing French hostility to the bombing. Churchill's fear was that this would now get much worse. The air plan favored by Eisenhower advocated using bombers to maximize disruption to the transportation infrastructure before, during, and after D-Day. The aim was to buy the Allied troops crucial time to secure their positions by preventing the Germans from moving vital reinforcements and supplies toward the Normandy beachheads. This plan put a particular emphasis on the bombing of railway hubs and marshaling yards, where troops and equipment were likely to assemble. Unfortunately, these also tended to be located in densely populated urban areas.

By the end of February, Churchill was aware that the Allied air staffs were divided. Support for the transportation plan was balanced by those who argued strongly for the bombing of sites connected with the German Air Force or enemy oil supplies. There was criticism of the "transportation plan." It would divert resources from other targets; it would be ineffective unless all rail facilities were destroyed; and "attacks on the scale proposed would have an adverse effect on the French."

The War Cabinet, concerned with minimizing the loss of civilian life, had initially imposed operational restrictions on the targets that could be attacked from Britain. This meant that only thirteen of the seventy-four French and Belgian railway centers identified by Eisenhower as critical to the success of his plan could be bombed. Eisenhower wanted them all attacked "by day or night without any operational restrictions." As chief of the Air Staff, Portal wrote to Churchill on March 29 confirming that it had been agreed that "the so-called Transportation Plan was the best way for the strategic bombers to pave the way for a successful Overlord" while also warning that "in the execution of this plan very heavy casualties among the civilians living near the main railway centres in occupied territory will be unavoidable, however careful we may be over the actual bombing." The Ministry of Home Security estimated that, without evacuation, the number of civilian casualties would be between 80,000 and 160,000, "of which a quarter would be killed." The chiefs of staff felt such action needed the prime minister's approval and argued that the French civilian population and especially the railway workers should be warned. Portal brought Eisenhower's request before the War Cabinet on April 3.

Churchill immediately expressed "some doubts as to the wisdom of this policy." He referred the matter to the Defence Committee and wrote to Eisenhower expressing his concerns in no uncertain terms:

> The Cabinet today took rather a grave and on the whole an adverse view on the proposal to bomb so many French railway centres, in view of the fact that scores of thousands of French civilians, men, women and children, would lose their lives or be injured. Considering that they are all our friends, this might be held to be an act of very great severity, bringing much hatred on the Allied Air Forces.

He worried that the plan would provide a gift to enemy propaganda and suggested that General de Gaulle be notified. Eisenhower was uncompromising in his reply, arguing that "we must not fail to make such preliminary employment of this [air] force as will later help us in our moment of crisis." He believed that the probable casualties had been exaggerated and argued that, ultimately, "the French people are now slaves. Only a successful Overlord can now free them."

The British Defence Committee met late on April 5 with Churchill in the chair. It brought together the leading politicians with the chiefs of staff and was attended by a number of the relevant air experts, including Tedder, Norman Bottomley (deputy chief of the Air Staff), and Sydney Bufton (director of Bombing Operations). The scientists were represented by Lord Cherwell and Solly Zuckerman (scientific director of the British Bombing Survey Unit). The meeting exposed deep divisions, not just between the military and the politicians, but also within the military and scientific ranks over whether the Transportation Plan was the most effective bombing strategy.

The prime minister set the scene by announcing his fear that "even if the casualties were not so great as was estimated, they might well be sufficient to cause an unhealable breach between France and Great Britain & USA." He also questioned whether

the effect which would be achieved by bombing attacks on railway centres, would justify the slaughter of masses of friendly French allies, who were burning to help us when the day came, and who showed their friendly feelings by giving unstinted help to any of our airmen forced down among them. It was one thing to launch attacks which would result in heavy loss of civilian life during the hot blood of battle; it was quite another to begin, when no fighting was going on, a policy which was bound to result in the butchering of large numbers of helpless French people.

These were strong words and were most likely even stronger in the meeting itself, where Churchill's draft of the minutes shows his deletion of the phrase "in cold blood."

The prime minister questioned whether bombing the railway lines was the right strategy. He felt that it would be just as easy for the enemy to move troops and materials by road. The issue divided the room. The two scientists took opposing views. Cherwell felt that the attacks were unlikely to do sufficient damage to disrupt enemy transportation and that other alternatives had not been adequately explored. Zuckerman, on the other hand, defended the study he had undertaken on the Tunisian and Sicilian campaigns, which had shown that the greatest effect on disrupting enemy communications had been achieved by systematic attacks on the railway centers. The air men present were similarly divided: Portal, Tedder, and Leigh-Mallory spoke in favor of the plan while Commodore Bufton argued for more direct attacks on the aerodromes, repair facilities, and factories of the German Air Force, as well as the bombing of military training centers. Among the politicians, Attlee was worried about the antagonism that would be aroused in the French, while Eden felt that the attacks might drive the French and Belgians away from the British and Americans and into the arms of the Russians. "After the war we would have to live in a Europe which was already looking more to Russia than he would wish." When Churchill suggested bombing the Romanian oil fields as an alternative, thereby depriving the Germans of much needed fuel, Portal countered by pointing out that it would not impact Overlord, as the Germans already had sufficient fuel stocks in France to sustain operations for several months.

An impasse was reached. It was decided to continue with experimental attacks against three railway centers where there was a reduced risk of civilian casualties. Brooke's diary records his frustration at being kept up until 12:45 a.m. by this discussion. He would endure a similar fate on April 13 and 19 as the matter was returned to the Defence Committee for consideration on a weekly basis. At each meeting, similar arguments were made, and, on each occasion, Churchill deferred a final decision while allowing the bombing to continue on a temporary basis. He would not let his concerns drop and returned repeatedly to his main worry. On April 13, he complained that:

This slaughter was likely to put the French against us and he was doubtful if the results achieved by the plan would justify this. There was a limit to the slaughter and the resulting anger and resentment which it would arouse among Frenchmen beyond which we could not go.

By April 26, he was concerned that continuing the attacks over a long period would build up a volume of dull hatred in France which would affect relations with that country for many years to come and would lead to the Royal Air Force, which had hitherto been regarded with admiration, being looked upon with odium and accused of killing friends by blind night bombing attacks.

At the War Cabinet meeting the following afternoon, it was agreed that the plan for bombing targets in enemy-occupied territory should be limited to attacks on those railway centers with low estimated casualties and that consideration should be given again to attacking ammunition dumps, military camps, and vehicle parks. Churchill now accepted that the total casualties from the program would be much lower than originally envisaged, perhaps twelve thousand people, but he still felt that it was offering an advantage to German-controlled Vichy propaganda. The bombing was also falling disproportionately on the Royal Air Force, who, bombing at night, had dropped twelve times the weight of bombs than their American counterparts and Churchill feared the loss of life would "be blamed on blind night bombing carried out by the British." On balance, he felt that the bombing "might well do more evil than good," and he undertook to discuss the matter with Eisenhower and to prepare a telegram for the president. The chiefs of staff disagreed and appended their own paper to the official minutes endorsing the bombing as the only effective plan for supporting the troops and preventing a German counteroffensive.

By this time the bombing had started, and Churchill was getting daily intelligence updates on its impact. These only reinforced his anxiety. The report on reactions to bombing in the twenty-four hours up to 13:30 hours on April 29, 1944, confirmed that "the raids in the Paris area have not been satisfactory, as there were too many civilian casualties. Those on Rouen, Lille and Villeneuve-St-Georges have been 'Catastrophic' for French morale." The underlining was Churchill's and was accompanied by his handwritten note "General Eisenhower to see."

He got short shrift from Ike who wrote to Churchill on May 2 pointing out that "casualties to civilian personnel are inherent in any plan for the full use of Air power to prepare for our assault." The Supreme Commander argued that, "Railway centres have always been recognized as legitimate military targets, and attack on them is clearly obvious to the general population as a strictly military operation." In his view, and that of the chief of the Air Staff, there was "no effective alternative plan" and, if operations were limited in the way now being suggested, it "would emasculate the whole plan."

On the same day, Churchill received a note from Brendan Bracken, his close friend and minister of information, warning him that:

We are shouldering a grim responsibility in consenting to constant raids on a town like Malines which, as a centre of Belgian religious and educational life, has great spiritual significance for the Belgian people. There can be no doubt that the odium which we are incurring will be intense and lasting.

Churchill was caught between the operational needs of Overlord and a possible political breach with France and Belgium, which might lead to those countries emerging from the conflict with hostility toward Britain. Their workers might be driven toward communism.

That evening at the War Cabinet, Churchill reported on Eisenhower's strong response. While recognizing that "very great consequences might follow from interference with his [Eisenhower's] plan on political grounds," he ruefully remarked that he had not "fully realized that our use of air power before Overlord would assume so cruel and remorseless a form," and he suggested that "these air operations should be governed by some laws of war laid down by the War Cabinet and accompanied by an immense programme of leaflet dropping, to warn the inhabitants of the threatened areas, even if this involved some additional risk to our airmen."

The Defence Committee reconvened the next day. There was now about a month to go before D-Day. Churchill wanted to look again at the level of bombing against railway targets as a proportion of the total bombing effort between now and three months after the invasion. Faced with his rebuff from Eisenhower, he was keen to use the meeting to gather views for a communication to President Roosevelt. He also wanted to ensure that the Americans "accepted their share of responsibility for the heavy casualties that would be inflicted on the friendly civilian population of the occupied countries."

Portal and Leigh-Mallory set out the plans for the air campaign. It would evolve over four phases. First, the attacks on railway targets, then strikes on tactical targets—enemy units and fortifications, starting about three weeks before the assault, then supporting operations for the landings themselves, and finally tactical support for the ensuing campaign. In the run-up to the invasion, about 35 to 40 percent of bomber effort would be directed against the railway targets, with 30 percent against airfields and 15 percent focused against batteries dominating the assault area. To preserve secrecy over which beaches were to be used, and to reinforce the deception plans, attacks would also be mounted against batteries in other coastal areas.

Other targets scheduled for attack included ammunition dumps, military transport hubs, and radar stations. Those most likely to involve heavy civilian casualties were the telephone exchanges, transport hubs, ports, and headquarters. Churchill said that, with the exception of the railway centers, no one could reasonably object to the other targets being attacked, as they were clearly of a military nature. But he feared that enemy and foreign propaganda would contrast the German and Russian armies, fighting "bravely despite the lack of air superiority" with the "ruthless employment of air power" by the British and Americans "regardless of the cost in civilian casualties." He remained particularly worried that the British would be singled out as the "greatest offenders" for their bombing by night, which was less accurate and scattered the bombs over a wide area, "whereas the Americans carried out precision bombing in daylight." He called for a special study of the case for and against using delayed action bombs and for special attention to be paid to warning the French civilians "which areas were dangerous."

Returning to his concern over the bombing of railway centers, Churchill once again tried to limit civilian casualties, asking Tedder if he would approve a plan that would restrict them to ten thousand. Cherwell jumped in, pushing for alternative attacks on ammunition dumps and bridges. Tedder refused to be drawn on casualties, estimating the number killed to date at between three thousand and four thousand. He defended the Railway Plan. In attacks on bridges, a large number of bombs missed and were completely wasted; in attacks on railway centers, "every bomb which fell within the area of the centre did some damage of military value."

The politicians present, Clement Attlee, Anthony Eden, and Oliver Lyttelton, all shared Churchill's reservations. Attlee was worried that the Railway Plan would "spoil our political future in Europe." He felt that "the political disadvantages of the plan outweighed its military advantages." This was a point that the prime minister was particularly keen to emphasize, and it was agreed that he would draft a letter for the American State Department, to be communicated to the president. One more appeal would also be made to Eisenhower to try to limit civilian casualties to under ten thousand.

By this point, the bombing campaign had been running for weeks, and it was probably too late to reverse it. In any event, the air offensive would shortly be switching to its tactical phase, which included hitting the railways alongside other targets.

The prime minister was running out of time and options. On May 7, he wrote to Roosevelt informing him of the divisions within air circles over the Railway Plan. He was at pains to point out that these cut across national divisions and that his concerns were shared by some Americans, before confirming that he was "personally by no means convinced that this is the best way to use our Air Forces in the preliminary period and still think that the G.A.F. [German Air Force] should be the main target." He feared that by pursuing their existing plan the Allies might "leave a legacy of hate behind them":

> It must be remembered on the one hand that this slaughter is among a friendly people who have committed no crime against us, and not among the German foe with all their record of cruelty and ruthlessness.

Though, aware perhaps of growing American concerns about his own level of commitment to Overlord, he ended with a note of reassurance:

> On the other hand we naturally feel the hazardous nature of Operation Overlord and are in deadly earnest about making it a success.

Roosevelt's reply came on May 11 and was unambiguous in its support for Eisenhower:

> However regrettable the attendant loss of civilian lives is, I am not prepared to impose from this distance any restriction on military action by the responsible commanders that in their opinion might militate against the success of Overlord or cause additional loss of life to our Allied Forces of invasion.

This effectively brought the political debate to an end. The episode shows the limits of Churchill's power to influence the military strategy. On the eve of the largest Allied operation yet undertaken, when faced with a determined Supreme Commander who ultimately had the backing of the Combined Chiefs of Staff and the president of the United States, Churchill had no option but to approve the military plans, whatever the level of his personal reservations. His intervention had ensured that the matter had been thoroughly debated and may have played a small role in reducing French casualties by limiting the initial onset of the bombing and by his insistence throughout that appropriate warnings be issued. On the other hand, the delay in making a firm decision and extensive debate occupied the key commanders—Eisenhower, Tedder, and Leigh-Mallory—at a time when they were already very busy finalizing their preparations.

Unfortunately, bombing in early 1944 was not all one way. Faced with the obvious buildup of Allied forces, Hitler unleashed a mini-Blitz on Britain, which clearly added to Churchill's concerns. Between January and May 1944, German bombers returned to the skies above the United Kingdom and particularly London, though not in the same numbers as in 1940. Harry Butcher recorded a thousand-kilo bomb hitting St. James's Square in central London and damaging the windows at Norfolk House, where some of the Overlord planning staff were still based. He was responsible for finding a suitable air raid shelter for Eisenhower near his London headquarters. His choice of a basement in a house owned by the Oxford Group, which preached Christian fellowship, proved somewhat controversial. It quickly led to an offer of alternative accommodation from Churchill when Eisenhower pointed out to the prime minister that "it seemed a bit incongruous for him as a military leader to seek safety in an air raid shelter run by pacifists." This was not quite fair to the members of the Oxford Group, many of whom had taken up arms against fascism.

With hindsight, the German campaign achieved little, though there must have been initial fears about the vulnerability of some of the Allied invasion forces being assembled on the south coast. Fortunately, the Luftwaffe was not the force it had been, and disruption to Overlord preparations was minimal. But the bombing was a further trial for the civilian population and impacted negatively on morale. Ultimately, it helped to wear down German air forces ahead of the cross-Channel operation, as every bomber lost over Britain would not be available to counterattack in France. But that was only apparent with hindsight. At the time, the threat was made worse by a growing fear that this renewed German air attack was a precursor for Hitler's release of his new secret weapons.

From late 1942, the Allies started to receive intelligence that the Germans were trialing long-range rockets (later to be known as V2). These were quickly linked with a research center at Peenemünde on the German Baltic coast. By April of the following year, the prime minister had been notified and a special investigating committee established under the chairmanship of Duncan Sandys. Intelligence was gathered from photographic reconnaissance, interrogation of prisoners, and analysis by British scientists, but details of the weapon remained elusive. In June, the Ministry of Home Security estimated that a rocket containing ten tons of explosive might devastate a radius of 850 feet, and Churchill was subsequently informed that "if one such rocket fell in the

London area every hour for thirty days the cumulative casualties might be 108,000 killed and as many seriously injured." Churchill turned to Cherwell, who was skeptical, correctly questioning whether such weapons could be produced in sufficient numbers and even wondering if this might be an elaborate hoax. But the government could not afford to ignore a potential threat on this scale. Peenemünde was the target for a massive raid on the night of August 17, 1943, RAF Bomber Command using 597 aircraft to drop 1,937 tons of bombs. Rocket production was disrupted and slowed but not halted.

Then came news of a second possible weapon. By September 1943, it was known that the Germans were also developing pilotless aircraft (V1), though there remained significant confusion as to exactly what was being produced. The Defence Committee met on October 25. Scientists were galvanized, photographic reconnaissance was increased (Sarah Churchill was among those analyzing the photographs), and bombing raids against possible production sites were intensified. The pressure was mounting. Construction sites now began to appear in northern France, including "ski sites" with ramps pointing at London. By the end of 1943, eighty-eight had been identified and at least fifty more were suspected. Photographic reconnaissance and other intelligence sources soon linked them to the pilotless flying bombs, which now replaced the rockets as the most immediate threat. The new German weapons were given the codename Crossbow, and bombing operations commenced against the launch sites, but they were not easy to pinpoint and destroy.

All of this added to the prime minister's burdens during this crucial period. If the flying bombs and rockets could be unleashed in significant numbers, they might lead to huge dislocation in London or the southern ports; displacing large numbers of the population, further disrupting production and transportation (which were already stretched by the Overlord requirements) and threatening the required concentration of ground troops and naval forces. In his broadcast to the nation on March 26, Churchill warned that Britain might become "the object of new forms of attack from the enemy." Here was an additional threat that had to be watched on a daily basis. It also resulted in the diversion of some strategic bomber forces away from other targets.

It was against this backdrop that Roland MacKenzie was assigned to 166 Squadron and arrived at RAF Kirmington on April 2, 1944. From then until June 6, he undertook eighteen sorties in his Lancaster Mark III. They illustrate the range of hazardous missions being required of the strategic bomber forces in the run-up to Overlord. On the nights of April 9, 10, and 18, he bombed French marshaling yards at Villeneuve-Saint-Georges outside Paris, Aulnoye, and then Rouen. These raids were conducted as part of Zuckerman's Railway Plan ahead of the Normandy landings. Then, on April 20, 22, 24, and 27, he was hitting targets in Germany at—respectively—Cologne, Düsseldorf, Karlsruhe, and Friedrichshafen. These were part of Bomber Command's strategic air campaign against German industry, with some of the targets linked to probable production centers for the V-weapons. The risks were high. Roland's logbook entry for Cologne noted that, "The Kitchen Sink Came Up But Missed Us." Then it was back to France to provide tactical support for the impending invasion by attacking an ammunition dump near Rouen (April 30), the German panzer military camp at Mailly (night of May 3)—at which forty-two Lancasters, including three from his squadron, were lost—the ammunition dump at Rennes (May 7), and the coastal defenses at Dieppe (May 10). May 12 found him laying mines in the North Sea, while on May 19, he attacked the marshaling yards in Orléans. His next three missions were in Germany, but on June 2, he was attacking defenses in Calais as part of the Overlord deception plan, before flying over the invasion fleet en route to Cherbourg on D-Day itself.

Tedder sent a report on the operation against Mailly to the prime minister, prompting a note from Cherwell on May 25 that, despite the heavy losses, it had been an outstanding success. Even now, Cherwell refused to let go of his arguments against the Railway Plan, arguing that, "Such direct results are surely much to be preferred to the individual and debatable consequences of the attacks on marshalling yards, particularly as few, if any, French casualties are involved." Churchill clearly agreed, replying to Tedder on May 29:

It would seem right as we urged to give a high priority to operations of this sort which contribute directly towards the disorganisation of the German armies and involve no French casualties. You are piling up an awful load of hatred. I do not agree that the best targets were chosen. Have you exceeded the 10,000 limit?

While French civilian casualties from the bombing campaign never approached the levels of Churchill's worst fears, losses still ran into the thousands. Churchill did not know it in May 1944, but the worst was still to come. He probably took small comfort from the note he received back from Tedder on July 13:

I don't believe the figure of 10,000 which you gave was greatly exceeded. I am afraid, however, that those casualties are being dwarfed by the casualties involved in the liberation of Caen and other Normandy towns and villages.

It was a small piece of a grim picture. The total figures for civilians killed by Allied bombs in German-occupied countries during the war would ultimately reach 75,000.

Churchill was exhausted by the wait. He had been fighting hard and often unsuccessfully to make his voice heard on the military plan. He was worried about the ratio of frontline troops to vehicles and support services, concerned about the political and ethical implications of aspects of the bombing policy, and troubled by last-minute security breaches. The country was in a state of semi-lockdown, its transportation and production capacity stretched to their limit, with normal communications and diplomatic relations suspended and facing the risk of direct attack from new weapons of unknown proportions. The weather also remained an unpredictable variant, one that Churchill was watching closely. From the end of May, he demanded daily updates from the Admiralty. Everything now hung on the next move, which lay with Eisenhower as Supreme Commander. Small wonder that he sought a temporary escape from Whitehall.

Churchill was already planning to visit the troops on the south coast prior to D-Day. He knew that his presence was important for morale and that the frontline troops would want to see their

commanders before embarking. King George VI, Eisenhower, and
Montgomery were all doing the same. Now he decided that he wanted
to take this a step further and actually accompany the Allied forces
across the Channel and see the battle for himself, writing, "I thought
it would not be wrong for me to watch the preliminary bombardment
in this historic battle from one of our cruiser squadrons." It was
probably at the final conference at St. Paul's School that he asked

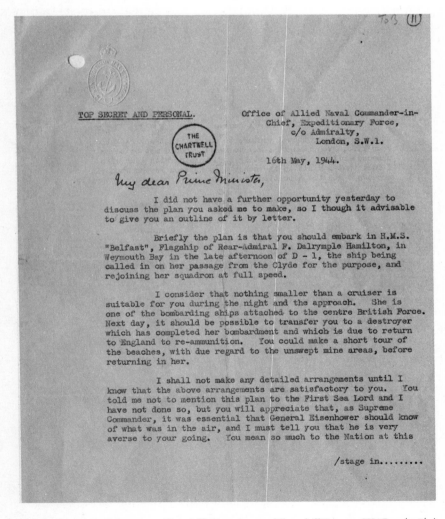

TOP SECRET AND PERSONAL.

Office of Allied Naval Commander-in-
Chief, Expeditionary Force,
c/o Admiralty,
London, S.W.1.

16th May, 1944.

My dear Prime Minister,

        I did not have a further opportunity yesterday to
discuss the plan you asked me to make, so I though it advisable
to give you an outline of it by letter.

        Briefly the plan is that you should embark in H.M.S.
"Belfast", Flagship of Rear-Admiral F. Dalrymple Hamilton, in
Weymouth Bay in the late afternoon of D - 1, the ship being
called in on her passage from the Clyde for the purpose, and
rejoining her squadron at full speed.

        I consider that nothing smaller than a cruiser is
suitable for you during the night and the approach. She is
one of the bombarding ships attached to the centre British Force.
Next day, it should be possible to transfer you to a destroyer
which has completed her bombardment and which is due to return
to England to re-ammunition. You could make a short tour of
the beaches, with due regard to the unswept mine areas, before
returning in her.

        I shall not make any detailed arrangements until I
know that the above arrangements are satisfactory to you. You
told me not to mention this plan to the First Sea Lord and I
have not done so, but you will appreciate that, as Supreme
Commander, it was essential that General Eisenhower should know
of what was in the air, and I must tell you that he is very
averse to your going. You mean so much to the Nation at this

                               /stage in........

Letter from Admiral Ramsay to Churchill, May 16, 1944. (Churchill Papers, CHAR 20/136/11)

Ramsay to draw up a plan. The naval commander did so, producing a schedule that would have seen Churchill embark on HMS *Belfast* on D-1, before later transferring to a destroyer to make a tour of the beaches on D-Day itself.

It is clear from the text that both Churchill and Ramsay knew how controversial this request was. Churchill specifically instructed Ramsay not to tell Admiral Cunningham, the First Sea Lord, who he knew would oppose it. Ramsay did not do so, but he felt compelled to tell General Eisenhower as the Supreme Commander with ultimate responsibility for all military aspects of Overlord, including the naval operation. Unsurprisingly, Eisenhower was against it. While recognizing that Churchill's request "was undoubtedly inspired as much by his natural instincts as a warrior as by his impatience at the prospect of sitting quietly back in London to await reports," the Supreme Commander could not risk the British prime minister becoming an accidental casualty, nor did he want others distracted from the operation at hand by the need to protect him. Churchill was not to be so easily put off, pointing out that Eisenhower did not have administrative control over the composition of any British ship's company and that if he made himself a "bona fide member of a ship's complement it would be beyond your authority to prevent my going."

Eisenhower had to concede, and there the matter rested until Tuesday, May 30, when Churchill went for his weekly luncheon with the king. In his diary, George VI recorded what happened next. He asked Winston

> where he would be on D-day or rather the night before & he told me glibly he hoped to see the initial attack from one of the bombarding ships. . . . I was not surprised & when I suggested that I should go as well (the idea had been in my mind for some time) he reacted well, & he and I are going to talk it over with Ad[miral] Ramsay on Thursday. . . . W[inston] cannot say no, if he goes himself, & I don't want to have to tell him he cannot. So? . . .
>
> I told E [Queen Elizabeth] who was wonderful & encouraged me. A.F.L. [Sir Alan Lascelles] was more reticent.

Perhaps Churchill felt he had no choice but to go along with the king's wishes; they being identical to his own. Perhaps he realized that, constitutionally, the monarch was the only person who could order him not to go. In his own memoirs, he said he would submit the request to the Cabinet after they had discussed the matter with Ramsay.

For Sir Alan Lascelles, the king's Private Secretary, this would never do, and his diary entry describes his response:

> I think I shook the King by asking him whether he thought the project would be quite fair to the Queen; and whether he was prepared to face the possibility of having to advise Princess Elizabeth on the choice of her first Prime Minister, in the event of her father and Winston being sent to the bottom of the English Channel. Another point, of course, is the paralysing effect which the presence on board of either the Sovereign or the PM, or both, would inevitably have on the unfortunate captain trying to fight his ship in the middle of what can only be an inferno.

By the following day, Lascelles had talked the king down but persuaded him of the necessity of restraining his prime minister. George VI sent a handwritten letter to Churchill, urging him to reconsider his plan, lest "a chance bomb, torpedo or even a mine should remove you from the scene."

Churchill and the king met with Ramsay, Lascelles, and Ismay in the Map Room at Churchill's Treasury Annexe at quarter past three on the afternoon of June 1. The admiral outlined his plan for the prime minister but "reacted violently" when informed that the king might want to go too. Churchill now said that this would require the approval of the Cabinet but refused to apply such restrictions to himself. Lascelles tried to convince Churchill of the risks, warning of the difficulty of changing prime minister in the middle of the largest military operation of the war, and arguing that he would need the sovereign's consent to leave the country. Churchill brushed these objections aside. Arrangements were in hand for his successor (presumably Anthony Eden, the foreign secretary), and he would be

BUCKINGHAM PALACE

May 31st 1944

My dear Winston,

I have been thinking a great deal of our conversation yesterday & I have come to the conclusion that it would not be right for either you or I to be where we planned to be on D day. I don't think I need emphasize what it would mean to me personally, & to the whole Allied cause, if at this juncture a chance bomb, torpedo or even a mine should remove you from the scene; equally a change of Sovereign at this moment would be a serious matter for the country & Empire. We should both I know love to be there, but in all seriousness I would ask you to reconsider your plan.

Letter from King George VI to Churchill, May 31, 1944.
(Churchill Papers, CHAR 20/136/10)

on board a British ship. For all of his persistence, it was clear that he was now in a minority of one—the king, Lascelles, Ramsay, and even Ismay were against his going. But still he insisted. Lascelles felt that "Winston knows perfectly well that he oughtn't to do this, but when he gets these puckish notions, he is just like a naughty child." He felt it could be self-defeating. If the prime minister was killed in the early stages of Overlord, "the news of his death might easily have such an effect on the troops as to turn victory into defeat."

One of those troops preparing to go was the young naval officer Tony Hugill. He had been recruited by naval intelligence, and specifically by Ian Fleming, into a special unit (30 Assault Unit) that would go into Normandy on D-Day to seek out and secure German military technology. His camp for 3,500 men near Felixstowe, which he nicknamed the "cage," brought back memories of his Officer Training Camp—"same smell of grass trodden down, same toughness in the meat, same latrines." He sought to distract himself from impending events, throwing himself into the routine of camp life, organizing his small group of marines, and trying not to dwell on the dire warnings of casualty levels as high as 60 percent.

D-Day was now imminent. The king left for Windsor. Churchill headed for the south coast. Whether he would get farther still hung in the balance.

June 5ᵗʰ 1944

10, Downing Street,
Whitehall.

Good morning

My Darling
I feel so much for
you at this agonising
moment — so full of suspense
which prevents me from rejoicing over Rome!
I look forward to seeing
you at dinner —
Write a nice letter to
the poor King —
Tender Love from

Clemmie

(I've sent suches
to Margaret)
Alexander

Just off to her Hospital

Clementine to Winston Churchill, June 5, 1944.
(Baroness Spencer-Churchill Papers, CSCT 1/28/2)

Chapter 9

On the Eve

*"Do you realize that by the time you wake up in
the morning 20,000 men may have been killed?"*

FRIDAY, JUNE 2. D MINUS 3. JUST FORTY-EIGHT HOURS TO GO BEFORE
the launch of the proposed liberation of France, now scheduled for
Monday, June 5. The United Kingdom was in a state of virtual lockdown.
But where was the prime minister? He was not to be found in 10 Downing
Street or his offices in Parliament or even in the Treasury Annexe. At a
time when travel around England was being severely restricted, Churchill
had made his way to the south coast in his private train. He could not bear
to be away from the center of events and still harbored dying hopes of
being allowed to accompany the assault force across the Channel.

Accompanied by his friend, South African prime minister Field
Marshal Smuts, and by Minister for Labour Ernest Bevin, he then
transferred from train to car and spent some time on Friday trying to
see some of that force for himself before dropping in on Eisenhower's
headquarters at Southwick House, located about five miles north of
Portsmouth. It did not prove easy to locate the action. According to
Eisenhower's naval aide Harry Butcher, the prime minister's motorcade
"had bad luck hitting the right loading places at the wrong time," and

as a result Churchill's naval aide Commander Thompson told Butcher
his boss was "peevish."

Churchill was a man of action who liked to be at the center of events.
He was aware that there was a high chance that many of the troops he
was about to see boarding would not return. He still felt compelled to
try to share some of their risks and had not yet responded to the king's
handwritten letter. We can assume, therefore, that he had not been best
pleased on receiving a second communication from his sovereign just
before leaving London on Friday. In it, George VI made "one more appeal
to you not to go to sea on D-Day," pointing out that:

> You will see very little, you will run a considerable risk, you will
> be inaccessible at a critical time when vital decisions might have
> to be taken, and however unobtrusive you may be, your mere
> presence on board is bound to be a very heavy additional respon-
> sibility to the Admiral and Captain.

So nervous was the king that Churchill might still go that Lascelles
then followed up with a late-night telephone call to Churchill's carriage.
The conversation was apparently friendly, and Churchill finally and
grudgingly deferred to the king's wishes, admitting to Lascelles that "if
that poor ship should go to the bottom, you will all say, 'I told you so.'"
His written reply, dictated in the early hours of that Saturday morning
and taken back to London by a motorcycle dispatch rider, was more
revealing of his mental state. Though couched in suitably deferential
language, in which he reluctantly deferred to "Your Majesty's wishes
and indeed commands," the prime minister made it clear that

> as Prime Minister and Minister of Defence, I ought to be allowed
> to go where I consider it necessary to the discharge of my duty
> and I do not admit that the Cabinet have any right to put restric-
> tions on my freedom of movement. I rely on my own judgement,
> invoked in many serious matters, as to what are the proper lim-
> its of risk which a person who discharges my duties is entitled
> to run.

His strong words hinted at his irritation. Churchill was now as close to the front line as he was going to get, at least for the time being. His office and bedroom were a railway carriage; his hotel a secluded, wooded siding outside the sleepy Hampshire village of Droxford. Today the tracks have disappeared and become a footpath; the line a victim of Dr. Beeching's cuts to the British railway network in the 1960s. The station is now a private house; the wartime role of the site marked only by a small round plaque beneath a post box. At first glance, it seems an incongruous location for the prime minister's headquarters at such a time, but in fact it had been carefully chosen precisely because its location combined both isolation, and therefore security, with close proximity to the main D-Day embarkation points. To Churchill, this was his "advance headquarters," but the prime minister's desire to get close to the action imposed huge practical difficulties on his staff and did not make things easy for himself.

On Saturday morning, General Ismay awoke to find himself faced with a prime minister who wanted to speak to everyone—"to the President in the White House, to Eden at the Foreign Office, and to the Chiefs of Staff in Whitehall"—from a train in a remote siding that was only connected to the outside world by a single line through the local exchange. He complained to Joan Bright back in London:

It's hell here—impossible to get a moment to oneself, and ONE telephone, very inefficiently staffed, in a room four feet by three feet occupied by three people. . . . No bath, except for a very poor shower—damned stuffy; and no privacy. . . . We are hopelessly out of touch here; and there are vital decisions to take which can only be properly taken if we get around a table and assemble all the relevant facts and arguments. How I've hated the last forty-eight hours.

When Duff Cooper visited with General de Gaulle on the following day, he described the prime minister's temporary accommodation as a "perfectly absurd scheme," noting in his diary that one of Churchill's team had told him "that he intended to lead a reformed life in future because he now knew what hell was like." The gravity of the moment combined with the chaos of the new surroundings meant that everybody was on edge. Churchill was clearly at his worst, complaining about the delays, but when Ismay suggested "in desperation that it might be better to get back to civilisation," his "head was bitten off. Were we not next-door to Eisenhower and at the very centre of affairs?"

During the day, Churchill traveled from Droxford to the port city of Southampton. There, with Smuts and Bevin still in tow, he witnessed the huge armada assembled in the Solent, ships of all sizes and functions filling the narrow stretch of water between the mainland and the Isle of Wight and stretching away as far as the eye could see. He watched the embarkation of Tyneside troops, part of the Fiftieth Northumbrian Division, shortly to land on Gold Beach. He was there to lift their morale, but their cheers must have been equally helpful in lifting his troubled spirits. His bodyguard Inspector Thompson recalled one soldier asking Churchill if he had his ticket. When Churchill asked what ticket, the man held up a piece of paper claiming it entitled him to a free trip to France. "I wish I had. If only I were a few years younger . . ." replied Churchill. The soldier did not realize how hard Churchill had tried to gain just such a ticket. The prime ministerial party then took to the water, traveling by motor launch to Portsmouth to view the assembly of landing craft, before once again visiting the Supreme Commander at Southwick House. Winston arrived back at Droxford anxious but amiable.

For Tony Hugill, embarkation was also taking place and was proving a slow process. It had all begun on Friday. The troops had made their way to the landing craft, waved off by the local population. Hugill had sought to grasp comfort from "a final familiar sight—an early 19ᵗʰ century house with roses on it. Magnolia by the road, a mother holding her children's shoulders." Sixty-six men and extra vehicles had then been crammed onto a landing craft and had been shoved off by two bulldozers. The troops had bedded down wherever they could find space with a can of self-heating soup to help send them to sleep. They had spent Saturday waiting in harbor, expecting to sail early on Sunday. But during the day, the weather outlook steadily worsened.

By the time Churchill and his party sat down for dinner on board his train on that Saturday evening, the hour was late, and the storm clouds were already gathering. The latest news from Eisenhower's headquarters was not good. The weather forecast for the following night was for high winds, rough seas, and low clouds. Halfway through the meal, Ismay took the call confirming that a postponement seemed very likely and that a final decision would be taken by Eisenhower in the early hours of Sunday morning. Some ships were already at sea, many troops were already embarked and waiting to go. You would expect the mood to have darkened, but this is where Churchill and his choice of traveling companions came into their own, Eden now joining Bevin and Smuts. They dined with 1926 champagne and brandy while Smuts reminisced about the two most difficult moments of his life: urging that the Boers surrender to the British in 1900 and then convincing the South Africans to fight alongside Britain in 1939. His choice of subject was clearly designed to distract Churchill. Talk of the Boer War must surely have led Winston to recall his own escape from Boer captivity in 1899. There had been a train then too; an armored troop carrier. Churchill, aged just twenty-four and in South Africa as a war correspondent, had been captured when it had been ambushed. He had not remained a prisoner for long, escaping over his prison wall and making his way to safety through a series of adventures, coincidentally involving two further trains. No doubt, the conversation was a chance to briefly escape into the past from the pressures of the day. Revived by alcohol and conversation, the prime minister even indicated that he would be happy to relinquish office to either Bevin or Eden. Though presumably not quite yet. The party broke up after midnight and when asked if he wanted to be woken with the news of Eisenhower's decision, Churchill replied, "Of course not. . . . What can I do about it?"

Churchill needed the refreshment of action and the consolation of sharing some of the risks faced by those he was sending into danger. It is the same spirit, the same impulsive side of his character, that saw him want to escape Boer captivity in 1899, personally supervise the siege of anarchists within a house in London's Sidney Street when Home Secretary in 1911, take command of the defenses in Antwerp while still First Lord of the Admiralty in 1914, and resign from the government and command a battalion on the Western Front in 1916. He hated waiting on events. The truth was that there was no longer anything he could do to influence the final stages of the D-Day operation. The decision to go rested with its Supreme Commander. Churchill's Droxford excursion was about maintaining his visibility, impressing his presence on the military commanders, and staving off his personal frustrations.

The provisional postponement of twenty-four hours was confirmed in the early hours of Sunday morning. Perhaps predictably, Churchill summoned and berated Ismay for not waking him: "I suppose it never occurred to you to let me know at once. I suppose you think you are running this war?" The anxiety was back. Those ships already at sea were being recalled, while troops already embarked (like Tony Hugill and his comrades) faced a long and unpleasant day of rolling in the waves while waiting anxiously on board for further news. What was worse was the continuing uncertainty. There seemed little hope that the weather would get better sufficiently quickly. The window of opportunity provided by a full moon and low tide might be lost.

This had huge implications for Churchill. How long could effective security measures and deception plans be maintained? What would happen if the operation were undertaken at a later date in suboptimal conditions? Was there now an increased risk of failure? To make matters worse, there followed the news that a female typist working for the Associated Press, while practicing, had accidentally placed a statement on the live tape that the Allies were invading France. The story had been quickly canceled, but not before it had gone around the world. But this was not the worst thing facing the prime minister on that uncertain morning. Churchill's mood, by all accounts already "peevish" and frustrated, was about to be further tested by the arrival of General Charles de Gaulle.

De Gaulle had flown in "bristling" from his headquarters in Algiers, then part of French North Africa, at Churchill's personal request and on board the prime minister's luxury Avro York aircraft. As leader of the Free French forces, he clearly had to be briefed on the liberation of French soil, especially as the Ministry of Economic Warfare and Special Operations Executive felt that a personal broadcast by the general on D-Day would have an "immense psychological effect" on the resistance movements in France, telling the prime minister that, "There is no getting away from the fact that his personal influence with the fighting elements among the French is of the highest importance." But there were huge difficulties and the conversation had been left to the last possible moment. While the British and Americans feared that Free French communication channels were not secure, and that their headquarters in Algiers leaked like a sieve, the real tensions were political. President Roosevelt still remained firmly opposed to any formal recognition of de Gaulle's Committee of National Liberation as the provisional government of France and continued to advocate free elections after the restoration of France, which made de Gaulle extremely reluctant to assist the Anglo-American allies with the post-liberation civil administration of Normandy.

Churchill was caught between his American and French allies. Roosevelt was adamant that his US representatives in Britain could not talk to de Gaulle about any future political arrangements for France. Nor was the president prepared to issue an invitation to the French general to visit Washington, DC, as de Gaulle was only the head of a committee, not a head of state. His one concession was that he was prepared to extend "an immediate and cordial affirmative" should de Gaulle request such a visit to America. That seemed unlikely. It would de facto involve de Gaulle recognizing that he was not the leader of France, something that de Gaulle would clearly see as an affront to his position, especially as his Committee of National Liberation had pointedly decided just before his departure to adopt the title of Provisional Government of France. De Gaulle's visit had hung in the balance till the last moment, with telegrams flying back and forth between Churchill and Duff Cooper, the British representative to the Free French Committee in Algiers. Aware of the lockdown in Britain, de Gaulle was insisting on complete freedom to communicate with his African headquarters in cypher and to leave Britain whenever he wished. He had also made it clear that he wanted to talk with the British and Americans about the government of France.

Valentine Lawford, Eden's Private Secretary, got up early to collect de Gaulle and his party from Northolt airport. Their convoy of cars swept into Carlton Gardens, the Free French headquarters in London, before heading off in search of Churchill's carriage in the Hampshire countryside. To Lawford the English landscape looked "green and wonderfully beautiful," but like Hugill he became sentimental as they raced past lorries carrying soldiers toward the coast:

> Their features were young and plebeian, but there was a strained, set impression upon them the result of knowing what they were in for in the next few days.

An awkward Sunday lunch on the train inevitably ensued. Duff Cooper, Smuts, Bevin, Anthony Eden, and Pierre Viénot (Free French ambassador to the United Kingdom) were all in attendance along with French generals Béthouard, Billotte, and Koenig. Despite the dire weather predictions for the forthcoming night, it was a hot summer's day, and the carriage must have been crowded.

The two leaders exchanged greetings and got down to business. De Gaulle, tall and taciturn: Churchill, short, voluble. Both men under pressure. Churchill aware that the operation had been delayed by at least twenty-four hours, perhaps longer, and fearful that any information supplied to the French party might leak out from Algiers; de Gaulle determined to ensure that the Free French would not be ignored. Refusing to rely on Lawford's interpretation, and insisting on speaking in his best pidgin French, Churchill made some attempt to be conciliatory. He drank to the health of France, but as Lawford noted:

> Luncheon was long and not genial. . . . De Gaulle has no small talk . . . and declined to respond to W[inston]'s badinage. . . . Those two will never be happy together.

The official Cabinet record of the conversations is revealing. The contemporary diaries of Lawford and Duff Cooper suggest it conflates into one document talks that took place before and after lunch. It certainly captures Churchill's concerns. He emphasized the scale of the military operation in terms of ships, assault troops, and follow-up divisions and talked at length about the reasons for the postponement, which he felt might be as long as ten to twelve days, in which case he feared the Allies might lose "the advantages of moon, tide, weather and wind. . . . As he had recognised General de Gaulle as the head of a Great Empire, he felt it would be impossible for him not to have free right of communication," but this did not stop him repeatedly requesting an assurance that "no military details of the operation should be imparted by the General to any of his colleagues except those at the meeting." De Gaulle in turn expressed his gratitude to the prime minister for inviting him, stressing that, "It was important for the future of both our countries that we should be together when the operation began."

So far, so good, but thereafter things went downhill. When Churchill urged de Gaulle to go to Washington and seek recognition from Roosevelt, de Gaulle replied that the French government already existed and that "I have nothing to ask, in this respect, of the United States of America nor of Great Britain." According to de Gaulle's later account, his subsequent refusal to recognize the "so-called French currency" being issued to the British and American troops prompted an outburst from Churchill in which the British leader declared:

> We are going to liberate Europe, but it is because the Americans are in agreement with us that we do so. This is something you ought to know: each time we have to choose between Europe and the open sea, we shall always choose the open sea. Each time I have to choose between you and Roosevelt, I shall always choose Roosevelt.

The British official version records slightly different words but with the same meaning. While de Gaulle professed himself "quite content

with the battle, which he felt showed that the United States, Great
Britain and France were all together . . . on the practical question of
administration of territories he had difficulties." To which Churchill
responded by stating, "The United States and Great Britain were two
great nations who were willing to risk the loss of scores of thousands of
their men in an operation designed to liberate France. . . . He must tell
him [de Gaulle] bluntly that, if after every effort had been exhausted
the President was on one side and the French National Committee of
Liberation on the other, he, Mr. Churchill, would almost certainly side
with the President and that anyhow no quarrel would ever arise between
Britain and the United States on account of France." Moreover, he was
certain that this view would be endorsed by the House of Commons.
In this, he may well have been wrong. It is clear that not all Churchill's
colleagues shared such a binary, pro-American and anti-French line.
Anthony Eden later wrote, "I did not like this pronouncement nor did
Mr. Bevin, who said so in a booming aside. The meeting was a failure."
The two leaders went together to see Eisenhower after lunch, which
must have been an awkward meeting, but damage had been done, and
they dined separately; de Gaulle refusing to travel back to London in the
prime ministerial train that evening, leaving the prime minister brooding and nursing ill feeling toward his erstwhile ally. The hot weather
deteriorated into a howling gale.

Churchill's departure from the coast was clearly welcomed by Ismay
and the beleaguered private office team. It must have also taken pressure off Eisenhower and his staff, who had been subject to Churchill's
repeated visits over the course of that long weekend. The prime minister's place was in London, with the War Cabinet and Parliament. The
collapse of his plan to accompany the troops and the delay of the operation effectively forced him back to the capital. Once there, he worked
continuously until almost 4:00 a.m.

When Churchill awoke, one of the documents waiting for him was
this short and simple manuscript note written by his wife, Clementine.
Like many couples, they had pet names for each other. She would sign
off her personal letters to him with a drawing of a cat; he would often
reply with a hastily scrawled pug or pig. Her letter read:

June 5th 1944
10 Downing Street
Whitehall
Monday morning

My Darling,
        I feel so much for you at this agonising moment—so full of sus-
pense, which prevents me from rejoicing over Rome.
        I look forward to seeing you at dinner—write a nice letter to
the poor King—
        I've sent enclosed to Margaret Alexander
                                        Tender Love from
                                        Clemmie
                                        [Cat drawing]
                                        Just off to her Hospital.

Clementine was heading off for a routine committee meeting at the
Fulmer Chase Maternity Home, a hospital facility for the wives of officers of all three services and one of several wartime charities she supported. They were both aware that momentous events were imminent,
and, after nearly thirty-six years of marriage, Clementine understood
better than anyone what her husband was going through. She also knew
from long experience that he was much more likely to take notice of
something that she put in writing.

The British prime minister was wrestling with his usual large
in-tray, delivered to him by his Private Secretaries in his official dispatch boxes. His responses to the many minutes, telegrams, reports,
and papers were dictated to his personal secretary, who sat patiently
at the end of the bed. We must imagine him propped up on his pillows,
resplendent in his favorite red, green, and gold dressing gown and occa-
sionally puffing on his cigar; his flow of dictation interspersed with
moments of deep concentration or interrupted by his barking of sudden
orders. One contemporary account from around this period, by his personal secretary, Elizabeth Layton, has him reaching for the little white
telephone by his bed and, upon being connected to the duty Private

Secretary (the civil servant John Peck), gruffly demanding, "Gimme the moon." What he wanted was the chart depicting the moon's phases, vital for predicting the all-important tides that would dictate the timing of the D-Day landings on the beaches of Normandy. He sent a telegram to Stalin noting that "the difficulties of getting proper weather conditions are very great."

This was a global war and, as always, he was dealing with a range of issues, among them the future political government of Greece, the retreat of Tito and his communist Yugoslav partisans to the island of Vis, and improvements to aerial photography techniques. The previous night, before retiring late, he had received the news of the liberation of Rome by the Allied forces under General (soon to be Field Marshal) Alexander. On any other day, this would have been a cause for significant rejoicing. But on this morning Churchill was clearly distracted.

He now knew that Eisenhower's momentous decision had been made. At a further meeting at Southwick House on the evening of Sunday, June 4, British meteorologist Group Captain Dr. James Stagg had predicted a potential break in the inclement weather on the morning of Tuesday, June 6, and identified a narrow window for the landings. General Eisenhower had seized the opportunity and authorized Operation Overlord. Had he been right to do so? This was the question that inevitably dominated Churchill's waking thoughts that Monday morning.

Eisenhower's decision had set in play events that could not now be reversed, and that would see the British, American, and Canadian forces and their allies begin their attempt to liberate France the following day, Tuesday, June 6. As Churchill sat trying to focus on his papers, he was aware that the airborne troops were getting ready to embark in their gliders to seize key bridges, and that the vast armada was now preparing to set sail from the British south coast. The clock was ticking; the countdown had begun. This was the "agonising moment—so full of suspense" referred to in Clementine's letter.

Tony Hugill's landing craft was finally underway. The journey was not pleasant. "This old cow of a craft is chucking herself about a good deal." There would be much vomiting.

By lunchtime Churchill was in a bullish mood. His dining companions were the British chiefs of staff: Cunningham, Brooke, and Portal. All three were feeling the weight of the pending operation on their shoulders, but they could not refuse Churchill's summons. Cunningham recorded a "good lunch" at 10 Downing Street with "as usual lots of wine. PM very worked up about 'Overlord' and really in about a hysterical state. Much conversation. He really is an incorrigible optimist." Field Marshal Sir Alan Brooke noted the same, confiding to his diary that he found Churchill "over optimistic as regards prospects of the Cross Channel invasion."

Perhaps Churchill was just putting on a brave face in front of his most senior commanders. Those around him often noted that he was at his best in a crisis. Perhaps he was being swept along by the excitement of the moment and the possibilities that were now opening up. He liked nothing more than discussing military operations while eating, and we can imagine him moving the plates and cutlery to represent the military units. It was also surely a manifestation of a palpable sense of relief. A decision had been made. The period of waiting was over. The difficulties and dangers associated with delay had at least been lifted, even if plenty of other dangers remained.

As Hugill looked around him and saw a sea with convoys stretching to the horizon, the larger landing craft looking like Roman triremes, he reflected: "There must be a lot of people in the Whitehall area walking around with their fingers crossed."

The War Cabinet met at 18:30 hours. Leo Amery, the secretary of state for India, had known Churchill since their school days at Harrow. He thought that "Winston was evidently greatly stirred and also at the end of his tether nervously, and no wonder. It is the most anxious moment of the whole war." Churchill began by briefing his colleagues on the postponement. The formal agenda then started with the liberation of Rome, and there was agreement that Churchill should send a message of congratulations to General Alexander and make a statement in the House of Commons. Then followed a report of naval, military, and air operations over the course of the last six days. In the Home Theater (meaning northwestern Europe), Bomber Command had flown 2,550 sorties, the United States bombers 4,900, and the Allied Expeditionary Force and the Tactical Air Force 13,000. Between them they had dropped more than 22,000 tons of bombs, largely on the occupied territories (meaning France and Belgium). Churchill still entertained huge anxieties about the impact on the morale and support of the French civilians.

He was also still worried about German reprisals against the British mainland and must therefore have been gratified to learn that Crossbow targets had once again been attacked. Equally pleasing would have been the news that there had been no shipping losses to enemy action in June—at least thus far.

But the main discussion that evening clearly raised his blood pressure. De Gaulle was now refusing to broadcast after Eisenhower on D-Day unless the Free French were given control over reestablishing civil government in France. Arguing that the "effective civil administration of France must be provided by Frenchmen," he refused to send liaison officers to work alongside the Anglo-American forces. Even the diplomatic language of the official minutes fails to disguise Churchill's angry response:

> The PRIME MINISTER said that if General de Gaulle refused to agree to the liaison officers proceeding with Operation "Overlord" it would not be possible for us to have any further discussions with General de Gaulle on civil or military matters. It might even be necessary to indicate that an aeroplane would be ready to take him back to Algiers forthwith.

According to Sir Alexander Cadogan, undersecretary of state at the Foreign Office (the country's most senior diplomat) and another inveterate diary keeper, "We endured the usual passionate anti-de G[aulle] harangue from P.M. On this subject, we get away from politics, diplomacy and even common sense." Churchill certainly liked to have someone to rail against. At different points in the war, it was a role that would be filled by the Indian nationalist leader Mohandas Gandhi, or by the Labour politician and government critic Aneurin Bevan. In

June 1944, the intransigence of General de Gaulle provided an outlet for his pent-up anger and frustration.

In a letter to de Gaulle, which he drafted but ultimately did not send, Churchill let off steam. He complained that he had "tried very hard on many occasions during four years, to establish some reasonable basis for friendly comradeship with you. Your action at this juncture convinces me that this hope has no further existence." He railed against the "heinous character" of the general's actions and concluded, "I can conceive [of] no useful purpose in your staying longer, and that the aeroplanes will be at your disposal to-morrow night, weather permitting." Ultimately, de Gaulle did broadcast, and some French liaison officers joined the assault force, but Churchill's personal relationship with the French leader was at a low point.

Fortunately, the rest of the agenda was less controversial and probably seemed less relevant in light of the huge operation that was about to unfold. Preventing the export of Wolfram (the metal tungsten) from Portugal to Germany, determining the composition of the British delegation to the conference of the International Monetary Fund at Bretton Woods in the United States, creating a refugee camp in Tripolitania [Libya], and recognizing the constituent republics of the Soviet Union. These were all no doubt important issues, but in the minds of those gathered around the Cabinet table, they must have paled into insignificance beside the imminence of Overlord. It was clearly a long Cabinet meeting, but not yet the end of a long day.

Later that evening, Churchill dined alone with Clementine. Afterward, she joined him in his Map Room before retiring. Laid out before them both in great detail were the beaches. There may even have been a three-dimensional papier-mâché model provided by the Americans. Breaking off from his study of the final dispositions for D-Day, he turned to her and said, "Do you realize that by the time you wake up in the morning 20,000 men may have been killed?"

As we have seen, his worries were not limited to the military casualties. For weeks he had been exercised by the impact of Allied bombing on French and Belgian civilians. Southern England had been turned into an armed camp and areas of the coast completely sealed off. The levels of restriction in place could not be maintained for long. All this, and there were signs that the Germans were preparing to unleash deadly new weapons on the United Kingdom.

An often-overlooked fact is that Churchill also had an additional and very personal worry. His only son, Randolph, was serving as part of a British military mission to the headquarters of Marshal Tito, the leader of the Yugoslav partisans. But, as Churchill knew only too well from his daily telegrams, Tito's mountainous hideout in Bosnia had been stormed by German paratroopers and the Yugoslav guerrilla leader was now on the run and being relentlessly pursued by the Germans. Randolph's exact whereabouts were unknown and his safety in doubt.

The 2017 film *Churchill* depicts the British prime minister in these hours as a lonely leader plagued by doubts and haunted by the ghosts of the Dardanelles Campaign. Much has been written about Churchill's "black dog" of depression, a term that only appears in one of his letters. It is an aspect of his health that will no doubt continue to be debated by historians. The latest research by two eminent medical consultants has concluded that "Churchill suffered no major psychiatric disorder" and that "Churchill's despair—always in response to events—was quickly followed by recovery." There is no doubt that he struggled with periods of enforced inactivity and that he hated this period of waiting prior to D-Day—his mood was probably exacerbated by his fragile physical health, but his instinctive reaction was to visit the troops, to seek the solace of action, and to lash out against those he deemed to be obstructing him. On the eve of the landings, we can see him running a range of emotions; from over-optimism to anger with de Gaulle to anxiety over potential casualties. They are all surely symptoms of his overarching worry about the price of failure.

Was Churchill wrong to be worried? The consequences of failure were surely immense. If the Allies were unable to gain a foothold on the beaches, the war in the West would certainly be prolonged. The casualties would be high and the blow to morale huge. Would the public in Britain and the United States have the appetite to try again? Would Churchill and Roosevelt remain in office? Would pressure reemerge for some form of settlement, leaving Hitler in charge of swathes of Western

Europe? Would America abandon the continent and turn east against Japan? These were all imponderables, but they were all very real concerns to Churchill on Monday, June 5.

It is clear from the contemporary diaries and letters of all those around Churchill, both in his private office and among the ranks of the senior military commanders, that the success of the operation could not be taken for granted. Admiral Ramsay worried about "the critical period around H-Hour when, if initial flights are held up, success will be in the balance."

General Brooke wished "to God it were safely over" and later reflected that

> I knew too well all the weak points in the plan of operations. First of all, the weather, on which we were entirely dependent; a sudden storm might wreck it all. Then the complexity of an amphibious operation of this kind, when confusion may degenerate into chaos in such a short time. The difficulty of controlling the operation once launched, lack of elasticity in the handling of reserves, danger of leakage of information with consequent loss of that essential secrecy.

Even General Eisenhower, the Supreme Commander, wrote out and sealed a letter accepting responsibility in the event of failure:

> Our landings in the Cherbourg-Havre area have failed to gain a satisfactory foothold and I have withdrawn the troops. My decision to attack at this time and place was based upon the best information available. The troops, the air and the Navy did all that Bravery and devotion to duty could do. If any blame or fault attaches to the attempt, it is mine alone.

It was a long day for all concerned and a long night too. Sir Hari Singh, the forty-eight-year-old maharaja of Jammu and Kashmir, was in London as a representative of the imperial government in India. In this capacity, he had been invited to attend the evening's Cabinet meeting and so had learned of the imminence of the D-Day invasion. According to Churchill's Principal Private Secretary, John Martin, "such was the immediate effect upon his mind that he was unable to sleep and had to call for sleeping draughts." It seems unlikely Sir Hari slept for long. Joan Bright recorded hearing a deep throbbing in the dark hours that at 6:00 a.m. changed to a thunder. The planes were in the air. "It was on." Valentine Lawford heard them too, knelt by his bed, and prayed that "all this sacrifice and longing should not be in vain." It is difficult to imagine that anyone got much sleep thereafter.

Chapter 10

Storming Ashore

*"As it was in the beginning
so may it continue to the end."*

CONVINCED THAT THE WEATHER WAS TOO POOR FOR THE ALLIES TO
mount their attack on mainland Europe over the period of June 5 and
6, German commanders made various decisions that were to have catastrophic consequences for them. Field Marshal Erwin Rommel, the
commander of German Army Group B, defending the Atlantic Wall,
decided to go home to Germany to celebrate his wife's birthday. General
Friedrich Dollman, the commander in chief of the German Seventh
Army in northern France, decided to gather his divisional commanders
together in Rennes for a command post anti-invasion exercise. Major
General Edgar Feuchtinger, the commander of Twenty-first Panzer
Division, whose tanks were closest to the Normandy coast, decided to
spend the night with his mistress in Paris. Senior commanders were
not at their posts at a critical moment. Decisions have consequences.

As they crossed the French coast, the singing inside the Horsa
glider piloted by Staff Sergeant Jim Wallwork died away. The 139 soldiers of the Oxfordshire and Buckinghamshire Light Infantry under
the command of Major John Howard realized that the moment for

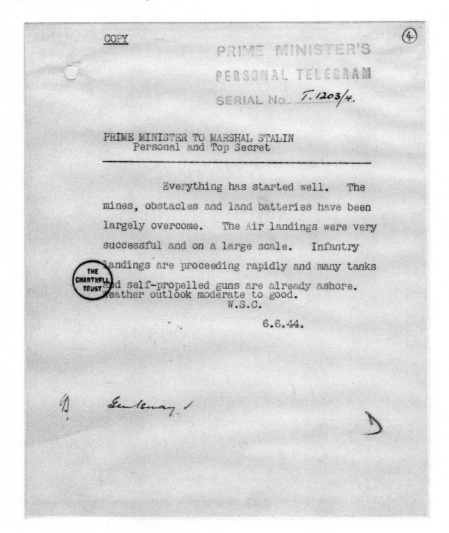

PRIME MINISTER TO MARSHAL STALIN
Personal and Top Secret

Everything has started well.   The
mines, obstacles and land batteries have been
largely overcome.   The Air landings were very
successful and on a large scale.   Infantry
landings are proceeding rapidly and many tanks
and self-propelled guns are already ashore.
Weather outlook moderate to good.
W.S.C.

6.6.44.

Telegram from Churchill to Stalin, June 6, 1944. (CHAR 20/166/4)

which they had been training was upon them. The silence intensified as their glider, along with the other five gliders carrying their
regimental comrades, parted company with their tug aircraft and
began the silent descent toward their objectives—the two bridges over
the Orne River and the Caen Canal. Capturing these bridges intact
was a key part of the overall Operation Overlord plan and would help

defend against a German counterattack into the left flank of the Allied invasion. The sky was clear and the moon bright as Jim Wallwork spotted the tiny strip of land between the two bridges and steered his heavily-laden glider toward his landing site—one so small that the German defenders had not bothered to erect anti-glider poles. In a feat of flying by the army's Glider Pilot Regiment that Air Chief Marshal Sir Trafford Leigh-Mallory later declared to be one of the "most outstanding flying achievements of the war," Jim Wallwork crash-landed his glider just yards from the bridge to be secured. He and his co-pilot, Johnny Ainsworth, were knocked unconscious by the impact of the landing, but the Ox and Bucks soldiers stormed across the bridge—known thereafter as Pegasus Bridge—and secured it within ten minutes. Lieutenant Den Brotheridge, leading the assault, was fatally wounded but the first ground objective of the Allied assault was a complete success. Moments later, the first French house to be liberated, the Café Gondrée, was entered, much to the delight of its owner, Georges Gondrée, who at once dug up a bottle champagne from his garden, hidden years before from the Germans, to celebrate with the British soldiers. To this day, his daughter, Arlette, then just five years old, opens champagne for British soldiers every year at midnight as June 5 gives way to June 6. But in 1944, the battle had just begun.

From airfields across Southern England, paratroopers from the British Sixth Airborne Division and the US Eighty-second and 101st Airborne Divisions flew through the night skies toward their objectives in Normandy as Allied minesweepers cleared pathways for the troop-carrying ships to approach the invasion beaches. The ships rolled and heaved, many of the soldiers were violently sick, regretting their early breakfast, but as dawn began to break, the stage was set for the largest amphibious operation that history had yet seen. Aircraft roared overhead as targets on the coast and inland were struck, and the Allied fleet belched forth its enormous firepower ahead of the landing craft and amphibious tanks as they made their way toward Sword, Juno, Gold, Omaha, and Utah Beaches. The overture reached a crescendo as the first assaults from the sea heralded the opening acts of the deadly adventure. Back in England, Churchill, Eisenhower, and Montgomery held their breath. Stan Hollis clambered down into his landing craft. The die was cast. There would be no second chance.

While the British Sixth Airborne Division secured objectives on the left flank of the Allied invasion, the US Eighty-second and 101st Airborne Divisions dropped inland of Utah Beach to secure the right flank and begin to threaten the German defenders of the Cotentin Peninsula and the key port of Cherbourg. The poor weather and intense antiaircraft fire caused many of the paratroopers' transport and glider-tug aircraft to take evasive action with the result that many of the American airborne troops were scattered widely over their objective areas, many tragically drowning in deliberately flooded marshes. Amidst the darkness and dispersion, the soldiers struggled to marry up with their own units; nevertheless a strong attack was mounted by various units of the Eighty-second Airborne Division on the key village of Sainte-Mère-Église. In among the real soldiers, dummy paratroopers with simulated gunfire devices were also dropped, which increased the confusion in the minds of local German commanders struggling to identify the strength and objectives of the airborne landings. As dawn broke, the amphibious assaults began.

Spearheaded by the heavy cruiser USS *Augusta*, a naval flotilla of some twenty Allied warships began their preliminary bombardment on the German positions of the 709th and 243rd Infanterie-Divisions and the Ninety-first Luftlande-Division defending Utah Beach. The assault wave of the Eighth Infantry Regiment of the US Fourth Infantry Division, supported by thirty-two special amphibious DD Sherman tanks, was scheduled to hit the beaches a half hour after dawn at 06:30 hours. Strong currents took the landing craft nearly a mile and a half farther east than intended, the navigation problem exacerbated by the loss of three of the four control vessels that were intended to act as guides. Fortune favored the Eighth Infantry Regiment as the beach on which they landed was less strongly defended than their original objective. Sensing some topographical confusion and doubt, Assistant Division Commander Brigadier General Theodore Roosevelt made his famously reassuring remark: "We'll start the war from here!" By noon, the forward troops had contacted the paratroopers of the 101st Airborne Division, and by the end of the day the Fourth Division had pushed inland by about four miles. The westernmost units were within a mile of linking up with the Eighty-second Airborne Division in Sainte-Mère-Église. The Fourth Infantry Division suffered only 197 killed or wounded on D-Day itself (lessons having been learned on Slapton Sands), though the two airborne divisions lost around 2,500 of their men, killed, wounded, or missing in the first twenty-four hours of Overlord.

Although the Fourth Division came ashore with very limited casualties, the picture on Omaha Beach for the US First and Twenty-ninth Infantry Divisions was very different. While a battalion of US Rangers heroically scaled the cliffs of Pointe du Hoc four miles to the west to silence a German gun battery, the first assault waves approached the beach to also land at 06.30 hours. From their landing craft, with the heavy shells of the naval bombardment screaming overhead from 05:50 hours, the waiting soldiers witnessed more than three hundred Fortress and Liberator bombers of the US Eighth Air Force drop more than a thousand bombs from 06:05 hours.

But the heavy bombers, more used to bombing large industrial targets in Germany, were incapable of the pinpoint accuracy required, and their bombs fell not on the beach defenses of the German 716th Infanterie-Division and forward elements of the more experienced 352nd Infanterie-Division, but farther inland. The complaint on the landing craft was that all the bombing had done was wake up the Germans. Worse still, despite the very choppy sea conditions, some of the tank-landing craft commanders stuck rigidly to their original orders and paused more than two miles from the shore to launch the thirty-two amphibious DD Sherman tanks of the 741st Tank Battalion. Of those tanks, twenty-seven foundered with the loss of their crews and only two tanks of that battalion landed successfully. In contrast, the officers controlling the launching of the tanks of the 743rd Tank Battalion decided to take their thirty-two amphibious tanks right onto the beach. Caught up in the subsequent mayhem of the infantry landings, nine members of the 743rd were to be awarded the Distinguished Service Cross for their actions on D-Day.

From the original beach reconnaissance, it was always known that the fight on Omaha would be tough with only five possible exits off the beach through gaps in the cliffs. For most of D-Day, the outcome on this beach hung in the balance. Some three hours after the initial landings, General Leonard T. Gerow, commanding the US V Corps, painted such a bleak picture to US First Army Commander General Omar Bradley, anxiously awaiting reports on the command ship USS *Augusta*, that Bradley began to consider suspending further landings on Omaha. Eventually by nightfall, through heroic leadership and selfless determination amid the bloodshed and chaos, the beach was secured, and the forward troops began to move inland. The beach itself remained under German artillery fire while demolition teams continued to destroy the vicious beach obstacles and clear the battlefield debris to allow reinforcements and supplies to get ashore. Casualties on Omaha Beach on D-Day were initially reported at around 2,300 of which 1,465 were killed. At ten times the casualty rate at Utah Beach, it is not surprising that the US government later decided to place its national memorial in Normandy on the high ground above Omaha Beach.

Farther east, it was the comparative success of the British Fiftieth (Northumbrian) Division landing on Gold Beach that took some of the pressure off US forces on Omaha. Brigadier Dietrich Kraiss, commanding 352nd Infanterie-Division, felt obliged to order one of his reserve battalions to block the British at Crepon, some six miles inland, rather than counterattack toward Omaha. Landing an hour later than the Americans due to tidal differences, the assault brigades of Fiftieth Division began to land at 07:30 hours. The 231st Brigade landed at Le Hamel supported by two squadrons of DD Sherman tanks of the Sherwood Rangers Yeomanry, which had also ignored the five-thousand-yard launch order and took to the water only a thousand yards offshore. However, even that shorter run meant delay and First Royal Hampshires had a tough fight around Arromanches-les-Bains. Supported by First Dorsets and Second Devons, they eventually secured their objectives by the end of the day. Also landing on Gold Beach were the Royal Marines of No. Forty-second Commando who pushed west toward Port-en-Bessin and would be the first British troops to join up with the American First Infantry Division from Omaha. Farther east, it was Stan Hollis's Sixth Green Howards alongside Fifth East

Yorks that approached La Rivière supported by the tanks of the Fourth and Seventh Dragoon Guards, again launching only yards offshore. Lieutenant Colonel Robin Hastings of Sixth Green Howards knew that his battalion was landing exactly in the right place, because a house with a prominent circular drive, which had featured in all the briefing photographs, was immediately inland from where his landing craft hit the beach. Unlike the intense machine gun fire that wrought such havoc as the landing craft ramps came down on Omaha, the experience on Hastings's vessel was different. The landing craft's ramp jammed. It took a huge shove from two burly Royal Marines to open it. Not sure how deep the water was in front of the craft, Hastings dangled his feet over the edge. The water only came up to his knees, so he and his command group took off up the beach. The fighting intensified inland, and in the course of the day Company Sergeant Major Stan Hollis carried out the two actions that were to win him the only Victoria Cross awarded on D-Day. By nightfall the Second Essex and the tanks of the Sherwood Rangers were just short of Bayeux. The Fiftieth Division suffered around 1,100 casualties on D-Day, of which 350 were killed.

Farther east still, the Canadian Third Division was determined to put the ghosts of the failed Dieppe raid behind them as they prepared to come ashore on Juno Beach. At 05:30 hours, the cruiser HMS *Belfast* and an international flotilla of British, French, Norwegian, and Canadian warships began their bombardment. Much to his chagrin, Prime Minister Churchill had bowed to his sovereign's wishes and had not embarked on HMS *Belfast* to witness proceedings. In the first wave, the Canadian Seventh Brigade headed toward Courseulles-sur-Mer and the Eighth Brigade toward Saint-Aubin-sur-Mer, supported by the swimming tanks of the First Hussars and the Fort Garry Horse (a Canadian armored regiment). Despite the overwhelming weight of incoming fire, the German defenders of two battalions of the 716 Infanterie-Division held their fire until the ramps of the landing craft came down. As the troops rushed ashore, the machine gun and artillery fire was intense. The Canadians suffered 961 casualties, of which 340 were killed. The shoreline was largely a built-up area of houses and commercial buildings that afforded the Germans considerable protection. Tanks were needed to blast exits inland off the beaches. Although the beaches were cleared only slowly, the reinforcement waves and logistic supplies kept coming forward. This produced considerable confusion on the beaches, which slowed the move inland. Nevertheless, by the end of the day the Canadians were some seven miles inland at Le Fresne-Camilly and Villons-les-Buissons—the farthest inland of any Allied troops—but were short of their objective to cut the Caen-Bayeux road and capture Carpiquet Airfield. Whether this degree of exploitation inland on the first day was ever achievable has remained an open question. It would be another month of fierce fighting against the Twelfth SS Panzer Division "Hitlerjugend" before Carpiquet Airfield was taken.

Farthest to the east were the landings of the British Third Division that Bernard Montgomery had commanded in France and at Dunkirk in 1940. To this division he gave the most ambitious task of D-Day—to capture Caen. Unlike the Fiftieth Division landing on Gold Beach, which had fought with Montgomery across the North African desert, into Sicily and Italy, the Third Division had been out of combat in England and training for future operations. Their moment came on June 6, 1944.

As with the other assault divisions, Major General Tom Rennie's Third Infantry Division was supported by a huge naval bombardment led by the British battleships HMS *Warspite* and HMS *Ramillies,* and eighteen other warships including one from Poland. Not only did they fire over the heads of the soldiers of Eighth Infantry Brigade and Royal Marine Commando units in the assault wave, but also in support of the swimming DD tanks of the Thirteenth and Eighteenth Hussars and the Staffordshire Yeomanry. Common sense was applied to the launching into the sea of the tanks with the majority surviving the five-foot-high waves during their run in, a few arriving ahead of the assaulting infantry. With the capture of Caen as the prize objective of D-Day, doubt has lingered over whether enough planning had focused on how to exploit the initial successful landings by the Third Division. Strongpoints, codenamed Morris and Hillman, held by the German 736th Grenadier Regiment, had to be seized by Eighth Brigade before 185 Brigade could pass through them on the Périers Ridge to launch their attack on Caen itself. Congestion on the beach delayed the tanks of the

Staffordshire Yeomanry getting ahead to support the First Battalion, Suffolk Regiment, to secure Hillman. Worse still, the naval gunfire support officer had been killed, the initial bombardment had left Hillman intact, and intelligence had failed to identify this position as the strongly held headquarters of the defending regiment. Despite individual acts of heroism, including that of Private "Tich" Hunter (later awarded the Distinguished Conduct Medal), Hillman was not subdued until late afternoon. The First Norfolks of 185 Brigade, eager to press the attack on Caen, bypassed Hillman too soon and suffered more than 150 casualties from unsuppressed German positions. By nightfall the Third Division, despite having suffered more than a thousand casualties during the day, had not been able to attack Caen and fulfill that part of Montgomery's Overlord plan. It would take another six weeks and huge Allied and French loss of life before Caen was liberated on July 19.

Reports and news about the landings in Normandy filtered back slowly during the morning and afternoon of June 6. Public announcements needed to be cautious as Operation Fortitude was still running to persuade the Germans that Normandy was not the main Allied landing and that they should keep their eyes firmly on the Pas-de-Calais. Nevertheless, the peoples of Europe and North America needed to know what was happening.

Churchill spent the morning of Tuesday, June 6, in his Map Room trying to interpret the latest information about the landings ahead of his midday statement in the Commons. The fog of war still shrouded everything in uncertainty, but the initial reports seemed good. The Germans had failed to correctly interpret the increased traffic signals coming from the Allied fleet and had missed an early warning when some advance ships had been called back after Eisenhower's initial postponement in the early hours of Sunday morning. Their own meteorological services had failed to spot the gap in the weather. Tactical surprise had been achieved.

Bletchley Park was reading the German naval communications in almost real time, though not quite quick enough to prevent the loss of the Norwegian destroyer HNoMS *Svenner*, which was sunk by E-boats operating out of Le Havre. The American destroyer USS *Corry* was also lost to enemy action, most probably hit by fire from a shore battery, but the fleet had got across the Channel almost unscathed. Air superiority seemed absolute. News was filtering back about the difficulties of the Americans on Omaha Beach, but landings on the other beaches appeared to be progressing well. The casualties were still unclear, but they were far lower than the twenty thousand Churchill had feared.

The prime minister took lunch with George VI at Buckingham Palace. Sir Alan Lascelles felt the full force of Winston's glare on first meeting. He concluded he had not yet been forgiven for his role in preventing Churchill's trip to France. Thereafter, the prime minister accompanied the king to Leigh-Mallory's headquarters at Stanmore and then to Eisenhower's at Bushy Park, where the two men could follow the action on the large maps and charts on which progress was being plotted. There were no satellite communications, no real-time images, but the intelligence was continuing to flow in. A picture was emerging. The weather had caught the Germans off guard, but it had also created some difficulties for the Allies. The overcast sky had limited the effectiveness of the huge naval and air bombardment preceding the assault, while the onshore wind had created a higher-than-expected tide, making the approach to the beaches more difficult, especially for the swimming tanks, hiding some of the deadly obstacles that now became real death traps. And yet, the Allied troops were clearly getting ashore. There were also encouraging signs that their enemy was confused. Key panzer divisions had not yet been released for the battle.

For his part, Lascelles noted with wry amusement that, "Though they [the king and Churchill] had lunched together, and driven a number of miles in the same car, neither of them, apparently, made any allusion to their recent exchange of letters!"

While Churchill toured the headquarters, his Private Secretary, Jock Coville, now serving with his RAF squadron and finally allowed to fly over France, was taking part in two reconnaissance flights, looking down on "a sea boiling with ships of all kinds heading for the landing beaches" and part of "a vast aerial armada, bombers and fighters thick as starlings at nesting-time." For once, he probably had a better overview than his boss.

On the military front, at least, there seems to have been a palpable sense of relief. The Allies were ashore. The worst-case scenario had not come to pass, and Lascelles observed that "all those who have been entrusted with the very well-kept secret, look ten years younger." Churchill received a note from Montgomery on June 6, sent before the general crossed over to France, admitting that, "The past 5 months have not been an easy time for any of us. But I have always felt that you would see that all was well, and that your support was available at all times." Of course, that support may have sometimes bordered on interference.

A sense of relief can certainly be seen in the telegram that Churchill fired off to Marshal Stalin. Finally, after years of delay and changes to strategy, he delivered on his promise of a Second Front in northwest Europe. Finally, he was able to hold his head up and report an Allied operation on a scale comparable to the great battles of the Eastern Front.

> PRIME MINISTER TO MARSHAL STALIN
> Personal and Top Secret
> Everything has started well. The
> mines, obstacles and land batteries have been
> largely overcome. The Air landings were very
> successful and on a large scale. Infantry
> landings are proceeding rapidly and many tanks
> and self-propelled guns are already ashore.
> Weather outlook moderate to good.
>
> W.S.C.
>
> 6.6.44.

The prime minister had promised to report back to the British Parliament before the end of the daily session. He did so on his return to central London, addressing the House of Commons at 18:15 hours, just before it adjourned:

I promised to report to the House later on in the Sitting. I have been at the centres where the latest information is received, and I can state to the House that this operation is proceeding in [a] thoroughly satisfactory manner. Many dangers and difficulties which at this time last night appeared extremely formidable are behind us. The passage of the sea has been made with far less loss than we apprehended. The resistance of the batteries has been greatly weakened by the bombing of the Air Force, and the superior bombardment of our ships quickly reduced their fire to dimensions which did not affect the problem. The landing of the troops on a broad front, both British and American—Allied troops, I will not give lists of all the different nationalities they represent or the States they represent—but the landings along the whole front have been effective, and our troops have penetrated, in some cases, several miles inland. Lodgments exist on a broad front.

The outstanding feature has been the landings of the airborne troops, which were on a scale far larger than anything that has been seen so far in the world. These landings took place with extremely little loss and with great accuracy. Particular anxiety attached to them, because the conditions of light prevailing in the very limited period of the dawn—just before the dawn—the conditions of visibility, made all the difference. Indeed, there might have been something happening at the last minute which would not have enabled airborne troops to play their part. A very great degree of risk had to be taken in respect of the weather.

But General Eisenhower's courage is equal to all the necessary decisions that have to be taken in these extremely difficult and uncontrollable matters. The airborne troops are well established, and the landings and the follow-ups are all proceeding with much less loss—very much less—than we expected. Fighting is proceeding at various points. We have captured various bridges which were of importance, and which were not blown up. There is even fighting proceeding in the town of Caen, inland. But all this, although a very valuable first step—a vital and essential first step—gives no indication of what may be the course of the battle in the next days and weeks, because the enemy will now probably endeavour to concentrate on this area and in that event heavy fighting will soon begin and will continue without end, as we can push troops in and he can bring other troops up. It is, therefore, a most serious time that we enter upon. Thank God, we enter upon it with our great Allies all in good heart and all in good friendship.

Churchill may have been relieved on the military front, but his anger toward de Gaulle had not abated. If anything, it seemed to have intensified. The general was still refusing to cooperate over the civilian administration of France and the bitter row continued to rage over whether he would broadcast to the French people. The Allies felt this to be essential for mobilizing the resistance and encouraging French support for the operation, but they also sought to retain control over the symbolism and content of the moment. De Gaulle would only be allowed to speak after Eisenhower and not as head of the French state.

To make matters worse, Eisenhower had shown de Gaulle the content of his broadcast. It ordered the French people to follow Allied military instructions. De Gaulle was not mentioned by name. Existing French officials were to be kept in place for the time being, and it repeated Roosevelt's line that the French would choose their own government after the liberation. In short, it made no recognition of de Gaulle's authority or the legitimacy of his newly self-declared Provisional Government of France. His reaction was not surprising:

> By speaking immediately after Eisenhower, I should appear to sanction what he said—of which I disapproved—and assume a place in the succession unsuitable to the dignity of France. If I were to make a speech, it could only be at a different hour.

To Churchill, concerned to minimize Allied casualties and maximize French support, this seemed a betrayal of their alliance. In the early hours of June 6, as the operation began, the angry prime

minister berated Pierre Viénot, de Gaulle's Free French ambassador
to the British government, for his leader's intransigence. In the end,
de Gaulle got his way and broadcast individually at 18:00 hours on
D-Day, stating that, "The orders given by the French Government and
by the leaders which it has recognized must be followed precisely."
Here was a very different emphasis. De Gaulle was deliberately giving the impression that Eisenhower derived his authority from the
French Provisional Government. For Churchill, this was a red rag to
a bull. De Gaulle had no great forces in the battle, the liberation was
being led by the Anglo-Americans, and the French general's authority
was entirely dependent on British and American patronage and support. Moreover, the president had been clear about not recognizing de
Gaulle's Provisional Government.

As foreign secretary, Anthony Eden had seen the text of de Gaulle's
broadcast before delivery. He had considerably more sympathy for
the general's position than his prime minister and was actively trying
to engineer a compromise that would allow the Americans to sit in
on British discussions about civil affairs with representatives of de
Gaulle's committee. It prompted two angry phone calls from Churchill,
working from bed: the first just after de Gaulle's radio message and
the second, lasting a full forty-five minutes, after midnight. Unable
to influence military events in France, Churchill was clearly brooding
on the political row and accused Eden of trying to turn the Cabinet
against him:

> He [Churchill] said that nothing would induce him to give way,
> that de Gaulle must go. Said I had no right to "bully" him at a time
> like this and much more.

When Eden refused to budge, Churchill vented his wrath on
Brendan Bracken. It was becoming increasingly clear to Churchill that
his hard-line position against de Gaulle did not command the agreement
of a majority of his Cabinet colleagues. Attlee, Bevin, and Eden were all
sympathetic to the position of the general and in favor of trying to talk
de Gaulle round.

It was at this point that two telegrams arrived from Roosevelt. The first, dated June 4, but delayed in the sending until D-Day, wished Churchill "all good luck in your talks with Prima Donna [de Gaulle]" and, referring to Churchill's previous communications on the matter, added, "Please for the love of Heaven do not tell de Gaulle that I am sending him a 'friendly message to come over to see me.' The whole point of it is that I decline absolutely as Head of State to invite him to come over here." This was a reiteration of the president's earlier line.

Fortunately, things had changed, and de Gaulle had grudgingly reached out to Roosevelt. The June 4 message was immediately super-seded—indeed, due to the delay possibly preceded—by a further com-munication from the president announcing that, "I have sent word to de Gaulle that in view of his expression of hope that I will see him over here, I shall be very glad to do so." Here was the prospect of a softening in the relationship between Roosevelt and de Gaulle that might take the pressure off Churchill, who remained caught in the middle. The pres-ident's first message of June 4 also referred to his pleasure on hearing that "Randolph got out of the cave safely," referring to Tito's dramatic escape from the Germans in Bosnia. The Yugoslav leader had had to scale a cliff after German paratroops had surrounded his forest hideout. The president knew that Randolph had been with Tito. Here at least, for Churchill, were some positives at the end of a long day.

It had also been a long day for Tony Hugill, waiting on board his cramped landing craft. Disembarkation did not come until the morning of June 7 after four days on board. The crowded scene that greeted him, with boats of all sizes trying to get on and off the beach, was an "absolute skipper's nightmare," but the actual coming ashore was an anticlimax. There were British and German bodies and burned-out equipment, but the battle had already moved inland.

For Churchill, any respite was short-lived. By the time the War Cabinet met at 18:00 hours on June 7, a new complication had arisen. In addition to withholding his liaison officers and refusing to discuss civil affairs, de Gaulle was now refusing to recognize the special French cur-rency that Eisenhower was proposing to issue to enable the Allies to pay for goods and services in liberated France. Churchill was not impressed by these new notes that he thought "singularly silly" because of their poor design, which made it hard to differentiate between amounts, but his bigger concern was that de Gaulle was attempting to use the issue to get himself recognized as the head of the French Provisional Government. There was also a related question of financial liability. Would the British and American governments be liable for redeeming these notes if they were not officially recognized in France? Churchill spoke about the deterioration of relations with de Gaulle and accused him of "a most non co-operative attitude" and being "primarily concerned with his personal position." His Cabinet colleagues, while sympathizing with Churchill's difficulties, encouraged the more conciliatory Eden to reach out to de Gaulle and persuade him to send commissioners to discuss these civil issues. They perhaps wisely sensed that their prime minister was still too emotive on this issue.

Churchill wrote to Roosevelt on June 8 summarizing the position as he saw it and concluding that if de Gaulle refused

> to send for the commissioners, we shall suggest he had better go back to Algiers. . . . I have repeatedly told de Gaulle and he acknowledged it without irritation that failing an agreement, I stand with you.

At the end, he added, probably only half in jest, "I think it would be a great pity if you and he did not meet. I do not see why I should have all the luck." Under increasing pressure from his own Cabinet members for a clearer American policy toward de Gaulle, he followed this up with further telegrams to the president on June 9 and 10, pressing him for an early answer on the currency issue. It finally came on June 13, when Roosevelt replied:

> If for any reason the supplementary currency is not acceptable to the French Public, General Eisenhower has full authority to use yellow seal dollars [specially produced dollars for military operations overseas] and British Military Authority notes. . . . It seems clear that Prima Donnas do not change their spots.

This did not allay all British worries about their liabilities, but Churchill refused to take the matter further with the president. The issue was a source of internal tension within the British Cabinet and took up a significant amount of the prime minister's time in the crucial first days of Overlord. He faced questions from the Australian government and murmurings in Parliament about the lack of rec- ognition for the Free French and their leader. When de Gaulle gave an interview with a news agency on June 10, criticizing the lack of French authority and officials in the liberated area and openly deny- ing the value of the Allied currency, Churchill minuted to Bracken that it would

> be well for you to warn the press that there are two sides to this story, and that a Government statement may easily be forthcom- ing when the time is ripe. One tale is good till another is told.

Churchill's pro-American stance had been made very obvious to everyone, including de Gaulle and those around him. This would inev- itably affect longer-term, Anglo-French relations.

It is ironic that just as Churchill's relationship with de Gaulle reached its lowest point, his hitherto uneasy correspondence with Stalin suddenly became extremely friendly, at least superficially. The Soviet leader responded immediately to Churchill's D-Day message, writing that "It gives joy to us all and hope of further successes," while confirming that the simultaneous offensive by Soviet forces, which he had promised to deliver at the Tehran Conference, would begin toward the middle of the month. Keen to exploit the opportunities provided by this friendly overture, and to use it to find out more about Soviet intentions, Churchill fired off a minute to Ismay on June 7 asking for further information that he could send to Stalin. He explained that he was trying to "extract a voluntary statement from the Bear [Stalin] of what he is going to do. Thus we must give something which is real and novel to him."

What Churchill gave, in a long telegram to Stalin dictated later on June 7, was detailed figures on the initial success of the Overlord operation. Twenty thousand airborne troops had safely landed behind the flanks of the enemy's lines, overall losses had been small, and by the end of the day the Allies hoped to have the best part of a quarter of a million men ashore. He gave news of the special tanks that had swum onto the beaches by themselves, though admitted that there had been "a good many casualties" as result of some being overturned by the waves, especially in the American sector. He proudly reported on the success of British armor in a tank battle with the Twenty-first Panzer-Grenadier Division "late last night near Caen" and announced that, "All the Commanders are satisfied that in the actual landing things have gone better than we expected." The novel element, which he reserved till last, was the news that two large synthetic harbors were about to be constructed on the wide sandy bay of the Seine estuary. "Nothing like these have ever been seen before. Great ocean liners will be able to discharge and run by numerous piers supplies to the fighting troops." He confirmed that the Allies expected to have twenty-five divisions deployed by D + 30 (July 5) and to have captured the port of Cherbourg, "But all this waits on the hazards of war which, Marshal Stalin, you know so well."

The correspondence between the two leaders continued in a similar vein over the course of the next few days. On June 9, Stalin confirmed that the Soviet summer offensive would open the following day on the Leningrad front. The next day, Churchill reported that, "By to-night, 10th, we ought to have landed nearly 400,000, together with a large superiority in tanks and a rapidly growing mass of artillery and lorries." Suddenly, the prime minister seemed more positive about the number of vehicles accompanying the assault. From the British ambassador in Moscow came the news that Churchill had been presented with a sketch of Stalin inscribed to him with the message, "In memory of the day of the invasion of Northern France by Allied British and American troops from his friend Joseph V. Stalin." What Churchill clearly liked more, and proudly shared with President Roosevelt, was the telegram he now received from the Soviet leader. It had clearly been specially crafted by Stalin and his advisers to appeal to Churchill's love of history and sense of destiny:

My colleagues and I cannot but admit that the history of warfare knows no other like undertaking from the point of view of its scale, its vast conception and its masterly execution. As is well known, Napoleon in his time failed ignominiously in his plan to force the Channel. The hysterical Hitler, who boasted for two years that he would effect a forcing of the Channel, was unable to make up his mind even to hint at attempting to carry out his threat. Only our Allies have succeeded in realising with honour the grandiose plan of forcing the Channel. History will record this deed as an achievement of the highest order.

This correspondence probably marks the high point in the wartime relationship between Churchill and Stalin. The promise to deliver the Second Front in Europe had finally been fulfilled. Behind the scenes, Churchill was pushing for the quick resumption of the Arctic convoys to Russia (which had been suspended in order to prioritize the Overlord operation). Yet the very success of Overlord and the rapid advances of the Soviets in the east were already threatening to create new tensions over the future of Poland, Germany, the Balkans, and Greece. The seeds of discord were already there. As Churchill received these glowing telegrams from Stalin, he was worried about communist infiltration of the government in Italy, was attempting to broker a deal between communist and royalist forces in Yugoslavia, was worried about the rise of communism in Greece, and was increasingly frustrated by American opposition to his desire to negotiate spheres of influence with Stalin in the Balkans. The quicker the German collapse, the more important these issues would become.

An insight into Churchill's real mindset is provided by the American war correspondent Virginia Cowles. She was part of a small luncheon party for the prime minister on June 7, a gathering that was presumably intended to take his mind off the huge pressures of the moment. Arriving in a blue siren suit (his zip-up overalls), the prime minister seemed "worried and preoccupied." But over food he launched into an angry diatribe against the "parlour pinks" who were criticizing his foreign policy in supporting the current regimes in Spain and Italy. "When this war is over," he growled, "England will need every ally she can get to protect herself against Russia." Churchill still believed that Britain could emerge from the conflict as a world power, but the country's position in the Mediterranean and influence in Europe would be threatened by Soviet expansion in southern and eastern Europe.

The immediate priority was to win the battle in Normandy. Churchill could offer support through his words in public and private. He was quick to send out a message to those who had made the artificial harbors possible:

> This was a fine feat. . . . The production of this novel and complicated equipment and its towing to the final erection sites and thence to the assembly areas, has been a very considerable undertaking. I feel that all Departments concerned are to be congratulated on the completion of the work.

Churchill may have been relieved by the launch of the operation, and even more so by its initial success, but he was also frustrated by not being able to do more. He could study the latest reports, monitor the casualty figures, follow the progress of the troops in his Map Room, and seek information from the chiefs of staff and the various military headquarters in the United Kingdom, but he chafed at not being able to influence events on the ground.

By June 8, Brooke was having to talk Churchill out of plans for additional landings on the west coast of France. By then, Churchill would have been aware of Montgomery's initial impressions of the battlefield, which—while generally good—included reference to the high casualties on Omaha Beach.

This top copy of the general's telegram of June 7 survives in the papers of John Selwyn Lloyd, who was then serving as deputy chief of staff to General Dempsey of the Second Army.

Handwritten telegram from General Montgomery to Chief of Staff,
June 7, 1944. (Selwyn Lloyd Papers, SELO 3/39)

The initial assault was just that. It was clear that weeks of serious fighting in Normandy lay ahead. On Thursday, June 8, Churchill addressed the Commons ahead of the weekend, sounding a note of caution and realism:

I earnestly hope that when Members go to their constituencies they will not only maintain morale, so far as that is necessary, but also give strong warnings against overoptimism, against the idea that these things are going to be settled with a run, and that they will remember that although great dangers lie behind us, enormous exertions lie before us.

Edgar Granville, the Liberal MP for Eye in Suffolk, responded by asking the prime minister whether he could give an assurance that the reason why he is not going to make any statement in the immediate future is not that he is going to make a visit to the coast of France?

No response is recorded. But for those who knew him well, it was obvious that it was going to be impossible to keep Churchill away from the scene of the action for long, and Brooke cannot have been surprised to get a minute from Churchill on June 9 telling him to make the necessary arrangements for a visit to the bridgeheads in France on Monday, June 12 (D-Day + 6). Churchill specified the wording his CIGS should use when informing Montgomery:

We do not wish in any way to be a burden on you or your headquarters, or in any way to divert your attention from the battle. All we should require is an A.D.C. [Aide de Camp] or other staff officer to show us round. We shall bring some sandwiches with us.

Montgomery replied to Brooke, not realizing his message would be copied to the prime minister, stating that:

Will meet you and give you full picture. Road not (repeat not) 100 per cent safe owing to enemy snipers including women. Much enemy bombing between dusk and dawn. Essential P.M. should go only where I take him and you must get away from here in early evening. Am very satisfied with progress of operations.

And so it was that the prime minister, accompanied by Brooke, Field Marshal Smuts, and his personal assistant, Commander "Tommy" Thompson, finally crossed the Channel on board the Royal Naval destroyer HMS *Kelvin*. The presence of Smuts is significant. Churchill trusted his judgment, particularly on military issues, and used him as a source of independent advice. The South African premier had been skeptical about D-Day, at one point warning Hughes-Hallett that it was the only operation the Allies could undertake that might lose them the war. He was there to act as Churchill's expert adviser and to play devil's advocate.

Sailing from Portsmouth at 08:00 hours, in good weather on calm water, the party enjoyed a panoramic view of the intense Allied activity, the culmination of so much preparation. The water was full of landing craft, minesweepers, supply ships, and tugs towing steel and concrete parts for use in the artificial harbors; above them, the air was a mass of Allied planes. Arriving at a Gooseberry formed from the sunken block-ships, the prime minister's party was met by Admiral Vian, commander of the eastern naval task force for the British and Canadian beaches, who transferred them into his barge and then into an amphibious DUKW (a six-wheel-drive amphibious vehicle sometimes called a "duck") for the drive ashore. Here, they were greeted by General Montgomery who whisked them inland by Jeep to his headquarters for a briefing and lunch.

For Churchill it was a moving experience. It was almost exactly four years since he had last set foot in France, at that fateful meeting with Reynaud at Tours on June 13, 1940. It had been a long road back. Both he and Brooke were struck by the beauty of the countryside. Churchill later described the scene:

We drove through our limited but fertile domain in Normandy. It was pleasant to see the prosperity of the countryside. The fields were full of lovely red and white cows basking or parading in the sunshine. The inhabitants seemed quite buoyant and well nourished and waved enthusiastically.

He tuned to Brooke and told him, "We are surrounded by fat cattle lying in luscious pastures with their paws crossed!" Brooke agreed about the cattle, but not about the attitude of the French people. To him, they "did not seem in any way pleased to see us arrive as a victorious country to liberate France. They had been quite content as they were, and we were bringing war and desolation to the country." This is not what Churchill wanted to see or remember.

Lunch was taken in a tent outside Montgomery's chateau looking toward the front, which was about three miles away. When Churchill asked about the risk of an incursion by German armor, Montgomery casually dismissed the threat. Yet, if one account is to be believed, the threat may have been much closer at hand than they realized. Tommy Thompson's memoirs describe a strange incident when, upon emerging from Montgomery's caravan, Smuts sniffed the air before telling the astonished aide de camp, "There are some Germans still here—quite close to us."

> Standing bare-headed in the sunshine, Smuts continued to frown in a puzzled way, staring suspiciously at the clumps of laurels and rhododendrons which almost surrounded the caravans, but he said no more, and they followed Montgomery into his Mess tent.

Two days later, two German paratroopers, long since cut off from their unit, emerged bedraggled and exhausted but still armed from their hiding place in the very same bushes and surrendered. If the story is true, they could have killed Churchill, Brooke, Smuts, and Montgomery, but it is a tale that does not appear in the memoirs of Churchill or Montgomery and so may well be embellished or apocryphal.

What is clear is that Churchill enjoyed the stimulus of travel and risk. Inspecting the British landing zone at Arromanches, he caused alarm by climbing to the top of a small lighthouse, tried unsuccessfully to board a Monitor (a small warship carrying large guns), which was bombarding the coast, before persuading Admiral Vian to allow HMS *Kelvin* to fire its guns in anger on the enemy before departing for home. After which, he slept soundly on the return trip: "Altogether it had been a most interesting and enjoyable day." The simple note he left in Montgomery's visitors' book read:

As it was in the beginning so may it continue to the end.

It had also been an educational experience. Churchill had spent time touring the British beachhead. He had seen the artificial break-water in operation and the ongoing preparations for construction of the full Mulberry harbor. He had also been pleased to learn about the three local ports of Port-en-Bessin, Courseulles, and Ouistreham, which were playing a far-larger-than-anticipated role in bringing in materials. On arrival back in Portsmouth, Winston met up with the American chiefs of staff—Marshall, King, and Arnold—who were visiting the United Kingdom and had also just crossed the Channel and toured the American positions. They all dined together in Churchill's railway carriage, and Marshall wrote out a message for Admiral Mountbatten, now Supreme Allied Commander in Southeast Asia, which they all signed, acknowledging that the "success of the venture, has its origin in developments effected by you and your staff of Combined Operations." Churchill must have retired with a sense of things having come full circle.

The timing of Churchill's trip was carefully calculated. He made sure that he got to Normandy before de Gaulle, who traveled across on June 14, and King George VI, who visited troops there on June 16. News of the prime minister's visit spread rapidly and was noted by Hugill in his diary.

De Gaulle's return to France was also symbolic and led inexorably to the recognition he wanted. By June 16, even Churchill was prepared to write to him in slightly more conciliatory tones, declaring:

> Ever since 1907, I have in good times and bad times, been a sincere friend of France, as my words and actions show, and it is to me an intense pain that barriers have been raised to an association which to me was very dear.

It was now time to tie up loose ends. Back in London on June 13, the prime minister chaired a Cabinet meeting, which agreed to extend the ban on private diplomatic communications. Eisenhower had requested an extension until D+15 (June 21) in order to protect Overlord security.

So far, the Germans had held forces back in the Pas-de-Calais area believing that further attacks might still come. The Bodyguard deception plan was working, and there remained a fear that neutral diplomats based in the United Kingdom might be able to convey information to the enemy that would undermine this. The government was unsure. Churchill and Eden had a strong desire to normalize diplomatic relations as quickly as possible. Indeed, the prime minister was aware that his intelligence services believed that diplomatic communications could be used to feed misinformation to the enemy and thereby enhance deception. In the end, it was agreed to lift the ban starting Monday, June 19. The visitors ban to the coastal areas and the travel ban to Ireland were also to be lifted by the end of the month.

A week after the landings, Churchill could take comfort from the fact that the initial assault had succeeded. The beachheads had been established and the initial losses had been significantly less than expected. The United Kingdom had risen to the challenge of the immense dislocation. The transport system had not crashed under the additional strain, and troops and material were being successfully delivered to their disembarkation points. Production targets for the Mulberries had been met and the artificial ports were now coming on stream. Relations with Roosevelt and Stalin were good, even if de Gaulle was proving problematic.

In spite of several near misses, security had not been compromised, deception had worked, and tactical surprise had been achieved. For more than a month after D-Day, the Germans continued to hold significant forces in the Pas-de-Calais area, expecting a second invasion. The teams of deceivers in Britain worked hard to maintain the pretense, and Churchill wrote to Eisenhower on July 15 to urge continuation, stating that, "Uncertainty is a terror to the Germans. The forces in Britain are a dominant preoccupation of the Huns."

On the personal front, Randolph had reached the safety of Vis and subsequently returned to Britain, though Churchill had been clear that his son should not be given any special consideration. His relief may have been short-lived. By July 11, Mary Churchill's diary was recording that "RANDOLPH—is, as usual, a bone of sorrow & contention, behaving with such odious unkindness, rudeness and heartlessness to Papa & Mummie." Winston's relationship with his oldest son was always complex.

By then he had other problems. It was on June 13 that the first V1 self-propelled flying bombs fell on the country, eclipsing the success of D-Day in the public mind and replacing any relief with a visceral new threat. Today, a blue plaque on Grove Road, East London, commemorates the site of the first explosion, which killed six, injured forty-two, and destroyed a bridge on the railway line from London Liverpool Street to Stratford. Losses and damage in the coming weeks would be significant, but at least Churchill knew that Hitler's new weapon had come too late to affect D-Day itself. If the Allies could break out in Normandy, then these firing sites in northern France and Belgium could be quickly overrun and neutralized. But worries remained. What of the other weapon, the liquid fuel rocket that the Nazis were developing? When and where might this be deployed? And how dangerous might it prove?

And what of the Normandy breakout? When would it come? The town of Caen had been a final objective for the British and Canadian forces on June 6. The first week of Overlord had passed, and the town was still in German hands. Churchill was once again left studying the mounting casualty figures, military and civilian, and his worries about high losses were returning.

For TL Rodgers, it was already too late. Deployed as an elite pathfinder, he was one of the first Americans to parachute into Normandy, dropped into Sainte-Mère-Église behind the American beaches an hour before the main airborne assault to set up beacons to guide his comrades in. Like so many, the exact circumstances of his death are unclear. One account has him killed on landing, dropped into the courtyard of a farmhouse hosting a German garrison, another dying days later in a firefight around an orchard. His story here stands as just one tale of bravery and loss. By all accounts, he was a giant of man, physically and also in his moral stature. Sainte-Mère-Église was the first French town to be liberated.

K.1.

A volume would be required to recount the story of the crossing of the Channel and the landing of the Armies of Liberation on the soil of France.   I have only a few minutes. In _April_, 1943 General Morgan of the British ~~Service~~ Army became the head of a British and American Planning ~~Committee~~ Staff which surveyed the whole ~~scene~~ layout.   ~~That Committee~~ They made a plan which I took with me last year to Quebec, where it was submitted to the President and to the ~~American~~ Combined Chiefs of Staff. This plan selected the beaches for the attack and presented the ~~simple~~ outlines with a mass of detail to support them. It received in principle complete agreement.   At Teheran we promised Marshal Stalin we would put this plan or something like it into operation at the end of May or the beginning of June, and he for his part promised that the whole of the as indeed they have been Russian Armies would be thrown into general battle in the East.

(L)   In January the Commanders were appointed.   We took over the command of the Mediterranean and General Eisenhower in Britain assumed the command of the Expeditionary Force, ~~with General~~ Montgomery in command of the invading troops.   For more than a year past American stores, equipment and men had been

Draft for Churchill's speech to House of Commons, August 2, 1944.
(Churchill's Papers, CHAR 9/200A/18)

Chapter 11

Tyranny of Overlord

*"All right, if you insist on being damned fools,
sooner than falling out with you, which would
be fatal, we shall be damned fools with you,
and we shall see that we perform the role
of damned fools damned well!"*

WITH THE BENEFIT OF HINDSIGHT, WE KNOW THAT D-DAY LED TO
the liberation of France, but success was not immediate. For the first
three months, the Allied armies faced a tough battle of consolidation
and attrition.

Set against the 19,240 British fatalities on the first day of the Somme
offensive on July 1, 1916, the success of the D-Day landings came at a
terrible but comparatively much lower cost. There were just under
11,000 Allied casualties, including around 3,800 killed, of which slightly
more than a thousand were British. By the end of June 6, 1944, more
than 5,000 ships had landed 133,000 Allied troops, supported by 14,674
air sorties and immense naval gunfire. However, D-Day was only the
first day of the extended Normandy Campaign, which continued until
August 30, 1944, with the crossing of the river Seine and the liberation
of Paris. Although the fighting on D-Day was fierce, much worse was

to follow in the close bocage (terrain of mixed woodland and pasture) country of Normandy, characterized by sunken lanes and high hedges, during the battles for Caen and in the eventual breakout toward Paris. As Stan Hollis's commanding officer, Lieutenant Colonel Robin Hastings of Sixth Green Howards, records: "On the first day, we suffered about ninety casualties, a comparatively low figure but one which included two company commanders and several of our best NCOs. We lay down with a feeling of relief at having achieved a landing without excessive cost. Little did we know what we had to look forward to."

And there was much "to look forward to," or put with less British understatement, there was a tremendous amount to be done. If the Allies were successfully ashore by nightfall on June 6, their toehold in Europe was precarious. At the final briefing presentation in front of King George VI and Winston Churchill at St. Paul's School on May 15, Montgomery had set out his plans for the land campaign in Normandy. Although the tri-service planning for the initial landings was meticulous, Monty set out in stark terms that the real challenge would be the rate at which the Allied forces could build up their strength compared to the Germans. Having assumed initial operational surprise, Montgomery predicted that by D+8 (June 14), the Allies would have eighteen divisions ashore but would be faced by twenty-four enemy divisions of which ten would be panzer divisions. Knowing that his old rival Erwin Rommel would try to defeat the landings as close to the beachheads as possible, his design for battle was to contain, absorb, and reduce the German counterattack capability before breaking out decisively to the south and east—ultimately toward Germany. Turning to a large map on the paneled wall of his old school's lecture room, Montgomery set out his intentions for the development of operations up to D+90. Although there has been much criticism subsequently that Monty revised the outline of his plan afterward to secure his place in history, nevertheless events on the ground broadly followed the outcome that he had predicted, albeit not at the speed that he anticipated. Caen was captured on D+33, not on D-Day, Cherbourg on D+22, not on D+8, and Falaise on D+71, not on D+17.

Many factors affected the way in which the campaign unfolded. The success of Operation Fortitude continued to keep doubt in the minds of the German High Command as to whether the landings in Normandy were the Allied main effort or a feint. Although Hitler himself seemed to have a two-way bet on which location was his enemy's main focus, he nevertheless was reluctant to release the panzer reserves, despite pressure from Rommel to do so. Even when the German armor was ordered to attack, the Allied domination of the skies confined their movement to the hours of darkness or in bad weather. Daylight moves incurred huge casualties to men and vehicles. However, the weather had a major effect on the Allies too. Having nearly caused a two-week postponement of D-Day itself, on the night of June 19, the most violent storm in forty years struck the Normandy coast, exacerbating the effects of a spring tide. Both Mulberry artificial harbors were destroyed, the one at Omaha beyond repair with the one off Arromanches-les-Bains out of commission for many days. The storm finally blew itself out by June 22. Although it had a major delaying effect on the manpower and logistic buildup, Eisenhower reflected that had he ordered the fortnight's postponement, the armada would have been at sea when the storm struck. In a note to Group Captain Stagg, the senior meteorological officer, he wrote: "I thank the gods of war we went when we did."

With a growing force ashore, Montgomery and his senior commanders were faced with how to develop their operations to maintain the momentum that the landings had achieved. The capture of Caen on D-Day had proved to be an objective too far. The hapless inhabitants of Caen were to be subjected to horrendous bombing attacks in which, over the next six weeks, much of the ancient city was destroyed, many citizens were killed, and others suffered at the hands of the Gestapo, keen to cover their tracks before they withdrew. As the first major French city to be liberated, the cost at three thousand citizens killed was a devastatingly high one. Through June and July, the battle ebbed and flowed around Caen. General progress by the Allied armies was severely impeded by the nature of the terrain over which they had to fight. Inland from the sandy assault beaches, they found themselves in the lush cornfields and thick hedgerows of the Normandy bocage. Fields were typically about the size of a football field, separated one from another by high, thick hedges and deep ditches or sunken lanes. This was the ideal environment for the defending Germans to site anti-tank and machine guns to cover any possible path to advance. Allied casualties were heavy, and the manpower drain on the attacking infantry was becoming a significant factor. The attacking armies needed to adapt, and rapidly. Although many tanks had been adapted to swim ashore, others now needed to be given the means to bulldoze their way through the hedges and across the ditches to provide firepower support to the infantry. Field workshops quickly devised metal battering rams to be welded onto the front of tanks, some made from the metalwork of Rommel's beach defenses. In the detailed study of the landing beaches, it had to be acknowledged that insufficient thought had been given to fighting in the close country inland.

As the overall commander of the Allied landings, it was Montgomery's responsibility to orchestrate the defeat of the German forces in Normandy and set up General Eisenhower to begin the liberation of Europe. Although Churchill's first fear of the landings being a failure had been removed, there was, nevertheless, the nagging worry that the invasion force could be marooned as in Gallipoli in 1915–1916 or as at Anzio in 1944. The bloody battles around Villers-Bocage on June 11–14 added to that fear. Montgomery resolved that he must wear down the defending Germans' strength by drawing them onto the British Second Army on the Allied left around Caen to provide the opportunity for Bradley's US First Army, and later Patton's US Third Army, to break out on the Allied right. Montgomery's first major attack was Operation Epsom to the west of Caen from June 26 to July 1, but this was contained by First and Second SS Panzer Corps after intense fighting. The concern over infantry manpower grew. General Miles Dempsey's British Second Army was, however, not short of tanks. Dempsey persuaded Montgomery that an attack by three armored divisions preceded by a heavy bombing strike could achieve a breakthrough to the east of Caen. At 05:30 hours on July 18, 2,500 British and US bombers began two and a half hours of aerial attack on the defending Germans, dropping nearly 8,000 tons of bombs. Despite the devastating effect of the bombing, the British armor was slow to follow up. When it did so, it faced surprisingly stiff resistance particularly from German anti-tank guns, which had survived the onslaught from above. The so-called death ride of the British armor in Operation Goodwood failed to achieve the breakout promised by Montgomery to Eisenhower.

Tensions on Downing Street by the end of June were once again running high. The initial relief on getting ashore had worn off. Everyone was tired after the stress of the last few weeks; a situation only made worse by the arrival of the V-weapons in the skies above London and the return of terror to the streets of the capital. General Brooke admired Churchill's staunch response to the flying bombs, praising the firm way in which the prime minister slapped down his Home Secretary, Herbert Morrison, for expressing doubts that London could take such a renewed attack, noting at the Cabinet meeting on June 19 that "Winston was in very good form, quite 10 years younger, all due to the fact that the flying bombs have again put us into the front line!!"

But such moments were not typical. More often, Brooke found dealing with Churchill to be frustrating during this time. When discussing strategy, he felt Winston was meandering, "producing a lot of disconnected thoughts which had no military value," was guilty of "strategic ravings" and of "giving one strategic lecture after another." For the prime minister, it seemed that the relief at getting safely ashore, and the excitement of seeing the beachheads for himself, had given way to uncertainty about the next steps and renewed argument about the best way of exploiting Overlord.

The prime minister's thoughts kept returning to Italy. Hitler's decision to contest the Italian peninsula had served to keep German forces away from Normandy in the run-up to D-Day, effectively replacing the delayed Anvil assault on the south of France as a diversionary campaign, but Eisenhower now wanted Alexander's operations scaled back. More troops and resources were to be diverted to France and a new version of Operation Anvil, rebranded for security reasons as Dragoon, was to take place as soon as possible. This would open up a new route into northern France from the south, thereby taking pressure off the beachheads.

Initially, Churchill seemed torn. He briefly toyed with further operations against the west coast of France, returning to the strategy of widening the assault front that he had first advocated in 1942. The problem was that he still wanted the best of both worlds. He wanted to ensure the success of the operation in France, but he also wanted to continue to fight in Italy.

On June 21, he met with Brooke and Smuts to discuss options. Influenced by the positive reports he was receiving from General Alexander in the aftermath of the capture of Rome, Churchill was now excited by the idea of being able to strike northward from Italy into Austria via Trieste and the Ljubljana Gap. Smuts too was attracted by this idea but spoke in favor of a new cross-Channel assault at Calais. To Brooke, both ideas seemed hopelessly overoptimistic. The Allies did not have the capacity to launch and sustain another major invasion of France from Britain (though they were continuing with the deception plans to try to convince the Germans they did) while Alexander was unlikely to cross the Italian Alps before the onset of winter, which would then make further operations impossible until the spring. Brooke did not want to see Alexander denuded of troops, he favored continuing to wear the Germans down in Italy, but in the course of repeated conversations about strategy over the next few days he found it hard to make Churchill "realize that if we took the season of the year and the topography of the country in league against us we should have 3 enemies instead of one."

Churchill's desire to continue the fight in Italy was entirely consistent with his policy prior to Overlord. He still did not want to risk everything on one throw of the dice in Normandy. It was already clear that as the campaign in France developed it would become more and more of an American show. In contrast, the Mediterranean theater under its Supreme Commander General Wilson and the Italian campaign, under soon-to-be Field Marshal Alexander, were British-led operations that he could present as an important counterweight to growing American and Soviet influence in Europe. With the Red Army now advancing rapidly toward Austria and Germany from the east, and the postwar settlement of Europe now in sight—a matter of when, not if—he felt it vital for Britain to end the war in a strong geopolitical position on the continent. While the soldiers were quite rightly focusing on the military defeat of the enemy, the politicians were already thinking in terms of the political aftermath. For Churchill, this meant obtaining a stable Europe (which for him meant non-communist) while protecting British imperial interests in the Mediterranean; for Stalin, it meant establishing buffer zones of client states between the Soviet Union and other powers in Eastern Europe and the Balkans; while for Roosevelt, it was about the creation of the United Nations organization and a world order based on the values of the Atlantic Charter. It was increasingly obvious that these aims would conflict and pull in different directions.

The immediate fight was with the Americans over Anvil/Dragoon. At one of the rambling meetings about strategy, held in Churchill's Map Room on June 22, the prime minister and his chiefs of staff attempted to thrash out their own position before negotiating with their allies. Churchill was very keen that any troops in the Mediterranean theater that were surplus to the requirements of Alexander's main northern advance should be used for an amphibious assault in the Trieste area. He was proposing another operation in the style of Salerno or Anzio, speeding up progress on the peninsula by using the sea to leapfrog up the coast. He greatly preferred this to "an 'Anvil' type operation on the south coasts of France," which was too far removed from General Eisenhower's battlefront for an Allied landing there to have any tactical effect on "Overlord." The enemy would probably be more sensitive to a thrust developing from the head of the Adriatic than to an advance up the Rhone Valley.

Churchill also returned to a familiar theme, one calculated to annoy Brooke, when he made the further argument against Anvil that it would require an enormous "tail," necessitating a new base in the south of France. For his part, Brooke spoke in favor of Alexander advancing in northern Italy but recommended using any surplus forces that could be released to support a landing in the south of France rather than in the Bay of Biscay or Loire area. No firm decision was taken but Churchill dug in. He was encouraged by Smuts, who telegraphed from Italy backing Alexander and Wilson, the British commanders on the ground who were keen to push north.

In his war memoirs, Churchill would later present this as a straightforward clash between Eisenhower and the American chiefs of staff on the one hand, and himself and the British chiefs of staff on the other. As Brooke's more nuanced position makes clear, it was not quite that simple, but when the prime minister raised the issue with Roosevelt, the president once again made it very clear that he was backing Eisenhower. He wrote that the proposal,

> for continued use of practically all the Mediterranean resources to advance into Northern Italy and from there to the northeast is not acceptable to me, and I really believe we should consolidate our operations and not scatter them.

FDR then followed up with a second, much longer telegram a day later, on June 29, in which he outlined all his reasons for prioritizing operations in France that struck "at the heart of Germany." His "interest and hopes" centered "on defeating the Germans in front of Eisenhower and driving on into Germany, rather than on limiting this action for the purpose of staging a full major effort in Italy." Alexander would still have enough forces to hold the Germans, while the Allies already exercised mastery of the air and sea in the Mediterranean. Eisenhower regarded Anvil as being of "transcendent importance" and the plans were already well advanced and had been approved by Stalin. The president could not agree to the deployment of US troops into Istria as politically he would "never survive even a slight setback in 'Overlord' if it were known that fairly large forces had been diverted to the Balkans." The president's message called for the immediate withdrawal of five divisions, three American and two French, from Italy for use in the south of France.

Roosevelt's view was clear. Here was Churchill up to his old tricks of trying to divert American forces away from their prime focus and into the Balkans and, just as with Rhodes and the Dodecanese Islands in 1943, the president would not countenance it. The Americans wanted Anvil and they wanted it as soon as possible and on a scale that would inevitably weaken Alexander's ability to go forward in Italy.

Churchill was left fuming. He briefly contemplated flying over to Washington to argue his case in person, but, according to Brooke:

In the end we got him to agree to our outlook which is: "All
right, if you insist on being damned fools, sooner than falling
out with you, which would be fatal, we shall be damned fools
with you, and we shall see that we perform the role of damned
fools damned well!"

The episode is a clear illustration of the changed political dynamic
within the "Special Relationship." Once Overlord was launched, it's scale
and significance trumped all other operations in the European theater.
For Roosevelt, Marshall, and Eisenhower, winning in Normandy and
striking quickly and directly at Germany was the only game that mattered; Overlord and the strategic bomber offensive were their vehicles
for delivering victory. Everything else was now secondary.

Rather than risk an open breach, the prime minister phoned
Eisenhower agreeing to Anvil and informed him that General Wilson
would be authorized to make the attack on the south of France using
forces from the Mediterranean theater.

But it would not be his last word on the matter. By July 6,

he [Churchill] was in a maudlin, bad tempered, drunken mood,
ready to take offence at anything, suspicious of everybody, and
in a highly vindictive mood against the Americans.

Unfortunately, events on the ground in France only served to exac-
erbate the prime minister's ill mood. Contrasts were being drawn in
the Allied media between the advances of the American forces, who
were now sweeping across Brittany from their western beaches, and the
inertia of the British and Canadian forces, who were still stalled in front
of Caen in the east. To make matters worse, it seems that Eisenhower,
and perhaps Tedder and others, had begun to drop hints to Churchill
that Montgomery was being too cautious.

Matters reached a head at a meeting that evening. When Churchill
began to disparage Montgomery in front of the politicians present,
Brooke lost his temper and accused the prime minister of not being
able to trust his generals for five minutes and of "continuously abusing

them and belittling them." Churchill was furious. He kept "shoving his chin out" and protesting (perhaps too much) against the accusation.

Things then got worse when the prime minister decided to revisit the Normandy battlefield for himself. All hell broke loose on July 19. Brooke was summoned to Churchill's bedside, where he found the prime minister in "a new blue and gold dressing gown" and "an unholy rage." When Brooke finally managed to get a word in, he discovered the reason for the outburst. Eisenhower, in an apparently well-meaning but ill-thought-through conversation, had told Churchill that Montgomery did not want the distraction of visitors. Churchill assumed that this had come from Monty himself. As Minister of Defence, Winston did not consider himself an ordinary visitor and clearly felt that this was a conspiracy by his generals to stop him from exercising his rights to see what was really going on. Fortunately, it was a passing storm. After some frantic diplomacy by Eisenhower and Brooke, and an assurance by Montgomery that a visit would be welcomed, Churchill was appeased, and the trip went ahead on the following day.

Churchill flew first to the Cherbourg Peninsula, where he inspected a flying-bomb launch site and saw the extensive German damage to the harbor, admiring the bravery of the divers who were charged with clearing the deliberate German sabotage. Hugill had been there just days before him and observed the controlled destruction of the underwater minefield: "The domes of spray were lovely to watch, in the way a big underwater explosion always is." But it was clear that Cherbourg was not yet a working harbor.

There then followed a rather rough sea voyage to the British Mulberry—Port Winston—at Arromanches. According to Commander Thompson, Winston was bored and seasick en route (a version contested by Churchill, who later wrote that he did not suffer and slept soundly) "but as soon as we arrived at Mulberry Harbour he was in his element, for the port was seething with activity." Here he stayed for three days, observing the constant loading and unloading of supplies, and the "waddling" onshore of the amphibious DUKWs. On his last day, he visited Montgomery's headquarters before flying low over the Allied bridgehead in the general's captured German Fiesler Storch aircraft and visiting some of the air stations. Ismay and Thompson from his party made it to Caen and must have made Churchill aware of the scale of the utter devastation of the city.

As with his earlier visit, the trip seems to have had a rejuvenating effect. Back in London, Churchill had initially seemed "supremely happy" with the military situation, but there then followed a series of further conversations with Eisenhower and a lunch on July 26. The table talk turned on whether Montgomery was being too hesitant and whether the British Second Army could do more to take the offensive to the enemy. Churchill was highly sensitive to accusations that the British were not pulling their weight and were taking fewer casualties.

News of a plot was quick to reach Montgomery. It must have been unsettling. He knew that Churchill made a habit of dismissing generals whom he considered too cautious, most notably Montgomery's own predecessor in North Africa, General Auchinleck. That said, Monty's position was somewhat stronger. His reputation remained high after the victory at El Alamein, making him the most famous and recognizable contemporary British figure after Churchill, and any attempt to remove him at the height of the battle would have required the support of both Eisenhower and Brooke, which would not have been forthcoming. His disappearance would have been damaging to morale and a propaganda gift to the enemy.

Even so, such rumors were hardly the support that the commander in the field needed while in the throes of a major battle. Brooke rushed in to talk Winston down. This time, perhaps acknowledging the force of Brooke's previous arguments, Churchill was more receptive to his army head and even damned Brooke with faint praise, describing the CIGS as his "alter ego" on military matters. Ultimately, Churchill's reservations evaporated in the face of Montgomery's battlefield success. By July 20, the capture of Caen was complete, and German eyes were firmly fixed on containing the British.

While the British and American politicians and generals were sniping about one another politely over lunch, the real plotting was taking place in Germany. Encouraged by the prospect of a British breakout in Normandy, a group of German army officers now embarked on a daring but ill-fated assassination attempt on Hitler. On July 20, as Caen was finally being liberated, Colonel Claus von Stauffenberg flew to the Führer's secluded headquarters in East Prussia known as the Wolf's Lair (Wolfsschanze) to attend a military conference with Hitler. He then placed a bomb in a briefcase underneath the table in the wooden hut where the meeting was taking place, made his excuses, and left. The ensuing blast narrowly failed to kill Hitler, resulting in terrible reprisals as the conspirators were rounded up, tortured, and executed. News of this plot and its impact on the higher echelons of the German army was gradually filtering back to Churchill. What he did not know at this point was that Rommel himself would soon be implicated and forced to take his own life. Though from a strictly military perspective, this had ceased to matter. Rommel had been badly injured on July 17, when his car was strafed in Normandy by the RAF. For Germany's most famous general, the campaign and the war were over.

Field Marshal von Kluge, now commanding German forces in Normandy, remained convinced that any breakout attempt would come in the British sector. He was wrong. On July 25, First US Army launched Operation Cobra, its major assault being toward St. Lô and Avranches. Again, it was spearheaded by a heavy bomber attack but once more the lack of precision bombing skills by the aircrew caused casualties to both sides. Several aircraft dropped their loads short of their targets killing US troops on the ground, including Lieutenant General Leslie McNair who had gone forward to witness the opening of the attack. Nevertheless, First US Army pushed ahead and by August 1 had achieved their objectives. On that date, Patton's Third US Army became operational with four army corps under his command. Patton's first mission was to seize Brittany and the port of Brest in conjunction with the *Forces Francaises de l'Interieur*, who had been ordered onto the offensive by their headquarters in London. Events began to move quickly. The British VIII Corps struck south and west of Caen in Operation Bluecoat, which ran until August 7. That morning the most dominant feature in Normandy, Mount Pincon, was in British hands and German Army Group B reported that it taken over 150,000 casualties since June 6 with only 20,000 reinforcements coming forward. There was a growing inevitability about the outcome of the campaign, but it was not seen by Hitler in the *Wolfsschanze.*

With the Allied breakout, things were now moving in the right direction. By early August, Churchill felt confident enough to give a detailed report to the House of Commons. Speaking just before the summer recess, he was finally able to tell the whole story as he saw it. Addressing the critics who had wanted an earlier Second Front, he declared:

> I do not believe myself that this vast enterprise could have been executed earlier. We had not the experience. We had not the tackle. But, before we launched the attack in 1944 we had made five successful opposed landings in the Mediterranean, and a mass of wonderful craft of all kinds had been devised by our services and by our United States colleagues on the other side of the ocean.

He then went on to describe some of the wonderful equipment that he had seen in action during his trips to Normandy, the landing craft with drawbridges that could unload direct onto the beaches, the American amphibious DUKW, "a heavy lorry which goes at between 40 and 50 miles an hour along the road, and can plunge into the water and swim out for miles to sea," and the harbors that "had been created compared with which Dover seems small." His glowing tribute to the ability of these artificial ports to supply "the entire elaborate equipment of modern armies," which required one vehicle to four or five men, must have prompted raised eyebrows from Brooke, Montgomery, and those planning staff who had faced his previous harangues on the subject of there being too much transport.

He was drawing lines in the sand. What had been contentious issues were now part of the operation's successful history. At the request of the Air Ministry, he praised the "strategic bombing by the combined British and American Bomber Forces, and the use of the medium bomber and fighter forces" for providing "the essential prelude to our landing in Normandy." Prompted by the Foreign Office, he also sought to build bridges with the Free French, admitting his many differences with de

Gaulle but recognizing him as "the first eminent Frenchman to face the common foe in what seemed to be the hour of ruin of his country, and possibly, of ours."

He even used the occasion to restate his credentials as a lifelong friend of France.

> All my life I have been grateful for the contribution France has made to the culture and glory of Europe, and above all for the sense of personal liberty and the rights of man which has radiated from the soul of France. But these are not matters of sentiment or personal feeling. It is one of the main interests of Great Britain that a friendly France should regain and hold her place among the major powers of Europe. Show me a moment when I swerved from this conception, and you will show me a moment when I have been wrong.

Finally, he took the opportunity to emphasize that the British and Canadian troops were holding their own, and that "the losses of the British and Canada forces together are about equal to those of the larger United States Army in proportion to their relative strength." He was basing this on casualty figures supplied to him for the period up to July 23. These showed British and Canadian losses at 1 in 13 or 8 percent and American losses at 1 in 11.5 or 8.7 percent.

There was praise for the long-suffering General Brooke and even for the War Office, though Churchill did point out that, "To say this is by no means inconsistent with any criticisms that it may be necessary to put forward from time to time." Toward the end, there was even a brief mention of the Stauffenberg plot, with a passing reference to "the highest personalities in the German Reich . . . murdering one another."

There was more he would have liked to say and could not. He had wanted to include more about the logistical planning and mounting of the operation, but it was felt that this might prejudice Fortitude, as the deception operation was still running, and Eisenhower wanted the Germans to keep guessing about forces that might still be in Britain. He had wanted to celebrate the bravery of the divers he had

CASUALTIES.
NORMANDY

1st August, 1944.

Dear Martin,

At last night's Cabinet the Prime Minister stated that he proposed to refer to the Allied casualties in Normandy and in this connection asked my Secretary of State to furnish him with certain information.

~~In this connection~~ My Secretary of State *now* asks me to send you the following figures which are from the published casualty returns up to 23rd July last.

	Total Forces Landed	Casualties	Ratio
British and Canadian	653,950	49,280	1 in 13, or 8 per cent
American	809,440	70,300	1 in 11.5, or 8.7 per cent.

The ratio to total strength at a certain date is perhaps slightly misleading as the average strength is different; the British build-up started quicker and the Americans have a rather larger tail.

/The

J.M. Martin, Esq., C.V.O.

Material on casualties compiled for prime minister's speech, August 1, 1944.
(Churchill Papers, CHAR 9/200A/111)

seen clearing the harbor at Cherbourg, but it was felt that this might be to their disadvantage by causing the Germans to lay booby traps in the future.

The speech brought Churchill's D-Day campaign to an end, but there was still one battle left for him to fight. The recent success in Normandy meant that he now felt confident enough to return to the charge against Dragoon (formerly Anvil). For him, the tactical moment for an invasion of the south of France had passed. He later wrote that

> Once we joined battle in Normandy "Anvil's" value was much reduced, because Hitler was not likely to detach troops from the main struggle in the north for the sake of keeping his hold on Provence.

It was not just about Italy, though Churchill still favored operations there; it was also about the potential difficulty of opening a new front in the south of France, especially one that was so far removed from the main Overlord battlefield. Arguing that Eisenhower no longer needed reinforcements from the south of France, as these could now come directly into Brittany and Normandy and other French ports, he lost no opportunity to lobby the Supreme Commander.

Eisenhower described it as "one of the longest sustained arguments that I had with Prime Minister Churchill throughout the period of the war." It reached a head on Saturday, August 5, when Churchill used an aborted trip to France, canceled due to bad weather, to divert to Eisenhower's forward headquarters near Portsmouth and hold an impromptu conference. Accepting that forces would still have to be transferred from the Mediterranean theater, he advocated changing the plan to sail them through the Straits of Gibraltar and land them in western France. According to Harry Butcher, "Ike said no, continued saying no all afternoon, and ended saying no in every form of the English language at his command." The Supreme Commander was clear that he needed another port of entry into France (as many of those in the west were not yet fully operational or were already at capacity), was keen to open up a new flank that would further stretch the enemy, and relieve pressure on those fighting in Normandy, and—unlike Churchill—believed that results could be achieved quickly by an assault in the south.

Both men would later dwell on this row in their memoirs. Eisenhower would claim that he had recognized that Churchill's real concern was political; a desire to establish an Allied presence in the Balkans ahead of the Russians. Churchill would later deny it was about moving armies into the Balkans but would write of the lost strategic and political positions in Istria (now Croatia, Slovenia, and Italy) and Trieste, which "might exercise profound and widespread reactions, especially after the Russian advances." In both cases, of course, they were writing with the benefit of hindsight, as leaders in the Cold War, but in the summer of 1944, they were both astute enough operators to see the political as well as the military arguments. Their analysis with regard to the likely extent of Soviet expansion was probably similar, but their immediate priorities and solutions were very different. For Eisenhower, the protégé of Marshall, the surest route to victory was still Germany via France, and he was not prepared to be diverted.

Churchill appealed to Washington, DC, but Marshall and Roosevelt also continued to say no. Grudgingly, the British prime minister conceded and afterward reflected:

> It is worth noting that we had now passed the day in July when for the first time in the war the movement of the great American armies into Europe and their growth in the Far East made their numbers in action greater than our own.

At the time, he vented to his doctor, Lord Moran, complaining that the Russians were "spreading across Europe like a tide" and describing the impending landings in the south of France as "Sheer folly.... If only those ten divisions could have been landed in the Balkans" (a sentiment that—if true—confirmed American suspicions and gave the lie to his denials about wanting to dominate southeastern Europe).

Yet his response was typically Churchillian. Rather than sit at home and brood on his failure to influence his allies, he took himself off to

the Mediterranean to see the situation in the British theater firsthand
and to meet "the commanders and the troops from whom so much was
being demanded, after so much had been taken." For a man approaching his seventieth birthday, whose last bout of long-distance traveling
had brought him close to death, this was another epic trip. He flew first
to Algiers and then on to Naples, where he met with Marshal Tito and
urged him to form a combined front with the Yugoslav king against the
Germans. In rare moments of relaxation, he enjoyed the sunshine, swam,
and visited the islands of Ischia and Capri. But Churchill was never off
duty for long. When his barge encountered a large convoy of US troops
sailing toward the French Riviera to take part in Operation Dragoon, he
passed between the ships flashing his famous V for Victory salute and
receiving their cheers while thinking to himself that "they did not know
that if I had had my way they would be sailing in a different direction."

That did not stop him from wanting to get near the action and, on
August 15, he flew on to Corsica, birthplace of his great hero Napoleon.
On the following day, he boarded a destroyer to watch the American
landings on the French south coast. He was trying to do exactly what
he had not been allowed to do on D-Day, though in the event it proved
an anticlimax. The landings went in fairly easily and, much to his frustration, he was kept out at sea and away from the beaches, reduced
to reading the novel *Berlin Hotel* in the captain's cabin (a work by the
Austrian-born writer Vicki Baum about wartime life in a German hotel).
He described it all in a letter back to Clementine, which is featured on
the next page.

While conceding that the operation had gone like clockwork, he
confirmed his fears "that Eisenhower's operations have been a diversion
to this landing instead of the other way round," expressed his view that
these armies "now cast on shore 400 miles from Paris" should "have
come in at St. Nazaire [on the Atlantic coast] in about a week and greatly
widened the front of our advance with corresponding security against
German movement east of Paris," and ultimately complained that:

We have three armies in the field. The first is fighting under
American command in France, the second under General

PERSONAL

10, Downing Street,
Whitehall.

Italy.

17 August, 1944

My darling.

We have had a busy but delightful time since
we arrived here.   A very comfortable guest-house, formerly
the villa of a wealthy Fascist, now in a concentration
camp, was got ready for us.   I have here been able to
see or entertain all the principal officers of the Army,
also Kathleen Harriman and Dorothy Macmillan.   The few
days we spent in Naples were relieved by a lovely
expedition to the Island of Ischia on the first day, and
the second to Capri.   I thought the Blue Grotto wonderful.
We have had altogether four bathes which have done me all
the good in the world.   I feel greatly refreshed and am
much less tired than when I left England.

On the 14th I flew with two of my party to
Ajaccio.   (Do you remember when we went to see
Napoleon's house there in 1910 ?).   General Wilson and

-1-

First page of letter from Winston to Clementine Churchill, August 17, 1944.
(Baroness Spencer-Churchill Papers, CSCT 2/33/1)

Alexander is relegated to a secondary and frustrated situation by the United States' insistence on this landing on the Riviera. The third on the Burmese frontier is fighting in the most unhealthy country in the world under the worst possible conditions to guard the American air line over the Himalayas into their very over-rated China. Thus two thirds of our forces are being mis-employed for American convenience, and the other third is under American Command.

He also mentioned his ongoing frustrations with de Gaulle, who had refused to meet him, and his fear that a Gaullist France would be very hostile to Britain.

It was just before setting off for Corsica that Churchill revealed to his doctor that he had suffered from a period of depression during his early parliamentary career and that even now he did not like standing near the edge of a railway platform or the side of a ship, where "a second's action would end everything. A few drops of desperation. And yet I don't want to go out of the world at all in such moments." It was perhaps another indication of the stress he was under; another rare admission of his own mortality. Like all such moments, it passed quickly. He was soon set on visiting General Alexander, seeing the front line in Italy, and then traveling to North America to take up the big political and military issues with the president. But the very fact that his focus had switched to Italy is telling. He knew he would be received with full honors and warm hospitality by Alexander (while Montgomery did not drink or smoke) and believed that his voice and his presence could still count for something in the Mediterranean, where British support was vital to Yugoslavia and Greece. It was a recognition that control of the battle for France had passed into other hands.

In Normandy, the final throw of the dice by the German army was to mount a counterattack with most of its remaining panzer units. Operation Lüttich was to be a last throw counterattack from Mortain into the flanks of the US Thirtieth Infantry Division. The aim was to disrupt the US advance and buy time for the Germans to withdraw to the Loire, a move that Hitler had sanctioned. The main attack began early in the morning of August 7 and caught many of the Americans by surprise. The day before, the US Fourth Infantry Division had recorded in its operational log that: "The war looks practically over." But once again it was Allied air superiority that turned the battle. Reconnaissance aircraft had spotted German armor moving in the open to attack the Thirtieth Division. Eighteen squadrons of RAF Typhoon rocket- and cannon-equipped fighters were ordered into a relentless cycle of attack. Piloted by aircrew from a dozen nations, including from France, Australia, and New Zealand, the Germans were pounded from the air and by increasing batteries of artillery firing in support of Thirtieth Division. Worse was to follow for von Kluge as also just before midnight on August 7, Montgomery launched the First Canadian Army on Operation Totalise south toward Falaise. With Patton's US Third Army now threatening the German Seventh Army's supply base: "It was clear," a senior German officer reported, "that this was to be the knockout blow and the end of the army and the whole of the Western Front."

Although many German units still offered stiff resistance, morale was fragile, and ammunition stocks very low. On August 14, von Kluge ordered his troops to break out in a northeasterly direction. On August 15, some 150,000 Allied troops landed largely unopposed in southern France as part of Operation Dragoon, which, at a stroke, changed the strategic landscape. The German occupation of France was nearing its end, but the army was still in the field fighting. In a rather undignified set of exchanges, Montgomery and Bradley failed to coordinate closing the encirclement of the withdrawing Germans as soon as they might have done. Montgomery was initially keen to plan an encirclement of the Germans on the river Seine. He then changed his mind and belatedly ordered the closing of the Falaise Gap, which ensured the near destruction of the German Seventh Army; however, many units had escaped east before the encirclement was complete. On August 21, von Kluge, having been sacked by Hitler, committed suicide. With Field Marshal Model now in command of what was left of German forces in France, Montgomery issued a declaration to the Twenty-first Army Group: "The victory has been definite, complete and decisive.

The Lord mighty in battle has given us the victory." Not all shared that view. Between 20,000 to 30,000 German soldiers, albeit with only about twenty-five tanks, had escaped the encirclement and managed to cross the Seine. Monty's harshest critics were RAF Air Chief Marshal Tedder and Admiral Cunningham who believed that Monty had let too many Germans get away.

The final act of the Normandy Campaign was the advance toward the river Seine and the liberation of Paris. Hitler had ordered the new military commander of the city, Major General von Choltitz, to raze Paris to the ground and defend it from the ruins. Choltitz soon decided that this would serve no military purpose. The issue began to turn more political than military. Patton's Third Army was poised to push toward Paris, with General Philippe Leclerc, urging his army commander to allow the French Second Armored Division to be the first into Paris. Within Paris, tension was mounting between the communists and the Gaullists, while the remaining Germans streamed out of the city. On August 25, von Choltitz, after a final lunch with his senior staff, signed the surrender of Paris in a document presented to him by Leclerc whose troops, along with various US units, had begun to occupy the city earlier that day. De Gaulle arrived in Paris shortly after the surrender. Later he made his famous speech: "Paris. Paris outraged, Paris broken, Paris martyred, but Paris liberated!" And then in the style that would mark his subsequent leadership of France, he continued: "Liberated by herself, liberated by her people, with the help of the whole of France, that is to say of the France which fights, the true France, eternal France." No doubt when Winston Churchill read those words, he must have reflected on his final conversations with Prime Minister Paul Reynaud in Tours on June 13, 1940, shortly before France capitulated. The wheel had come full circle.

Chapter 12

Legacies

*"If we open a quarrel
between the past and the present,
we shall find that we have lost the future."*

THE SUCCESSFUL BREAKOUT IN NORMANDY, WHEN COUPLED WITH the Soviet advances against Germany in the east, led inexorably toward the Allied victory in Europe. The British and American commanders took private bets among themselves on how quickly the war would be over, now a matter of when, not if. But there were plenty of signs that the Germans were not going to give up easily. At the Casablanca Conference in January 1943, Churchill and Roosevelt had very publicly announced that they would only accept unconditional surrender from Germany. Then, it had been a way of signaling to Stalin that they would make no separate peace. But now—as the war in Europe entered its final phase—the policy was arguably helping to prop up the Nazi regime, removing any incentive for the German political and military elites to remove Hitler in the hope of negotiating better terms. Coupled with the failure of the Stauffenberg plot, which had resulted in a purge of the German army, the Nazi grip on power intensified, even as the Allied net closed in.

On Monday, May 15, three weeks before
D-Day, held a final conference in London at
Montgomery's Headquarters in St. Paul's School.
The King, Field-Marshal Smuts, the British
Chiefs of Staff, the commanders of the expedition,
and many of their principal staff officers were
present. On the stage was a map of the
Normandy beaches and the immediate hinterland,
set at a slope so that the audience could see it
clearly, and so constructed that the high
officers explaining the plan could walk about on
it and point out the landmarks. His Majesty
opened proceedings, with a short speech, and I
followed. In the course of my remarks I said,
"I am hardening on this enterprise." General
Eisenhower in his book has taken this to mean
that I had always been against the cross-Channel
operation, but this is not what I meant. Ismay
reminds me that I had often used this expression
to signify that the more I thought about it the
more certain I was of its success. Eisenhower
spoke next, and then Montgomery took the stage
and made an impressive speech. His theme was,
"We have a sufficiency of troops, we have all the
necessary tackle. We have an excellent plan.
This is a perfectly normal operation which is
certain of success. If anyone has any doubts
in his mind, let him stay behind." Perhaps he
had been reading Henry V before Agincourt:

He that hath no stomach for this fight
Let him depart.
His passport shall be made
And crowns for convoys put into his purse.

[Note on plan to follow]

Montgomery was followed by the
administrative staff officers, some of whom
dwelt upon the elaborate preparations that had

Draft of Churchill's text for his war memoirs, c. 1951.
(Churchill Papers, CHUR 4/335/57)

In Britain the V1 flying bombs continued to fall. As the Allies swept through northern France, many of the initial launch sites were overrun, but, after a short break, attacks resumed from Holland. The self-propelled V1 flying bombs were also launched from German aircraft. Countermeasures were deployed; launch sites and suspected production centers were bombed and incoming flying bombs were shot down, but a steady stream of casualties continued, especially in the London area.

Then, on September 8, 1944, four years after the start of the Blitz, the first two V2 rocket bombs fell on London, one of them in Churchill's own constituency of Epping (just to the northeast of the capital). These terrifying new weapons, carrying 1,600 pounds of high explosive, were fast enough to hit without warning, adding a terrifying new dimension to this final, desperate German bombing offensive. Casualties from individual blasts could be high. On November 25, at twenty-six minutes past twelve in the afternoon, a rocket hit a crowded Woolworths store in Deptford, southeast London, killing 168 and injuring nearly as many.

It was only in November, in response to German announcements, that Churchill publicly acknowledged the existence of the new rockets in Parliament, admitting that, "Because of its high speed, no reliable or sufficient public warning can, in present circumstances be given." The government was worried about increasing levels of civilian anxiety. Churchill could take comfort from the intelligence that the Germans could not deliver these weapons in sufficient quantities to cause real terror and dislocation, but he could not be sure that there would not be some last terrible chemical or nuclear surprise.

It was not until March 1945 that the threat to Britain was finally eradicated, with most launch sites captured and any remaining weapons now out of range. Between June 1944 and March 1945, nearly 2,500 V1 flying bombs fell on London, and almost 3,500 on other areas of the country. About six thousand people were killed and more than seventeen thousand injured. Then came the rocket attacks. The British home front was the other front line in the aftermath of D-Day. Servicemen abroad like Tony Hugill were naturally worried about

their families, while the continued attacks only intensified the growing war weariness and desire for peace and reconstruction among the
civilian population.

It is a sentiment that can be seen in this moving letter of February
1945, written from a concerned Chingford family to Churchill, as their
constituency MP, about the menace from the German V2 rockets:

> Do please tell us that some effective steps are being taken to put
> a stop to these murderous German rockets which are daily and
> nightly descending upon us Londoners, killing us and destroying
> our homes.
>
> So far we have had no assurance from any responsible
> Minister that anything is being done about it.
>
> We Londoners can still "take it," but after what we have already
> endured, why should we have to continue to "take it" at this stage
> of the War?

Joan Bright, still working in London as she had done through the
Blitz in 1940, confirmed that "real fear" accompanied the sudden arrival
of the V1s, as they came at a time when people were unprepared for
dangerous interruptions to their daily life. She found herself "always
listening; in the street I wished the traffic would stop, among my friends
that they would not talk, because there might be one approaching."
Then, if one was heard, listening for that terrible moment as the engine
cut out, followed by a "sickening moment of suspense, then 'CRRRRMP'
and silence again."

For Churchill, the last year of the war was not a time for celebration.
He was able to enjoy some peaceful moments that followed in the wake
of the advance of the Allied armies. In a day laden with symbolism, he
walked down the Champs-Élysées and placed a wreath at the Arc de
Triomphe with General de Gaulle on November 11 (Armistice Day from
the war of 1914–1918), their political differences temporarily put aside
in favor of a mutual celebration of victory. His daughter Mary described
the enormous crowds that had gathered in the cold, clear air—"people
had clambered into the trees—and were clinging to the chimney pots."

And later, on March 25, 1945, he triumphantly crossed the Rhine and strode purposefully onto occupied enemy soil.

But most of his time was now taken up with planning for the aftermath. A second Quebec Conference with Roosevelt in September 1944 was followed by a bilateral meeting with Stalin in Moscow in October and the second "Big Three" conference with the president and Stalin at Yalta in February 1945. His focus in all of them was on the impending European settlement. Britain had gone to war for the defense of Poland in 1939, but now the Soviet Red Army dominated the country. To Churchill's disgust, Stalin had refused to come to the aid of the Polish uprising against the Germans in Warsaw in August 1944. It was increasingly clear that the Russian leader favored establishing his own government, rather than allowing back the country's exiled leaders who had based themselves in Britain. Would Poland be lost to the Soviet sphere? What would a future Germany look like and how would it be governed by the victorious Allies? Would Greece and the Balkans be dominated by Moscow?

In April 1945, just before the final collapse of Nazi Germany and Hitler's suicide, came the news of President Roosevelt's death. What should have been a moment of jubilation was marred by uncertainty over the new direction in Washington, DC, and fear of the existing direction in Moscow. Even before the German surrender, Churchill was using terms in his private telegrams like "iron curtain" and "third world war" to refer to the declining international situation with Russia. In May 1945, as most of the country celebrated the end of five and a half long years of conflict, he asked the British chiefs of staff to draw up plans for a limited military campaign against the Soviet Union. Codenamed Operation Unthinkable, the plan considered the possibility of using British, American, Polish, and even some German divisions to overturn the Soviet position in Poland. Unsurprisingly, the conclusion was that it was truly unthinkable and would only have led to a further protracted and total war. Brooke described the whole idea as "fantastic and the chances of success quite impossible."

The plan was based on flawed assumptions. Such an operation would never have enjoyed the support of an American government that still wanted Stalin's help in the war in the Pacific. Nor would it have been supported at home. Public opinion in Britain and America still saw the Soviet Union as an ally, and one that had sacrificed much in defeating Germany. Churchill's plan was a nonstarter and remained secret until the end of the twentieth century, but it was revealing of the extent of his fears about the Soviet Union.

Change was in the air. Joan Bright took charge of the British administrative arrangements for the Washington, Quebec, Moscow, Yalta, and Potsdam summits, attending them all. In 1940, it would have been very rare for a woman to travel outside the country as part of an official delegation, and almost inconceivable that she would find herself in such a position of authority. At Yalta, Joan even pretended to be a major general in order to be taken seriously by the rank-conscious Russians (for contrast, the highest military rank achieved by Churchill was lieutenant colonel in 1916!).

Early 1945 was a period of rising international tension within the alliance, combined with war weariness and a growing desire for change at home. There had not been a general election in Britain since 1935, and the existence of the national coalition government had meant that there had been few outlets for real political opposition to Churchill's administration. The success of D-Day led to victory in Europe in May 1945, but it also led just as inexorably to the end of the wartime coalition and to the resumption of normal party-political strife. In the final months of the war in Europe, clear differences were emerging between the Conservative and Labour Parties. Churchill, his own health weakened, was finding it harder to manage the domestic political landscape. Condemned by the Labour Party for his policy of supporting the nationalists in Greece and attacked by his own Conservative backbenchers for not doing more for Poland, he remained determined to see the job through to completion and to finish the war in the Pacific, but—like all British prime ministers—he had to think about the optimum timing for a general election. Was it better to move quickly and hold an election in the immediate aftermath of victory in Europe, hoping to benefit from a victory bounce in the polls, or should he try to continue the coalition until after the defeat of Japan. In the case of Japan? the Allies were not yet certain of the atom bomb, and final victory might be a costly and protracted affair. In the end, his hand was forced. Both the rank and file of the opposition Labour Party and many of his senior Conservative political colleagues favored a quick election. It was clear that his coalition would not last.

Churchill tendered his resignation to the king on May 23, only a fortnight after VE Day, and was tasked with forming a caretaker government while the election campaign was conducted and the votes counted. Polling took place on July 5, but the additional difficulty of counting the large number of overseas service votes meant that the result of the ballot was not declared until July 26. The result was a Labour landslide, a majority of 146. Churchill was out.

To Mary Churchill, who was with her father in his Map Room as the results came in, this was a terrible humiliation and betrayal:

> Hot tears came & had to be hidden. Everyone looked grave and dazed. We lunched in Stygian gloom.

General Brooke, not always Churchill's greatest admirer, thought it a "ghastly mistake to start elections at this period in the World's history!" and the next day, when meeting with Churchill and the chiefs of staff, he almost broke down at "a very sad and very moving little meeting."

To Joan Bright, "They had not rejected Winston Churchill, they had rejected war and its leadership. He would remain for all time one of their greatest Englishmen; they would always be in his debt."

Clementine Churchill had a slightly different take. For her, this was a "blessing in disguise." She feared that if her husband continued in office, the continued burden might have killed him. It elicited the characteristically blunt reply from Churchill that it was "certainly very well disguised." Yet he put a brave face on the defeat. When Michael Parish, a friend of Mary's, told him he had won the race, he replied with a suitable horse racing analogy, "And in consequence I've been warned off the turf."

There are of course many complex reasons why Churchill lost the 1945 election, but there are a few that relate directly to the themes of this book.

The first is the impact of events on his own health. By the beginning of 1944, Churchill had already served as prime minister for three and a half years. The physical toll of holding high office for so long was inevitable and by the end of the war he did have recurring heart and respiratory problems. His sense of frustration and anxiety was at its highest during the enforced period of preparation immediately prior to D-Day. He chafed against being able to influence the military strategy, worried about the likely levels of Allied military and French civilian casualties, and wrestled with the difficulties of putting a country into virtual lockdown to facilitate and protect the Overlord operation. His energy levels never seem to have fully recovered, and this surely contributed to a lackluster and ill-judged performance in the election campaign. His decision to attack the Labour Party, rather than sitting above the political fray, allowed his opponents to exploit a distinction between Churchill the war leader and Churchill the party politician.

A second factor was the contribution of Overlord to the already changing mood of the British electorate. In the buildup to June 6, 1944, they had endured unprecedented levels of restriction to their daily lives—forbidden from visiting certain areas of the country, their internal travel restricted, their homes blacked out, food rationed, their mail censored, and the countryside turned over to barracks, bases, and airfields. The assault on Europe brought with it further separation and loss; it also brought direct retaliation through the onslaught of the V-weapons and the return of terror from the skies. All this reinforced a natural tendency to want to rebuild a better postwar world; one that would make such sacrifices worthwhile. Both Mary and Sarah Churchill, Winston's daughters, were serving in uniform. They sensed this mood in the young people surrounding them. Churchill apparently did not. Lord Moran recalled a conversation:

> "There are two opposing ideas in the country," I said to him. "There's pretty universal gratitude to you, and there's a notion about that you aren't very keen on this brave-new-world business." Winston answered: "The desire for a new world is nothing like universal; the gratitude is."

Churchill was wrong. He was too focused on his new fight against the Soviet Union to realize that not everyone shared his single-minded focus on the international scene.

But D-Day also weakened Churchill because it took the focus away from him. In 1940, Britain was on the defensive and under attack. Then, Churchill had harnessed the wider government information machine and used a series of set piece broadcasts to rally morale, establishing himself as a visual representation of the people's resistance. In 1944, it was not possible to do this. To broadcast in advance of D-Day risked giving away that the invasion was imminent; to do so immediately afterward risked compromising the deception plans that hinted that the Allies were yet to do more. Besides, this was now a multinational operation, and one that was increasingly dominated by the Americans. He lacked the freedom to speak about the military operation without coordinating his words through Roosevelt, the Combined Chiefs of Staff, and Eisenhower.

Churchill was not the contemporary voice of D-Day. Moreover, by the time he came to write about it—in volumes V and VI of his multi-volume history *The Second World War,* published respectively in 1952 and 1954—he was on the back foot, meaning he felt defensive—having to respond to suggestions already in print that he had never been a whole-hearted supporter of the operation. The race to publish had started as soon as the war had ended. Harry Butcher, Ike's naval aide, had published *Three Years with Eisenhower* in 1946. Read in full, the book is generally admiring of Churchill, but it included some very unflattering vignettes. An entry for August 26, 1942, recounts a report from General Clark regarding a meeting with the prime minister at which Churchill smashed a glass, changed his socks in front of guests, and later walked to the open door, put his back to its edge, vigorously rubbed his shoulder blades [sic] against it, and said: "Guess I picked 'em up in Egypt."

More damaging, perhaps, were the allegations in Eisenhower's own book, *Crusade in Europe,* published in 1948, that Churchill feared the seas would run red with blood and that the British leader was a late convert to Overlord, having announced as late as May 15 that he was "hardening toward this enterprise," suggesting of course that he had been soft on it up to that date. Then there was Alan Moorehead's biography of Montgomery, also published in 1946, which annoyed Churchill by recounting details of the prime minister's visit to Montgomery's headquarters on May 19, publishing their disagreement over Churchill's attempt to interrogate the staff and the general's threat to resign. As Moorehead had been given access to Montgomery's own papers, this led to a somewhat awkward postwar exchange between Churchill and Monty.

The fact that Churchill chose to respond to these issues in his own history showed how much these attacks had wounded him. But he also had to be careful how he responded. By the time he published, he was back in 10 Downing Street, Eisenhower was president of the United States, and Montgomery was NATO's Deputy Supreme Commander in Europe. He needed to work with both men and did not want a public row about the past. In his "Finest Hour" speech of June 18, 1940, he had warned that "if we open a quarrel between the past and the present, we shall find that we have lost the future." So, he was diplomatic in what he wrote, downplaying the disagreements. By "hardening on this operation," he had meant "wishing to strike if humanly possible"; and at no time did Montgomery threaten to resign and "nothing in the nature of a confrontation with his staff took place."

Churchill's protestations probably only added to stories of his wobbling over D-Day. Over time, more information was released about the debates at the top. The memoirs of General Brooke (later Lord Alanbrooke), General de Gaulle, Lord Moran, and Sir Alexander Cadogan added to a growing publication list, which was then further fueled by releases of more official records.

This book has not set out to exonerate all that Churchill did. It is impossible to know with certainty whether better or worse results could have been achieved if the British and American allies had followed a different strategy. What we have aimed to do is to put Churchill's decisions and actions in context and to show the many factors and individuals that colored his approach to this critical operation.

He was undoubtedly influenced by the First World War and a desire to avoid a repeat of the huge bloodshed of the trench stalemate in France, which would have been catastrophic for the country and almost certainly fatal to his own administration.

He was determined to preserve the British Empire. Any British prime minister in 1940 would have been forced to think about the defense of Egypt, Malta, and Palestine, and of routes to Canada, India, South Africa, Australia, and New Zealand, but Churchill was particularly driven by a desire not to preside over the Empire's liquidation and his Mediterranean and Balkan policies had both a clear imperial and anti-Soviet dimension. This was certainly a factor in Churchill's desire to keep fighting in these theaters, even after the final decision had been taken to attack in northwest France, and explains why he resented the "tyranny of Overlord."

Yet, for all this, as he told his friend Smuts, he regarded the relationship with the United States and the commitment to Overlord as the "keystone of arch of Anglo-American co-operation." The major decisions were discussed with Roosevelt and the Combined Chiefs of Staff and taken for sound strategic reasons. Operations in North Africa and Sicily took on their own momentum and further delayed D-Day, but they were launched because the preconditions for an assault on Normandy had not yet been met, because the risks of a frontal assault in France were deemed too high, and because to do nothing while preparing to attack France was politically and militarily unacceptable. The Battle of the Atlantic had to be won, mastery of the skies obtained, and the enemy isolated and weakened.

On D-Day itself, Churchill—in spite of his best efforts to get himself a front-row seat on board a British ship—had to wait for news of the battle in London. There is no doubt that the buildup to the launch had been a particularly stressful time. He did not have the same reserves of energy as in 1940, but neither was he a nervous wreck. The weeks leading up to Overlord saw him taking an active interest in all aspects of the operation and using his convening power to ensure that production targets were met and security was maintained. Though often portrayed as a warmonger, one of his consistent concerns had been to minimize military and French civilian casualties. Yes, he drove the War Cabinet and the chiefs of staff to distraction, challenging them on the number of vehicles, railing against de Gaulle, and refused to back down on his opposition to the bombing of the marshaling yards, but he did so out of a concern to reduce losses and ensure success. Surely that was his job?

Nowadays, Churchill is rarely talked about in connection with D-Day. The focus tends to be on his role in the events of 1940. Sometimes, he is mentioned in connection with his role in developing the Mulberry harbors; more often he is criticized for trying to delay or obstruct the operation. What we hope we have shown is that he played a key role in the timing and nature of Overlord. He was certainly not standing alone; he was working with others (not always harmoniously) and his moods and motivations shifted with events, but he played a vital role in creating the alliances and the framework that facilitated the liberation of France.

With hindsight, we can say that D-Day was successful. Churchill, Eisenhower, and the other commanders could not be so sure at the time. This was an enormous operation upon which so much depended. Surely, Churchill can be forgiven for hedging slightly and for not wanting to put all his eggs in one basket. Ultimately, Overlord can only be judged by its success, and Churchill was one of its architects.

And what of some of the others? Hughes-Hallett finished his career in 1954 as a vice admiral. Tony Hugill went on to marry one of Admiral Ramsay's Wrens, using the advance from his wartime memoirs to fund the engagement ring. Both Christian Oldham and Joan Bright gave up their jobs after marriage in accordance with the conventions of the time. Geoffrey Pyke continued to think outside the box but enjoyed little success. His suicide in 1948 prompted the *Times* newspaper to describe him as "one of the most original if unrecognised figures of the present century." Percy Hobart retired from the army. Churchill wrote an unsuccessful letter of reference for him to become the Chichele Professor of War at Oxford University. Basil Liddell Hart continued to enjoy a successful career as a historian and military commentator. The Liddell Hart Center for Military Archives at King's College, London is named for him and houses his papers alongside those of Alanbrooke, Ironside, and others. Jock Colville became Private Secretary to Princess Elizabeth, the future Elizabeth II, before returning to Downing Street to serve Churchill again as his Joint Principal Private Secretary from

1951 to 1955. Roland MacKenzie went home to Canada, resumed his career in banking, and rarely talked about his war. Stan Hollis became a publican. TL Rodgers was temporarily buried in a cemetery in France. His remains were eventually returned to Covington County, Alabama, where he was laid to rest in the family plot at the Carolina Baptist Church Cemetery. Their stories, like Churchill's, are all threads in the bigger tapestry.

Which brings us back to Churchill College in Cambridge. And to another work of art hanging on the wall, this time in the main library. In 1961, General de Gaulle presented the College with a large, magnificent, and colorful tapestry by the artist Jean Lurçat called *Etoile de Paris* (Star of Paris). Rich in imagery, the work celebrates the liberation of the French capital from the Germans in 1944. Sewn into the fabric, in a top corner, is the phrase *"Paris, soi-meme liberé"* (Paris liberated itself). While recognizing the role of de Gaulle and the French resistance, as well as the literal truth of French troops being allowed to enter the city first, Churchill would surely have disagreed. There were many threads that led to the successful liberation of France. He had played a key role in pulling them together.

If all Winston Churchill's worries and fears about launching a land invasion of Europe from Southern England could be summed up in one short sentence, it was the remark he made to his beloved Clemmie on the evening of June 5, 1944:

Do you realise that by the time you wake in the morning 20,000 men may have been killed?

These were the "black dog" anxieties borne of the scars and memories of Gallipoli in 1915–1916, of the ineptitude of the 1940 Norway Campaign, and of the 1942 disaster at Dieppe. Responsibility, not just for the security of the nation, but for other men's lives, weighed very heavily on Churchill's shoulders. Of the 133,000 men and women who landed on June 6, 1944, there were around 11,000 casualties of which some 3,800 were killed in the first twenty-four hours. Among the fatalities, there were just under a thousand British soldiers, sailors, airmen, and marine commandos. But as this narrative has described, June 6, 1944, was but the first of the ninety days of the Normandy Campaign. By the time the river Seine had been crossed and Paris liberated, there had been around a quarter of a million Allied casualties with nearly 45,000 British, US, Canadian, and Polish soldiers killed among the ground forces and a further 16,000 deaths among the Allied air and naval forces. The French civil population suffered about 12,000 dead or injured. The German army reported around 320,000 casualties of which about 150,000 became prisoners. The price in both blood and treasure for all sides was very high. Eighty years on to younger generations, that figure looks extraordinary, totally unbelievable.

D-Day has become a major landmark, not just in the accounts of the Second World War, but as a turning point in global history. Until the western Allies were able to return to France and pose the dilemma to the Germans of a war on two fronts in Europe, it is conceivable that Nazi Germany could have held its Eastern Front and prevented further Soviet expansion westward. In those circumstances, the Europe of today would have looked very different—a communist east and a national socialist west. It was by the steadfast determination of the western Allies, led by Britain, that Germany must be defeated first and then Japan second that brought about the successful conclusion of the Second World War. From standing isolated and alone in June 1940 and facing defeat, Churchill had orchestrated a successful alliance with the democratic United States and an accommodation with Stalin's communist Soviet Union such that the tyranny of German national socialism and Italian fascism could be expunged from Europe. Normandy was the turning point.

To the dismay of the British veterans who had fought in Normandy and to the disappointment of the families of those who had fought and fallen in the campaign to begin the liberation of Europe, until 2021 Britain had no memorial in Normandy to mark the service and sacrifice of those who fought from the landing beaches to the river Seine. Very belatedly this national omission has been corrected. The British Memorial in Normandy now stands on the coast by the village of Ver-sur-Mer on a site overlooking Gold Beach, where Stan

Hollis stormed ashore with his Green Howards comrades, and near Arromanches, through whose Mulberry harbor so much of the vital logistics flowed to sustain the campaign. The memorial includes the names of the 22,442 servicemen and -women, from more than twenty nations, who died during the Normandy Campaign under British command. And there is also a memorial to the French civilians who died in the fighting so that their country and Europe could be free. *"Liberte, egalite, fraternite"*—the national motto of the French. The memorial provides a quiet space to reflect on the sacrifice of those who died to bring peace and freedom to Europe. And it also tells the story of the British leadership of the Normandy Campaign—the strategic and political leadership of Winston Churchill, the operational leadership of Bernard Montgomery, and the determined tactical leadership on the battlefield of thousands of fighters like Stan Hollis.

Codenames and Acronyms

Codenames

ANVIL Initial codename for Allied liberation of south of France

ARCADIA Washington, DC, Conference, December 22, 1941–January 14, 1942

BAGRATION Soviet offensive on the Eastern Front, June–August 1944

BARBAROSSA German invasion of the Soviet Union, June 1941

BLUECOAT British offensive around Caen, July–August 1944

BODYGUARD Overarching codename for all deception plans to protect Allied liberation of Normandy in 1944

BOLERO Buildup of American forces in the United Kingdom

BOMBARDON Interlocking steel crosses used to construct artificial harbors

BONIFACE Cover name used to protect intelligence obtained from breaking the German codes

CHARIOT British raid against docks at St. Nazaire, March 1942

COBRA US offensive in Normandy, July 1944

COCKADE Overarching codename for a series of Allied deception operations in 1943

DRAGOON Final codename for Allied liberation of south of France, August 1944

DYNAMO Evacuation of British and French forces from Dunkirk, May–June 1940

EPSOM British offensive in Normandy, June 1944

EUREKA Tehran Conference, November 28–December 1, 1943

FORTITUDE NORTH Deception designed to suggest an Allied attack in Scandinavia, 1944; part of Bodyguard

FORTITUDE SOUTH Deception designed to suggest a second Allied landing in the Pas-de-Calais region of France, 1944. Part of Bodyguard

GOLD Beach between Arromanches-les-Bains and La Rivière, taken by the British in June 1944

GOODWOOD British attempt to break out of Normandy, July 1944

GOOSEBERRY An artificial breakwater

GYMNAST Initial British codename for operation against French North Africa

HABBAKUK Proposal to construct aircraft carriers from a floating ice/wood pulp mix known as Pykrete. Not implemented

HILLMAN German strongpoint defending Caen

HUSKY Allied operation against Sicily, July 1943

JUBILEE Unsuccessful British and Canadian raid on Dieppe, August 19, 1942

JUNO Beach between La Rivière and Saint-Aubin-sur-Mer, taken by the British and Canadians, June 1944

JUPITER British codename for proposed operation against northern Norway. Not undertaken

LILO Proposal for artificial breakwater created by piped air. Not implemented

LÜTTICH German counterattack near Mortain, August 1944

MINCEMEAT Deception plan involving documents planted on a dead body used to protect Allied landings in Sicily, April 1943

MORRIS German strongpoint defending Caen

MULBERRY An artificial harbor

NEPTUNE The naval operation to bring forces across the Channel, June 1944

OMAHA Beach between Vierville-sur-Mer and Colleville-sur-Mer, taken by the Americans, June 1944

OVERLORD The overarching codename for the Allied liberation of France via Normandy, June 1944

PHOENIX Large, hollow concrete units sunk to form artificial harbors and breakwaters

POINTBLANK Allied campaign for the strategic bombing of German military, industrial, and economic targets, 1943–1944

QUADRANT Quebec Conference, August 17–24, 1943

ROUNDUP Initial codename for large-scale Allied operation in Europe

RUTTER Superseded plan for operation against Dieppe, 1942

SLEDGEHAMER Codename for proposed Allied operation in France, 1942–1943

STARKEY Deception involving a large-scale, feigned attack against Boulogne, August—September 1943. Part of COCKADE

SWORD Beach between Saint-Aubin-sur-Mer and the Orne River, taken by the British, June 1944

SYMBOL Casablanca Conference, January 14 and 24, 1943

TENTACLE Proposed artificial floating runway. Not implemented

TIGER Large-scale rehearsal exercise for D-Day, April 1944

TINDALL Deception suggesting sailing of five divisions from Scotland against Stavangar in Norway, 1943

TORCH Final codename for Allied landings in French North Africa, November 1942

TOTALISE Canadian attempt to break out in Normandy, August 1944

TRIDENT Washington, DC, Conference, May 12–25, 1943

ULTRA Signals intelligence obtained by breaking German codes

UNTHINKABLE Plan for proposed military operation against the Soviet Union, May 1945. Not undertaken

UTAH Beach between St. Martin de Varreville and Pouppeville, taken by the Americans, June 1944

WADHAM Deception suggesting assault by two American divisions on Brittany, 1943

WESERÜBUNG German invasion of Denmark and Norway, April 1940

WHALE Steel pierheads and floating roadways used in artificial harbors

Acronyms and Terms Requiring Explanation

ADC Aide de Camp, a term for a personal assistant to a senior officer

BEF British Expeditionary Force

CAC Churchill Archives Centre, Churchill College, Cambridge

CIGS Chief of the Imperial General Staff (head of the British Army)

COHQ Combined Operations Headquarters

COS Chiefs of Staff

COSSAC Chief of Staff to Supreme Allied Commander

CSM Company Sergeant Major

D-DAY The day on which an operation commences. The D stands for day.

DD TANKS Amphibious duplex-drive tanks used by the Allies on D-Day

DUKW A six-wheel-drive amphibious vehicle

E-BOAT Small, fast, armed German attack ships

FUSAG First United States Army Group

H-HOUR The hour an operation commences. The H stands for hour.

LCS London Controlling Section (unit planning deception operations)

MI Military Intelligence

MI (R) Military Intelligence (Research)

MI5 Security Service of the United Kingdom, concerned with counterterrorism and home security

MI6 Special Intelligence Service of the United Kingdom, concerned with foreign intelligence

MP Member of Parliament

NCO Non-Commissioned Officer

PLUTO Pipeline under the ocean used to supply oil across the Channel

PWE Political Warfare Executive, responsible for British propaganda and damaging enemy morale

SHAEF Supreme Headquarters Allied Expeditionary Force

SOE Special Operations Executive, responsible for guerilla operations behind enemy lines

TNA The National Archives, Kew

U-BOAT German submarine

V1 A German pilotless flying bomb. The V stands for Vergeltungswaffe (vengeance weapon)

V2 A German rocket-powered missile

WREN Member of Women's Royal Naval Service

Allied Army Units

BATTALION Up to one thousand men, divided into companies and normally commanded by a lieutenant colonel

REGIMENT A permanent organizational unit within the army, normally divided into battalions and commanded by a colonel. Regiments will be combined for operational purposes to form brigades and divisions as circumstances require. In the British Army, the term *regiment* has two meanings. The peacetime organization of the infantry is within regiments, which can have many battalions. These battalions fight within brigades (see below). The second meaning applies to artillery, engineer, signal, and some logistic units, which are called "regiments" in the same way that the infantry refers to battalions.

BRIGADE Composed of two or more battalions or regiments and normally commanded by a brigadier or brigadier general

DIVISION Composed of several regiments or brigades and normally commanded by a major-general

CORPS Composed of two or more divisions and normally commanded by a lieutenant general

Acknowledgments

The letters and diary of King George VI are reproduced with permission from His Majesty King Charles III. Quotes from the speeches, works, and writings of Sir Winston Churchill are reproduced with permission of Broadwater Collection, London, on behalf of The Estate of Winston S. Churchill. © The Estate of Winston S. Churchill. The work contains public sector information licensed under the Open Government Licence v3.0 and parliamentary copyright materials licensed under the Open Parliament Licence v3.0. Images of documents from the Churchill Papers collection are reproduced with the permission of the Sir Winston Churchill Archive Trust. Images and quotations from other collections at the Churchill Archives Centre are reproduced with the permission of Churchill College, Cambridge, and the relevant copyright holders where known. Extracts from the Diaries of Sir Alan Lascelles are published here with grateful acknowledgment to and permission of the Estate of Sir Alan Lascelles. Substantial quotations from secondary sources are reproduced with the permission of the relevant copyright holders where known. In particular, thanks are due to the Trustees of the Alanbrooke Estate, David Eisenhower, Christian Lamb, the daughters of Hugh Lunghi, Roddy MacKenzie, the grandchildren of Admiral Sir Bertram Ramsay, Charles Tilbury, The Wavell Estate, and James Wilson. Quotes from *The Deception Planners: My Secret War* by Dennis Wheatley reprinted by permission of Peters Fraser & Dunlop (www.petersfraserdunlop.com) on behalf of the Estate of Dennis Wheatley.

The authors would like to thank Charlie Viney of the Viney Agency and Gordon Wise of Broadwater Collection. David Boler and Amanda Jones were kind enough to read the manuscript. Christopher Knowles at Churchill Archives Centre copied many of the images, Christian Lamb was kind enough to talk about her wartime experiences, and Russell Riley suggested the inclusion of his relative TL Rodgers.

Notes

Chapter 1: Hindsight Is a Wonderful Thing

1 "Are you going to lay there and get killed, or get up and do something about it?" United States Army, Center of Military History, https://history.army.mil/books/wwii/100-11/ch4.htm.

3 "I have also to announce to the House . . ." Churchill's statement to the House of Commons, June 6, 1944, Hansard, series 5, vol. 400, cc1207-11.

5 "The immense cross-Channel enterprise for the liberation of France had begun . . ." Churchill, W.S., The Second World War, vol.5, p.558.

14 "Without the title deeds of positive achievement no one had the power . . ." Churchill, W.S., The World Crisis, vol 2, p.498.

14 "The landing under cover of the guns of the Fleet . . .' A copy of the original paper can be found in the Churchill Acquired Papers at Churchill Archives Centre, CAC, Churchill Acquired Papers, CHAQ 1/5/3. An edited version is published in Churchill, W.S., The Second World War, vol. 2, p.215.

15 "the fearful price we had had to pay in human life and blood for the great offensives of the First World War was graven in my mind." Churchill, W.S., The Second World War, vol.5, p.514.

16 "essentially a government of committees . . ." Hastings, M., Finest Years: Churchill as Warlord, p.xx.

17 "In view of the many accounts which are extant and multiplying of my supposed aversion from any kind of large-scale opposed-landing . . ." Churchill, W.S., The Second World War, vol.2, p224.

Chapter 2: Dealing with Defeat

19 "He spoke in English, and evidently under stress." Churchill, W.S., The Second World War, vol.2, p.38.

20 "After this Norway breakdown there is of course a lot of criticism . . ." Unpublished diary of Leo Kennedy, May 4. 1940. CAC, Leo Kennedy Papers, LKEN 1/23.

21 "Churchill was so much larger in every way than his colleagues . . ." Wheeler-Bennett, J. (ed) Action This Day: Working with Churchill, p.161.

25 "Amphibious operations are a very specialised form of warfare . . ." Ismay, H., The Memoirs of General the Lord Ismay, p.120.

27 "almost impossible task . . . with absolute loyalty and apparent sincerity . . ." Nicolson, H., Harold Nicolson: Diaries and Letters 1930–1964, p.181.

31 "not to assign to this deliverance the attributes of a victory. Wars are not won by evacuations." Churchill, W.S. (ed), Never Give In, p.214.

33 "his confidence that Hitlerism would be smashed . . ." CAC, Churchill Papers, CHAR 23/2.

34 "However matters may go in France or with the French Government . . ." CAC, Churchill Papers, CHAR 9/140A, also reproduced in Churchill, W.S. (ed), Never Give In, pp.228-9.

36 "Today came the announcement that following Reynaud's resignation . . ." Soames, E. (ed), Mary Churchill's War, p.37.

37 "The completely defensive habit of mind which has ruined the French . . ." Churchill, W.S., The Second World War, vol. 2, p.214.

38 "With a shorthand pad and typewriter I could be a valuable . . ." Bright Astley, J., The Inner Circle, p.13.

Chapter 3: Arguments with Allies

43 "No lover ever studied every whim of his mistress as I did those of President Roosevelt." Colville, J., The Fringes of Power, p.624.

43 "Never in the field of human conflict was so much owed by so many to so few." CAC, Churchill Papers, CHAR 9/141A, also published in Churchill, W.S. (ed), Never Give In, p.245.

44 "If Hitler invaded Hell, I would at least make a favourable reference to the Devil in the House of Commons." Churchill, W.S., The Second World War, vol.3, p.331.

45 "So we had won after all!" Churchill, W.S., The Second World War, vol.3, p.539.

49 "What Harry and Geo. Marshall will tell you about has my heart & mind in it." CAC, Churchill Papers, CHAR 20/52/29.

49 "his lips are blanched as if he had been bleeding internally . . ." Moran, Lord, Winston Churchill: The Struggle for Survival 1940–1965, p.12.

50 "very upright man . . ." From unpublished transcript of interview with Joan Bright Astley. CAC, Brendon Papers, BREN 1/12.

52 "Western Europe is favoured as the theatre . . ." CAC, Churchill Papers, CHAR 20/52/33.

53 "our soldiers seem very incapable . . ." Dilks, D. (ed), The Diaries of Sir Alexander Cadogan, pp.432–33.

54 "Well I think 1942 was a horrible year . . ." From unpublished transcript of interview with Joan Bright Astley. CAC, Brendon Papers, BREN 1/12.

54 "he had no hesitation in cordially accepting the plan." TNA, Cabinet Office, Defence Committee (Operations) minutes, CAB 69/4.

56 "Unless we are prepared to commit the immense forces . . ." TNA, Prime Minister's Office, PREM 3/333/2.

57   "The Red Army is carrying the brunt of the battle." Butcher, H., Three Years with Eisenhower, p.7.

59   "he was the man to see first . . ." Butcher, H., Three Years with Eisenhower, p.20.

60   "owing to a recent re-estimate of the number of landing craft . . ." TNA, Prime Minister's Office, PREM 3/333/1.

63   "Mr. Churchill suddenly turned to me . . ." Memoir of Vice-Admiral John Hughes-Hallett. CAC, HHLT. Published as From Dieppe to D-Day, p.45.

64   "they were going to have to be very, very good." Kennedy, P., Engineers of Victory, p. 234.

64   Operation Jubilee box—". . . the very last thing they'd (the Germans) ever imagine is that we would be so stupid as to lay on the same operation again." Ziegler, P., Mountbatten, p.346.

67   "I do not like the job I have to do . . ." Humphrys, O., Ballade of the Second Front by General Wavell, Wavell in Russia, p.83.

68   "Stalin appeared quite at home . . ." CAC, Jacob Papers, JACB 1/16.

72   "preparing forces and assembling landing craft in England for a thrust across the Channel." TNA, Cabinet Office, Record of conference held at Casablanca, CAB 99/24.

74   "as the codeword implies, a landing to "round up" any German units . . ." Wheatley, D., The Deception Planners, p.122.

Chapter 4: Preconditions for Success

79   "all right if you won't play with us in the Mediterranean . . ." Danchev, A. & Todman, D. (eds), War Diaries 1939–1945: Field Marshal Lord Alanbrooke, p.472.

80   "There followed months of toil in an atmosphere of persisting doubt and uncertainty . . ." Morgan, F., Peace and War, p.155.

80   "A German collapse being extremely unlikely and not to be counted upon this year . . ." TNA, Prime Minister's Office, PREM 3/333/4.

80   "the creation of this vast complicated staff . . ." TNA, Prime Minister's Office, PREM 3/333/15.

81   "To this end the Combined Chiefs of Staff will endeavour to assemble . . ." Morgan, F., Peace and War, p.156.

86   "earned for himself the reputation in his own service of being "sold out to the British"...' Morgan, F., Peace and War, pp.158–59.

88   "whole basis of our higher organization was new . . ." Eisenhower, D., Crusade in Europe, p.99.

89   "The only thing that ever really frightened me during the war was the U-boat peril . . ." Churchill, W.S., The Second World War, vol.2, p.529.

90   "I had a feeling once about Mathematics, that I saw it all . . ." Churchill, W.S., My Early Life, p.27.

91   "How willingly would I have exchanged a full-scale attempt at invasion . . ." Churchill, W.S., The Second World War, vol.3, pp.100–1.

92   "We had to win the Battle of the Atlantic. Losing it would mean losing the war altogether." Lamb, C., Beyond the Sea: A Wren at War, p.119.

92   "measures to be taken to combat the submarine menace are a first charge . . ." TNA, Cabinet Office, Record of conference held at Casablanca, CAB 99/24.

93   "Signal after signal came in and the teleprinter buzzed on relentlessly." Lamb, C., Beyond the Sea: A Wren at War, p.184.

94   "That there must be a substantial reduction in the strength of the German fighter aircraft . . ." Churchill, W.S., The Second World War, vol.5, p.69.

96   "By February 1944, the Allies own analysis was that . . ." Figures taken from a paper of 1 March 1944. CAC, Bufton Papers, BUFT 3/44.

96   "29 years old, 5 foot ten . . ." MacKenzie, R., Bomber Command: Churchill's Greatest Triumph, p.28.

97   "Through Adversity to the Stars . . ." MacKenzie, R., Bomber Command: Churchill's Greatest Triumph, p.135.

98   "I deem it my duty to warn you in the strongest possible manner . . ." TNA, Prime Minister's Office, PREM 3/333/3.

98   "so very conscious of the poor contribution . . ." TNA, Prime Minister's Office, PREM 3/333/3.

99   "That there should not be more than twelve mobile German divisions . . ." Churchill, W.S., The Second World War, vol.5, p.69.

101   Figures for landing craft taken from Roskill, S.W, 'The War at Sea,' vol.3 part 2, p.19 & Barnett, C., Engage the Enemy More Closely, pp 813–14.

102   "We have victory—a remarkable and definite victory . . ." Churchill, W.S. (ed), Never Give In, p.341.

105   "Sicily, Salerno, Shrapnel Pass, the Plains of Naples . . ." Carter, R.S., Those Devils in Baggy Pants, p.159.

106   "this operation could be fitted in to our plan without detriment . . ." CAC, Churchill Papers, CHAR 20/120/45-46.

106   "Strategically, if we get the Aegean Islands . . ." CAC, Churchill Papers, CHAR 20/120/59-60.

110   "We have now been five days here . . ." Letter from Winston to Clementine Churchill, November 26, 1943. CAC, Baroness Spencer-Churchill Papers, CSCT 2/32. Published in Soames, M., Speaking for Themselves, pp.487–88.

111   "I hope you will realize that British loyalty to Overlord is keystone . . ." Churchill, W.S., The Second World War, vol.5, p.116.

111   "There I sat with the great Russian bear on one side of me . . ." Wheeler-Bennett, J. (ed), Action This Day, p.96.

Chapter 5: Bodyguard of Lies

115   "In wartime . . . truth is so precious that she should always be attended by a bodyguard of lies." Churchill, W.S., The Second World War, vol.5, p.338.

122   "I was given a carpet, a long polished table, wall maps, an easy chair . . ." Bright Astley, J., The Inner Circle, p.66.

123 "but with a strange quietness about his movements . . ." Wheatley, D., The Deception Planners, p.20.

125 "nearly everyone we approached scarcely bothered to conceal the fact that he thought this new-fangled deception racket a lot of nonsense." Wheatley, D., The Deception Planners, p.84.

131 "in order to deceive and baffle the enemy . . ." CAC, Churchill Papers, CHAR 9/204A/79.

Chapter 6: Mulberries and Gooseberries

133 "Gentlemen, I am hardening on this operation." Churchill, W.S., The Second World War, vol.5, pp.542–43.

136 "He was very breathless and anxious-looking . . ." Moran, C., Winston Churchill: The Struggle for Survival 1940–1965, p.151.

136 "Don't worry, it doesn't matter if I die now . . ." Churchill, S., A Thread in the Tapestry, p.77.

137 "When he [Montgomery] arrived at Marrakesh . . ." Churchill, W.S., The Second World War, vol.5, p.393.

138 "very serious criticism that the proposal to move so many divisions . . ." CAC, Churchill Papers, CHAR 20/179/15-17.

144 "A sufficient number of flat-bottomed barges or caissons . . ." A copy of the original paper can be found in the Churchill Acquired Papers at Churchill Archives Centre, CAC, Churchill Acquired Papers, CHAQ 1/5/3. An edited version is published in Churchill, W.S., The Second World War, vol. 2, p.216.

145 "They must float up & down on the tide . . ." CAC, Churchill Additional Papers, WCHL 13/4. Also published in Churchill, W.S., The Second World War, vol.5, p.66 with original document reproduced as an excerpt.

145 "we ought to have three or four miles of this pier tackle." TNA, Prime Minister's Office, PREM 3/216/1.

146 "This matter is being much neglected . . ." TNA, Prime Minister's Office, PREM 3/216/1.

146 "On Sunday, June 20, I went with Brian Egerton and Richard Fenning . . ." Memoir of Vice-Admiral John Hughes-Hallett. CAC, HHLT. Published as From Dieppe to D-Day, p.107.

147 "Our Army boys . . . are determined to have a port of their own . . ." Memoir of Vice-Admiral John Hughes-Hallett. CAC, HHLT. Published as From Dieppe to D-Day, p.118.

154 "to fit up a number of steam tractors with small, armoured shelters . . ." CAC, Churchill Papers, CHAR 2/103/53-56.

155 "A man of quite exceptional mental attainments . . ." CAC, Churchill Papers, CHAR 20/67/7.

160 "I do not agree with the loose talk which has been going on . . ." CAC, Churchill Papers, CHAR 20/161/113-114.

160 "the prime minister let go with a slow-starting but fast-ending stemwinder . . ." Butcher, H., Three Years with Eisenhower, p.463.

160   "one of his typical fighting speeches . . ." Eisenhower, D., Crusade in Europe, p.269.

162   "I may add however that I still consider that the proportion . . ." Churchill, W.S., The Second World War, vol. 5, p. 544.

Chapter 7: Lockdown

181   "We must beware of handing out irksome for irksome's sake . . ." & telegram from Churchill to Ismay, January 4, 1944. CAC, CHAR 20/179/34.

182   "telling them that there must be no attempt to forecast dates . . ." CAC, Churchill Papers, CHAR 20/137A/18-20.

184   "In particular I deprecate the wholesale character of these orders." TNA, Prime Minister's Office, PREM 3/345/4.

186   "the large number of Irishmen who are fighting so bravely in our armed forces . . ." Hansard, March 14, 1944, series 5, vol.398, cc36-8.

189   "our interests because it would leave us in the dark . . ." TNA, Prime Minister's Office, PREM 3/345/7.

192   "In the course of a general conversation about military matters . . ." TNA, Prime Minister's Office, PREM 3/345/8.

192   "that it was pretty clear that we would not undertake operations . . ." TNA, Prime Minister's Office, PREM 3/345/8.

193   "I think he should be frightened out of his wits . . ." TNA, Prime Minister's Office, PREM 3/345/8.

193   "from the time the Normandy landing was achieved . . ." Liddell Hart, B., 'The Military Strategist' in Taylor A.J.P. et al (eds), Churchill: Four Faces and the Man, p.196.

194   "You probably have no idea of the enormous inconvenience . . ." TNA, Prime Minister's Office, PREM 3/345/2.

195   "The first scene was 1938—back to Munich." Soames, E. (ed), Mary Churchill's War, p.259.

196   "Mon 20 March—P.M. looked flushed and was very woolly." Dilks, D. (ed), The Diaries of Sir Alexander Cadogan, pp.611 & 621.

196   "He said he could still always sleep well, eat well . . ." Danchev, A. & Todman, D. (eds), War Diaries 1939–1945: Field Marshal Lord Alanbrooke, p.544.

197   "he said it was inhuman to talk of soldiers in such cold-blooded fashion . . ." Eisenhower, D., Crusade in Europe, p.266.

197   "So there was a pregnant silence . . ." From unpublished transcript of interview with Joan Bright Astley. CAC, Brendon Papers, BREN 1/12.

Chapter 8: Bombing Civilians

203   "There was a limit to the slaughter and the resulting anger . . ." TNA, Prime Minister's Office, PREM 3/334/2.

205   "the only efficient support which Bomber Command can give to Overlord . . ." CAC, Bufton Papers, BUFT 3/44.

207 "but we must never forget that all the time, night after night . . ." CAC, Churchill Papers, CHAR 9/141A/57. Also published in Churchill, W.S. (ed), Never Give In, pp.244–45.

209 "The Cabinet today took rather a grave and on the whole an adverse view . . ." TNA, Prime Minister's Office, PREM 3/334/2.

210 "the effect which would be achieved by bombing attacks on railway centres . . ." TNA, Prime Minister's Office, PREM 3/334/2.

211 "This slaughter was likely to put the French against us . . ." TNA, Prime Minister's Office, PREM 3/334/2.

212 "be blamed on blind night bombing . . ." TNA, Prime Minister's Office, PREM 3/334/2.

212 "the raids in the Paris area have not been satisfactory . . ." TNA, Prime Minister's Office, PREM 3/334/1.

213 "casualties to civilian personnel are inherent in any plan for the full use of Air power . . ." TNA, Prime Minister's Office, PREM 3/334/2.

213 "we are shouldering a grim responsibility . . ." TNA, Prime Minister's Office, PREM 3/334/2.

213 "fully realized that our use of air power before Overlord would assume . . ." TNA, Cabinet Office, War Cabinet Minutes, CAB 65/16.

215 "It must be remembered on the one hand that this slaughter . . ." TNA, Prime Minister's Office, PREM 3/334/3.

216 "However regrettable the attendant loss of civilian lives is . . ." CAC, Churchill Papers, CHAR 20/164/77.

219 "It would seem right as we urged to give a high priority to operations of this sort . . ." TNA, Prime Minister's Office, PREM 3/334/4.

220 "I don't believe the figure of 10,000 which you gave was greatly exceeded." TNA, Prime Minister's Office, PREM 3/334/4.

222 "where he would be on D-day or rather the night before . . ." Royal Archives, PS/PSO/GVI/C/069.

223 "I think I shook the King by asking him whether he thought the project . . ." Hart-Davis, D. (ed), King's Counsellor, p.224.

225 "same smell of grass trodden down, same toughness in the meat . . ." CAC, Hugill Papers, HUGL 1.

Chapter 9: On the Eve

227 "Do you realize that by the time you wake up in the morning 20,000 men may have been killed?" Pawle, G., The War and Colonel Warden, p.302.

228 "one more appeal to you not to go to sea on D-Day . . ." CAC, Churchill Papers, CHAR 20/136/4.

228 "as Prime Minister and Minister of Defence, I ought to be allowed to go . . ." CAC, Churchill Papers, CHAR 20/136/6-8.

229 "It's hell here—impossible to get a moment to oneself . . ." Bright Astley, J., The Inner Circle: A View of War at the Top, p.144.

230 "a final familiar sight—an early 19ᵗʰ century house ..." CAC, Hugill Papers, HUGL 1.

234 "Their features were young and plebeian ..." CAC, Lawford Papers, LWFD 1.

234 "Luncheon was long and not genial ..." CAC, Lawford Papers, LWFD 1.

235 "We are going to liberate Europe ..." De Gaulle, C., War Memoirs: Unity 1942–1944 (translated by R. Howard), p.227.

235 "quite content with the battle, which he felt showed that the United States, Great Britain and France were all together ..." TNA, Prime Minister's Office, PREM 3/345/1.

239 "There must be a lot of people in the Whitehall area walking around with their fingers crossed.' CAC, Hugill Papers, HUGL 1.

240 "The PRIME MINISTER said that if General de Gaulle ..." TNA, Cabinet Office, War Cabinet Minutes, CAB 65/46.

241 "tried very hard on many occasions during four years ..." TNA, Prime Minister's Office, PREM 3/339/6.

243 "the critical period around H-Hour ..." Love, R. & Major, J. (eds), The Year of D-Day: The 1944 Diary of Admiral Sir Bertram Ramsay, p.83.

243 "General Brooke wished 'to God it were safely over ...'" Danchev, A. & Todman, D. (eds), War Diaries 1939–1945: Field Marshal Lord Alanbrooke, p.554.

243 "Our landings in the Cherbourg-Havre area have failed to gain a satisfactory foothold ..." Eisenhower Presidential Library, Online documents, accessed October 2023.

Chapter 10: Storming Ashore

245 "As it was in the beginning so may it continue to the end." Montgomery, B., Memoirs, p.253.

254 "Though they [the king and Churchill] had lunched together ..." Hart-Davis, D. (ed), King's Counsellor, p.231.

255 "The past 5 months have not been an easy time ..." TNA, Prime Minister's Office, PREM 3/339/13.

256 "I promised to report to the House ..." Churchill's second statement to the House of Commons, June 6, 1944. Hansard, series 5, vol. 400, cc1323-4.

257 "By speaking immediately after Eisenhower ..." De Gaulle, C., War Memoirs: Unity 1942–1944 (translated by R. Howard), p.230.

258 "He said that nothing would induce him to give way ..." Eden, E., The Reckoning, p.456.

260 "to send for the commissioners ..." CAC, Churchill Papers, CHAR 20/166/19-21.

260 "If for any reason the supplementary currency is not acceptable to the French Public ..." CAC, Churchill Papers, CHAR 20/166/82-3.

261 "be well for you to warn the press that there are two sides to this story ..." CAC, Churchill Papers, CHAR 20/152/6.

263 "My colleagues and I cannot but admit that the history of warfare . . ." CAC, Churchill Papers, CHAR 20/166/79.

263 "'When this war is over,' he growled . . ." Cowles, V., Winston Churchill: The Ear and the Man, Hamish Hamilton, 1953, p.344.

264 "This was a fine feat . . ." CAC, Churchill Papers, CHAR 20/152/6.

265 "I earnestly hope that when Members go to their constituencies . . ." Hansard, series 5, vol. 400, cc1522.

266 "We do not wish in any way to be a burden on you or your headquarters . . ." CAC, Churchill Papers, CHAR 20/152/6.

266 "Will meet you and give you full picture . . ." TNA, Prime Minister's Office, PREM 3/339/11.

267 "We drove through our limited but fertile domain in Normandy . . ." Churchill, W.S., The Second World War, vol.6, p.11.

268 "did not seem in any way pleased to see us arrive . . ." Danchev, A. & Todman, D. (eds), War Diaries 1939–1945: Field Marshal Lord Alanbrooke, p.557.

268 "Standing bare-headed in the sunshine . . ." Pawle, G., The War and Colonel Warden, p.303.

269 "Ever since 1907, I have in good times and bad times . . ." CAC, Churchill Papers, CHAR 20/137C/288.

Chapter 11: Tyranny of Overlord

274 "On the first day, we suffered about ninety casualties, a comparatively low figure . . ." Hastings, R., "An Undergraduate's War", p.126.

277 "Winston was in very good form, quite 10 years younger . . ." Danchev, A. & Todman, D. (eds), War Diaries 1939–1945: Field Marshal Lord Alanbrooke, p.560.

278 "realize that if we took the season of the year and the topography of the country . . ." Danchev, A. & Todman, D. (eds), War Diaries 1939–1945: Field Marshal Lord Alanbrooke, p.562.

279 "was too far removed from General Eisenhower's battle-front for an Allied landing . . ." TNA, Cabinet Office Papers, Chiefs of Staff Meetings, CAB 79/76. Published in Gilbert, M. & Arnn, L. (eds), The Churchill Documents, vol.20, pp.572–75.

280 "for continued use of practically all the Mediterranean resources . . ." CAC, Churchill Papers, CHAR 20/167/89.

281 "in the end we got him to agree . . ." Danchev, A. & Todman, D. (eds), War Diaries 1939–1945: Field Marshal Lord Alanbrooke, p.565.

281 "he [Churchill] was in a maudlin, bad tempered, drunken mood . . ." Danchev, A. & Todman, D. (eds), War Diaries 1939–1945: Field Marshal Lord Alanbrooke, p.566.

285 "I do not believe myself that this vast enterprise could have been executed earlier . . ." CAC, Churchill Papers, CHAR 9/200A/20-21 for early draft of speech. Published in Rhodes James, R., Winston Churchill: His Complete Speeches, vol. 6, p.6972.

286   "all my life I have been grateful for the contribution France has made . . ." CAC, Churchill Papers, CHAR 9/200A/47-48 for early draft of speech. Published in Rhodes James, R., Winston Churchill: His Complete Speeches, vol. 6, p.6980.

288   "once we joined battle in Normandy "Anvil's" value was much reduced . . ." Churchill, W.S., The Second World War, vol.6, p51.

289   "It is worth noting that we had now passed the day in July...' Churchill, W.S., The Second World War, vol.6, p.62.

290   "We have three armies in the field." CAC, Baroness Spencer-Churchill Papers, CSCT 2/33.

293   "The victory has been definite, complete and decisive . . ." cited in Beevor, A., D-Day, p.478.

294   "Paris. Paris outraged, Paris broken, Paris martyred . . ." cited in Beevor, A., D-Day, p.512.

Chapter 12: Legacies

295   "if we open a quarrel between the past and the present, we shall find that we have lost the future." Taken from Churchill's Finest Hour speech, June 18, 1940, see Churchill, W.S. (ed), Never Give In, p.221.

298   "Do please tell us that some effective steps are being taken . . ." CAC, Churchill Papers, CHAR 7/74B.

298   "always listening; in the street I wished the traffic would stop . . ." Bright Astley, J., The Inner Circle: A View of War at the Top, p.147.

301   "Hot tears came & had to be hidden . . ." Soames, E. (ed), Mary Churchill's War, p.349.

302   "'There are two opposing ideas in the country,' I said to him . . ." Moran, C., Winston Churchill: The Struggle for Survival 1940–1965, p.251.

303   "walked to the open door, put his back to its edge . . ." Butcher, H., Three Years with Eisenhower, p.64.

Illustrations

Cover Churchill arriving in Normandy, June 12, 1944. CAC, Churchill Press photographs, CHPH 1A/F3/73 (colorized).

Documents

Photographic Images for Centerpiece

Select Bibliography

1: PRIMARY SOURCES

Churchill Archives Centre (CAC)

AMEL   Papers of Leopold Amery

BREN   Papers of Dr. Piers Brendon (for interview with Joan Bright Astley)

BUFT   Papers of Air Vice Marshal Sydney Osborne Bufton

CHAQ, CHAR & CHUR   Papers of Sir Winston Churchill

CLVL   Papers of Sir John Colville

CSCT   Papers of Baroness (Clementine) Spencer-Churchill

HHLT   Papers of Vice Admiral John Hughes-Hallett

HUGL   Papers of John Antony Crawford Hugill

JACB   Papers of Sir Ian Jacob

LKEN   Papers of Leo Kennedy

LWFD   Papers of Valentine Lawford

MART   Papers of Sir John Martin

MISC 68   Copy of Operational Intelligence Centre Special Intelligence Summary: "The Use of Special Intelligence in connection with Operation Neptune January 1944–September 1944," 1945

PYKE   Papers of Geoffrey Pyke

SELO   Papers of Lord Selwyn Lloyd

WCHL   Churchill Additional Material

WDVS   Papers of Admiral Sir William Wellclose Davis

The National Archives

CAB 65   Minutes of the War Cabinet

CAB 69   Minutes of Defence Committee (Operations)

CAB 99/24   Record of conference held at Casablanca, January 1943

PREM 3   Prime Minister's Office operational correspondence and papers

Other

Hansard   Record of Parliamentary Debates

Royal Archives   King George VI correspondence with Churchill

2: PUBLISHED DIARIES, MEMOIRS & PRIMARY SOURCES

Bright Astley, J., *The Inner Circle: A View of War at the Top*, (Hutchinson, 1971).

Butcher, H., *Three Years with Eisenhower: The Personal Diary of Captain Harry C. Butcher, USNR, Naval Aide to General Eisenhower, 1942 to 1945* (Heinemann, 1946).

Carter, R.S., *Those Devils in Baggy Pants* (Revised edition, Jan-Carol Publishing, 2021).

Churchill, S., *A Thread in the Tapestry* (Deutsch, 1967).

Churchill, S., *Keep on Dancing* (Weidenfeld and Nicolson, 1981).

Churchill, W.S., *Never Give In! The Best of Winston Churchill's Speeches* (Easton Press, 2003)—edited by his grandson.

Churchill, W.S., *The Second World War*, 6 vols (Cassell, 1948–54).

Churchill, W.S, *The World Crisis*, 6 vols (Thornton Butterworth, 1923–31).

Colville, J., *The Fringes of Power. Downing Street Diaries 1939–1955* (Hodder & Stoughton, 1985).

Danchev, A. & Todman D. (eds.), *War Diaries 1939–1945. Field Marshal Lord Alanbrooke* (Weidenfeld & Nicolson, 2001).

De Gaulle, C., *War Memoirs*, Vol II, "Unity," Richard Harwood (trans) (Weidenfeld & Nicolson, 1959).

Dilks, D. (ed), *The Diaries of Sir Alexander Cadogan* (Cassell, 1971).

Eden, A., *The Eden Memoirs, The Reckoning* (Cassell, 1965).

Eisenhower, D., *Crusade in Europe*, (Heinemann, 1948).

Gilbert, M. & Arnn, L. (eds.), *The Churchill Documents*, vol. 20 (Hillsdale, 2018).

Grehan, J. (ed.), *Hitler's V-Weapons: The Battle Against the V-1 & V-2* (Frontline, 2020)—a published version of the official history.

Hart-Davis, D. (ed.), *King's Counsellor: Abdication and War: The Diaries of Sir Alan Lascelles* (Weidenfeld & Nicolson, 2006).

Harvey, J. (ed), *The Diplomatic Diaries of Oliver Harvey, 1937–1940* (Collins, 1970).

Hastings, R., *An Undergraduate's War* (Bellhouse Publishing, 1997).

Hickman, T., *Churchill's Bodyguard* (Headline, 2006)—Based on memoirs of Inspector Walter Thompson.

Hughes-Hallett, J., *From Dieppe to D-Day: The Memoirs of Vice Admiral Jock Hughes-Hallett* (Frontline, 2023).

Ismay, H., *The Memoirs of General the Lord Ismay* (Heinemann, 1960).

Lamb, C., *Beyond the Sea. A Wren at War* (Mardle, 2021).

Love, R. & Major, J. (eds), *The Year of D-Day: The 1944 Diary of Admiral Sir Bertram Ramsay* (Hull University Press, 1994).

Macleod, R. & Kelly, D. (eds.), *The Ironside Diaries, 1937–1940* (Constable, 1962).

Macmillan, M., *War Diaries: Politics and War in the Mediterranean 1943–1945* (Macmillan, 1984).

Montgomery of El Alamein, *The Memoirs of Field-Marshal the Viscount Montgomery of El Alamein* (Collins, 1958).

Moran, Lord., *Winston Churchill: The Struggle for Survival 1940–1965* (Constable, 1966)

Morgan, F., *Peace and War: A Soldier's Life* (Hodder & Stoughton, 1961).

Nel, E., *Mr. Churchill's Secretary* (Hodder & Stoughton, 1958).

Nicolson, H., *Diaries & Letters 1930–1964* (Penguin, 1984).

Norwich, J. J. (ed.), *The Duff Cooper Diaries* (Weidenfeld & Nicolson, 2005) .

Pawle, G., *The War and Colonel Warden* (Harrap, 1963)—Based on memoirs of Commander Thompson.

Rhodes James, R. (ed), *Winston Churchill: His Complete Speeches*, 8 vols (New York, Chelsea House, 1974).

Soames, E. (ed.), *Mary Churchill's War: The Wartime Diaries of Churchill's Youngest Daughter* (Two Roads, 2021).

Soames, M., *Speaking for Themselves: The Personal Letters of Winston and Clementine Churchill* (Doubleday, 1998).

Spears, E., *Assignment to Catastrophe*, 2 vols (London, Heinemann, 1954).

Wheatley, D., *The Deception Planners: My Secret War* (Hutchinson, 1980).

Wheeler-Bennett, J. (ed.), *Action This Day* (London, Macmillan, 1968)—Memoirs of Churchill's Downing Street team.

3: PUBLISHED SECONDARY SOURCES

Barnett, C., Engage the Enemy More Closely: The Royal Navy in the Second World War (Hodder and Stoughton, 1991)

Beevor, A., D-Day: 75th Anniversary Edition (Penguin, 2014)

Bishop, P., Operation Jubilee—Dieppe 1942: The Folly and the Sacrifice (Penguin Books, 2021)

Bowman, G., Empire First: Churchill's War Against D-Day (self-published, 2020)

Cowles, V., Churchill: The Era and the Man (Hamish Hamilton, 1953)

D'Este, C., Eisenhower: Allies Supreme Commander (Weidenfeld & Nicolson, 2003)

Gilbert, M., Winston S. Churchill, Vol VI, "Finest Hour" (Heinemann, 1983)

Gilbert, M., Winston S. Churchill, Vol VII, "Road to Victory" (Heinemann, 1986)

Hamilton, N., Monty: Master of the Battlefield 1942–1944, (Hamish Hamilton, 1983)

Hastings, M., Finest Years: Churchill as Warlord 1940–1945 (Harper Press, 2009)

Hinsley, F. H., British Intelligence in the Second World War, vol 3 pt.2 (HMSO, 1988)

Holt, T., The Deceivers: Allied Military Deception in the Second World War (Folio Society, 2008)

Humphrys, O., Wavell in Russia (privately published, 2017)

Kennedy, P., Engineers of Victory: The Problem Solvers Who Turned the Tide in the Second World War (Allen Lane, 2013)

Kiszely, J., Anatomy of a Campaign: The British Fiasco in Norway, 1940 (Cambridge University Press, 2017)

Knight, N., Churchill: The Greatest Briton Unmasked (David & Charles, 2008)

Lampe, D., Pyke: The Unknown Genius, (Evans Brothers, 1959)

MacKenzie, R., Bomber Command: Churchill's Greatest Triumph (Air World, 2022)

Mackesy, K. J., Armoured Crusader: A Biography of Major-General Sir Percy Hobart (Hutchinson, 1967)

Macrae, S., Winston Churchill's Toyshop (2nd edition, Amberley, 2010)

Milton, G., The Ministry of Ungentlemanly Warfare (John Murray, 2016)

Morgan, M., D-Day Hero, CSM Stanley Hollis VC (Sutton Publishing, 2004)

Olusoga, D., Black and British (Macmillan, 2016)

Overy, R., The Air War 1939–1945 (Europa, 1980)

Overy, R., The Bombing War: Europe 1939–1945 (Penguin, 2014)

Packwood, A., How Churchill Waged War (Frontline, 2018)

Packwood, A. (ed.), The Cambridge Companion to Winston Churchill (Cambridge University Press, 2023)

Prior, R., Conquer We Must (Yale University Press, 2022)

Reynolds, D., In Command of History (Allen Lane, 2004),

Roberts, A., Masters and Commanders (Allen Lane, 2008)

Roberts, A., Churchill: Walking with Destiny (Allen Lane, 2018)

Roskill, S., The War at Sea, 1939–1945, Vol. III, The Offensive, Part I, 1 June 1943 (HMSO, 1960)

Roskill, S., The War at Sea, 1939–1945, Vol. III, The Offensive, Part II: 1 June 1944, (HMSO, 1961)

Roskill, S., The Navy at War (Collins, 1960)

Ryan, C., The Longest Day (Victor Gollancz, 1960)

Soames, M., Clementine Churchill (revised edition, Doubleday, 2002)

Stafford, D., Churchill & Secret Service (John Murray, 1997)

Taylor, A.J.P. et al, Churchill: Four Faces and the Man (Allen Lane, 1969)

Thorpe, D.R., Selwyn Lloyd (Jonathan Cape, 1989)

Vale, A. & Scadding, J., Winston Churchill's Illnesses 1886–1965 (Frontline, 2020)

Ziegler, P., Mountbatten (Guild, 1985)

Index

ABOUT THE AUTHORS

GENERAL SIR RICHARD DANNATT became Chief of the General Staff in 2006, leading the British Army as it fought two wars in Iraq and Afghanistan. He handed over his position forty years to the day from when he first joined the Army. In 2009, Her Majesty The Queen appointed him Constable of the Tower of London, and in 2010, he was appointed as Crossbencher to the House of Lords. Richard Dannatt is also Chairman of Trustees of the British Normandy Memorial.

ALLEN PACKWOOD BA, MPhil (Cantab), is a Fellow of Churchill College at the University of Cambridge, the Director of the Churchill Archives Centre, and a Fellow of the Royal Historical Society. He was awarded an OBE for services to archives and scholarship in the 2016 Queen's Birthday Honors. His book *How Churchill Waged War* was published in 2018, and he has since edited the Cambridge University Press Companion to Winston Churchill and coedited *Letters for the Ages: The Private and Personal Letters of Sir Winston Churchill.*

THE BRITISH NORMANDY MEMORIAL

The British Normandy Memorial stands above Gold Beach. It is Britain's national memorial commemorating the names of the more than 22,000 men and women in British units who lost their lives on D-Day and during the Battle of Normandy.

For decades after the Second World War, the United Kingdom was the only principal Allied nation which did not have a national memorial in Normandy. In 2015, the Normandy Memorial Trust was set up to fulfill the hopes of Normandy Veterans to establish a British memorial in Normandy. The completed memorial was opened by the then Prince Charles, Prince of Wales, on June 6, 2021.

Close to the memorial is the Winston Churchill Centre, an exhibition and education centre developed to ensure that future generations remember the events of 1944 and understand their significance.

There are more details at www.britishnormandymemorial.org where you can find information about the Guardian scheme to support the memorial's care and maintenance.

**BRITISH
NORMANDY
MEMORIAL**

INTERNATIONAL CHURCHILL SOCIETY

Since 1968, the International Churchill Society (ICS) has been the world's preeminent organization educating and inspiring present and future generations to be outstanding leaders in their fields through the example of Sir Winston Churchill. By celebrating the timeless values of Sir Winston Churchill, ICS emboldens all generations to understand the historical context of Churchill's life and defend, enhance, and promote the values he embodied: freedom, democracy, and human rights.

ICS is a non-profit organization in the United States and a registered charity in the United Kingdom with over 3,000 global members on seven continents. It publishes its quarterly magazine *Finest Hour,* provides research funds to students and authors, and hosts an international conference, among many other activities and efforts. It has formal partnerships with the Royal United Services Institute, George Washington University, and America's National Churchill Museum. You can learn more and become a member by visiting winstonchurchill.org.